PRINCIPLES OF RELATIONAL DATABASE SYSTEMS

SITANSU S. MITTRA
TRW, Inc.
Northeastern University

PRENTICE HALL
Englewood Cliffs, New Jersey 07632

Library of Congress Cataloging-in-Publication Data

Mittra, Sitansu S.
   Principles of relational database systems / Sitansu S. Mittra.
      p.   cm.
   Includes index.
   ISBN 0-13-716796-2
   1. Relational data bases.   I. Title.
QA76.9.D3M58 1991
005.75'6--dc20   90-36361
                                                  CIP

*To Pranati, Partha, and Ansuman—in
deep appreciation of their willingness
to renounce the legitimate claim they
had on the many, many hours of our
family life that I stole from them while
writing this book.*

Editorial/production supervision
   and interior design: Bayani Mendoza de Leon
Cover design: Lundgren Graphics, Ltd.
Manufacturing buyer: Lori Bulwin

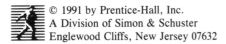

© 1991 by Prentice-Hall, Inc.
A Division of Simon & Schuster
Englewood Cliffs, New Jersey 07632

Printed in the United States of America

10 9 8 7 6 5 4 3 2 1

ISBN 0-13-716796-2

Prentice-Hall International (UK) Limited, *London*
Prentice-Hall of Australia Pty. Limited, *Sydney*
Prentice-Hall Canada Inc., *Toronto*
Prentice-Hall Hispanoamericana, S.A., *Mexico*
Prentice-Hall of India Private Limited, *New Delhi*
Prentice-Hall of Japan, Inc., *Tokyo*
Simon & Schuster Asia Pte. Ltd., *Singapore*
Editora Prentice-Hall do Brasil, Ltda., *Rio de Janeiro*

TRADEMARK INFORMATION

INFORMIX is a registered trademark of
Informix Software, Inc.

INGRES is a trademark of Ingres
Corporation.

LOGIX is a registered trademark of
Logical Software, Inc.

ORACLE is a registered trademark of
Oracle Corporation.

RIM is a registered trademark of Boeing
Computer Services.

UNIFY is a trademark of Unify
Corporation.

dBase III Plus is a trademark of Ashton-
Tate Corporation.

ASCENT is a trademark of Control Data
Corporation.

CONTENTS

3   RELATIONAL ALGEBRA   69

4   RELATIONAL CALCULUS   95

8   ENTITY–RELATIONSHIP DATA MODEL   190

Contents

9 DESIGN, IMPLEMENTATION, AND MAINTENANCE OF RELATIONAL DATABASES 208

10 CONTEMPORARY TOPICS IN RELATIONAL DATABASE SYSTEMS 238

11   RELATIONAL DBMS PACKAGES   287

12   EVALUATION AND SELECTION OF A DBMS   311

INDEX   318

PREFACE

The book provides a comprehensive coverage of the principles of relational database systems. Relational databases are widely used at present and their use will continue to grow in the future. They do not presuppose any rigid structure on the data and use the familiar notions of records and files. Their popularity as an alternative to nonrelational databases can be ascribed to the following two reasons:

1. The nonrelational databases impose a rigid structure on data in the form of owner–member relationships that new users find difficult to understand.
2. To formulate a query in a nonrelational database, users have to navigate through the schema and use a procedural language.

The book consists of twelve chapters. In Chapter 1 we introduce a database environment as an improvement over a file processing system. We explain how the three levels of a relational database together can achieve data independence. We then define a database management system (DBMS) and identify the components of a DBMS, such as data definition language (DDL), data manipulation language (DML), query language, data dictionary, and kernel.

In Chapter 2 we discuss the relational data structure by providing in-depth treatment of the DDL and DML, using System R as an example of a relational DBMS. In addition, we discuss the integrity rules, views or virtual relations, and dated relations.

In Chapter 3 we discuss relational algebra as a basis for defining query languages. The necessary mathematical tools needed for an understanding of our later discussion of relational algebra are provided. The notions of primitive and derived relational algebraic operations are discussed as a preparation for introducing the equivalence of relational algebra and relational calculus in Chapter 4.

In Chapter 4, relational calculus, both tuple and domain, is described. Mathematical prerequisites are provided at the beginning of the chapter. A complete proof is provided of the equivalence theorem, which shows that query languages based on relational algebra and the two types of relational calculus are equivalent in terms of their expressive power. The chapter closes with a discussion of the relational completeness of query languages and Codd's classification schemes of relational databases.

In Chapter 5 we provide a detailed treatment of the query optimization principles. Examples are used to show how widely the processing time of a given query can vary, depending on the actual formulation. Also examples are given of a variety of query languages, such as SQL, SQUARE, QUEL, QBE, and QBF.

In Chapter 6 we discuss the principles of functional dependency and normalization. The five normal forms and the Boyce–Codd normal form are introduced with examples. We close with a discussion of three relational data models: binary, irreducible, and functional. The use of functional data model in designing query languages is also shown.

In Chapter 7 we discuss three nonrelational data models in order to show how a relational database differs from a nonrelational database. These three data models are: hierarchical, network or CODASYL, and inverted file. For each data model, examples are given of its DDL and DML.

In Chapter 8 we introduce the entity–relationship data model of Chen. We provide the detailed syntax of the DDL proposed by Chen and show how this model can produce the relational and nonrelational data models as special cases. The chapter closes with a discussion of the use of the entity–relationship model in database design and overall business planning.

In Chapter 9 we discuss issues related to database administration, including a detailed treatment of the design, implementation, and maintenance of relational databases. The role of the database administrator (DBA) is emphasized as being critical for proper operation of the databases used in an organization. Copious examples of database maintenance–related issues are given using the ORACLE DBMS. The chapter closes with a discussion of the data dictionary, which is often described as a "database about the database."

In Chapter 10 we introduce a variety of contemporary issues in relational databases, such as distributed database, database machine, intelligent database, object-oriented database, and the use of natural language as a query language.

In Chapter 11 we provide an overview of seven relational DBMS packages: INFORMIX, INGRES, LOGIX, ORACLE, RIM, UNIFY, and dBase III Plus. The last is PC-based, whereas all the others are available on mainframes or superminis, although scaled-down versions of some of them are available on the PCs as well.

Finally, in Chapter 12 we provide a methodology for the evaluation and selection of a relational DBMS for use in an organization and describe how a score sheet can be used to make the final selection.

Special features of the book include:

1. Complete mathematical proof of the equivalence theorem on the expressive power of relational algebra and relational calculus
2. Technical problems and their solutions related to database maintenance
3. Discussion of a variety of contemporary issues in database systems, collected primarily from journals and technical reports
4. Overview of seven relational DBMS packages
5. Methodology for evaluation and selection of a relational DBMS

The book is intended for two types of users:

1. Business or computer science students who want to learn the techniques of relational databases
2. Computer system professionals who work with relational databases at the system end or application end

For the first group, the book can be used as a textbook for a one- or two-semester graduate course on database systems. In fact, I have used most of the material in the book to teach graduate courses on databases at Boston University and Northeastern University for students working toward an M.S. degree in computer science. The book contains more material than can be covered in depth in a single semester. This allows the instructor a considerable amount of choice in selecting topics to teach. For the second group, the book provides a "how to" compendium of information necessary to design, implement, and maintain a relational database. As such it can be used as a step-by-step procedure manual or as a reference text to address problems at the external, conceptual, or internal level of a database.

During the time that I was writing the book I got continuous support from my family—my wife, Pranati, being the cheerleader of the team. Without her unswerving enthusiasm this book could not have become a reality. My sons, Partha and Ansuman, appreciated their father's work and were eager to see the book in printed form.

I acknowledge the help I received from my students at Boston University and Northeastern University in shaping my ideas about relational databases. I have benefited from their questions and homework assignments in the courses I offered. I also acknowledge the help of my colleagues at TRW, Inc. in providing source materials and conducting illuminating discussions.

It is a pleasure to acknowledge the friendly support of the editorial staff at Prentice Hall. I sincerely thank the production staff, especially Mr. Bayani Mendoza de Leon, for making this book a success.

Sitansu S. Mittra

CHAPTER I

INTRODUCTION TO DATABASE CONCEPTS

1.1 FILE SYSTEM VERSUS DATABASE SYSTEM

An organization of any type (e.g., private industry, government agency, academic institution, hospital, etc.) generates information on a regular basis and uses it for its daily operation. With the introduction of computers to process data, the file management system has been used traditionally as the vehicle for storage, retrieval, and maintenance of data. However, the file management system does not provide an integrated view of data for the entire organization and cannot implement the independence of data from programs. This means that in a file-oriented system the programs depend on how data are stored and accessed by the file management system. A database system offers a significant improvement over the shortcomings of the file management system.

Database technique allows an organization's data to be processed as an integrated whole. It thereby reduces the fragmentation imposed by separate files designed and implemented for separate applications and enables users to access data from different parts of the database to suit their purposes. File processing systems are indeed predecessors of database systems.

Consider the situation shown in Figure 1–1. Three separate files are handled by three separate application programs (Customer Listing, Invoice, Inventory) to print three separate reports. Each program interfaces separately with the operating system during this process to generate the reports.

Look next at Figure 1–2. All the data needed by the three programs are stored in a single logical file or schema. The same reports that were generated using separate files can now be produced through small application programs using

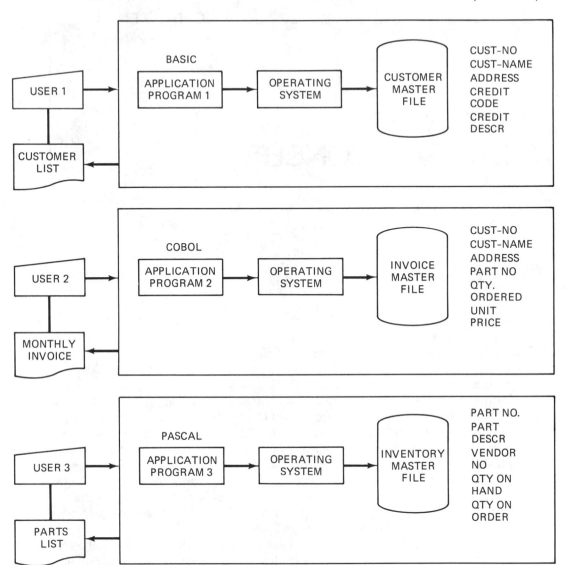

Figure 1–1 File processing system.

DML (Data Manipulation Language) commands and, if necessary, using statements from a host language such as FORTRAN, BASIC, or Pascal, or by using a query language such as SQL. These programs interface with a complex software called a database management system (DBMS), which, in turn, interfaces with the operating system to generate the necessary reports.

A file processing system, although an efficient data management tool for a specific application, has the following disadvantages:

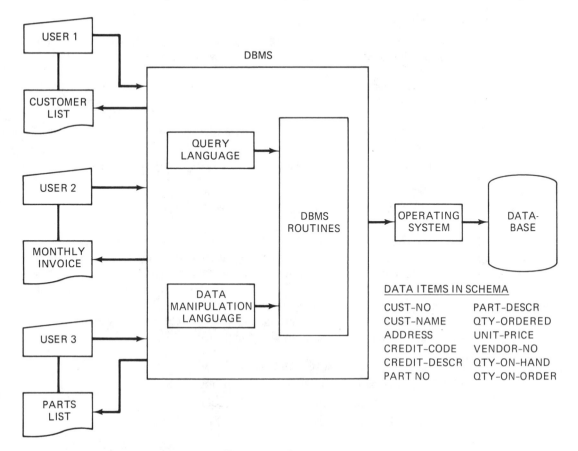

Figure 1-2 Database system.

1. *Redundancy of data.* Identical data are distributed over various files (e.g., Customer Number appears in Customer File and Invoice File).
2. *Multiple update.* One field may be updated in one file but not in others, thereby leading to lack of data integrity and production of conflicting reports.
3. *Waste of storage space.* When the same field is stored in four different files, the required storage space is needlessly quadrupled.
4. *The access language is normally unique to application programs and often not user friendly.*

A database system reduces or eliminates these problems significantly. Its advantages can be summarized as follows:

1. Reduction or elimination of data redundancy.
2. Maintenance of data integrity.

3. Reduction in wasted storage space.
4. Access to data through a query language that describes the information needed by the user but does not specify how the information is to be derived.

However, a database system is not an unmixed blessing. Some of its disadvantages are:

1. Installation and maintenance are more expensive than those of separate file systems.
2. Failure of one component of an integrated system may stop the entire system.

1.2 DATABASE MANAGEMENT SYSTEM

A *database* is a collection of related data that are used by application software. In a database the data definitions and their interrelationships are kept separate from the programs of the application. Multiple users may use the same database, and multiple applications may also use the same database. Thus a single database can offer multiple views of the same data.

A *database management system* (DBMS) is a complex and extensive unit of software that performs the following functions:

1. Creates and maintains the database.
2. Allows access to the database for an authorized user.
3. Retrieves data according to the user's request.
4. Updates (i.e., adds, deletes, or modifies) records in the database.

Consider the schema of Figure 1–2. To generate the Customer List from the underlying database, user number 1 can issue the following command in SQL, a widely used query language for relational databases (the details of SQL are discussed in Chapters 2 and 4):

```
SELECT CUSTNO, CNAME, CADDR, CRCODE, CRDESC FROM SAMPLE;
```

SAMPLE is assumed to be the name of the database. Then the following events take place:

1. The user types the instruction and presses RETURN.
2. DBMS intercepts the request and analyzes it.
3. DBMS recognizes that the query accesses the schema called SAMPLE and needs only five fields from it.
4. DBMS determines from the data dictionary the physical database descriptions and the disk files containing the necessary records.
5. DBMS transfers control to the operating system for reading the records.

6. Operating system retrieves the necessary data from the disk files, transfers them to the system buffers, and transfers control to the DBMS.

7. DBMS transfers data from system buffers to the user's work area.

8. The DBMS displays the customer list on the user's terminal.

Terms such as *database* and *data dictionary* will be described in more detail later. The eight steps listed above merely illustrate an operational scenario showing the interaction between a DBMS and an operating system supporting the DBMS.

Normally, user requests for ad hoc reports (i.e., reports that are not predesigned) are processed interactively, resulting in severe execution time overhead. However, complex queries may be stored in a command file, which may then be compiled and executed.

The interaction between the user and the system is handled by the DBMS, which provides the user interface to the database system. The user interface is a boundary of the system beyond which everything is invisible to the user.

A sequence of events similar to steps 1 through 8 takes place when the user wants to update the database instead of retrieving data therefrom. The command (e.g., in SQL) entered by the user first reads the designated records, then modifies the data in the user's work area, and finally, issues an instruction to the DBMS to write the modified data back into the database. The DBMS then issues the appropriate WRITE command to the operating system for implementing the modification.

1.3 DATA INDEPENDENCE

As noted in Section 1.1, one of the advantages of a database system is that different users can access the database for data retrieval and report generation without worrying about the data storage structure or access strategy. For example, to generate a customer list from SAMPLE (see Section 1.2), the user need not know if the field CUSTNO is a key (i.e., if each distinct value of CUSTNO corresponds to a unique record), and the form of the query will not change if CUSTNO is made a key. The access strategy is invisible to the user. On the other hand, if the report is generated using a file management system, the program must know how the file is structured: for example, as an indexed sequential file or as a direct file. Thus in a database system, any application is independent of the storage structure and access strategy. This feature is referred to as *data independence*. The provision of data independence is a major objective of database systems.

In a file management system it is usually the case that an application's logical record is identical to a corresponding physical record. This is not true, in general, in a database system, due to data independence. We shall see in Section 1.5 that this feature leads to the mutual independence of three levels of a database: the external, conceptual, and internal levels.

1.4 DATA MODELS USED IN DATABASE SYSTEMS

The logical structure or schema of a database can be described by using any one of three alternative data models: (1) hierarchical, (2) network, or (3) relational. The hierarchical model was introduced in the early 1960s. This model structures data in a rigid owner–member (also called parent–child) relationship. During the late 1960s the Conference on Data Systems Languages (CODASYL) Data Base Task Group (DBTG) started attempts to create the network model as an improvement over the hierarchical model. In April 1971 they published their recommendations, which established the foundation of the network model. (See Chapter 7 for a discussion of the hierarchical and network models.) The relational model was introduced by E. F. Codd in the early 1970s. It has become very popular because of its flexibility. As a result, many PC-based versions of relational DBMS packages are currently available in the market. A relational data model is often described as *the* natural way to look at data.

By way of comparison among the three data models, we can make the following comments:

1. Hierarchical and network data structures require a predetermined structuring of data links or paths.
2. The hierarchical and network data structures are good for a production environment but are less efficient for ad hoc queries.
3. A relational data structure is excellent for ad hoc queries but is less efficient for production settings, although improvements are continually being made to relational DBMS packages to reduce overhead and improve performance.

In a relational database, different files exist as separate relations, and therefore there is no structure such as that of owner–member relationships among these relations. The schema structure is not predetermined and relations can be added or deleted from the schema without affecting the other relations. This feature makes the relational database very suitable for relatively unstructured exploratory applications. Once we determine the precise structure of the data needed for producing the necessary reports, the relational database can be converted into a network database.

For the sake of completeness it must be mentioned that a fourth type of data model exists. It is called an entity relationship data model and can be regarded as a hybrid of network and relational data models. However, unlike the other three data models, which can be implemented by means of commercially available DBMS, the entity–relationship data model cannot be so implemented. Usually, a relational DBMS is used to implement this data model. We discuss the hierarchical and network data models in Chapter 7 and the entity–relationship data model in Chapter 8.

1.5 THREE LEVELS OF A DATABASE

The architecture of a database consists of three levels: (1) external, (2) conceptual, and (3) internal. The *external level* is closest to the users. It is concerned with the way users view the data for their own use. Thus each user accesses a separate external level of the database. The user can be an end user or an application programmer. Accordingly, the tools used for accessing each external level can be different. (See Section 1.7 for more details.)

The *conceptual level* involves a representation of the entire information content of the database. Each external level consists of some parts or all of the conceptual level. In this sense, the latter can be regarded as a set-theoretic union of all possible external levels. Hence for a given database there can be many external levels, but only one conceptual level. Some authors call it the logical level.

The *internal level,* also called the physical level, is the one closest to physical storage, where the data contents of the conceptual level are stored on disk files. Similar to the conceptual level, there is only one internal level for a database.

The contents of the conceptual level are often called *logical records*; those of the internal level are called *physical records.* From a user's viewpoint, the external levels offer high-level partial views of the database, while the internal level provides a low-level representation of the complete database. The conceptual level is intermediate between the two. Some authors use the terms *subschema, schema,* and *database* to refer, respectively, to the external, conceptual, and internal levels.

The three levels communicate with one another through two sets of mappings: (1) external/conceptual-level mapping and (2) conceptual/internal-level mapping. The first mapping defines the correspondence between a particular external level and the conceptual level. It maps each field referenced in the external level to its counterpart in the conceptual. Since there can be many external levels, this mapping is many-to-one. The second mapping specifies how the fields in the conceptual-level map onto their counterparts in the internal level. Since a database has only one conceptual level and only one internal level, this mapping is one-to-one; that is, each field in the conceptual level is mapped onto its stored version in the internal level. Figure 1–3 describes the architecture of a database and the two sets of mappings among the three levels.

The concept of independence (see Section 1.3) is directly related to the two sets of mapping described above. The external/conceptual-level mapping implements the *logical data independence.* As the database is used, it may become necessary to add information to the conceptual level. But such modification does not affect the existing external levels. Moreover, additional modifications can be made to the conceptual level if we redefine the mappings between the external and the conceptual levels. Similarly, the conceptual/internal mapping implements the *physical data independence.* This means that the internal level (i.e., storage

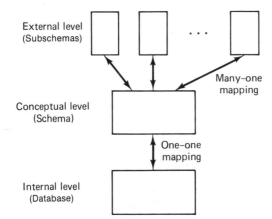

External level
(Subschemas)

Conceptual level
(Schema)

Many–one
mapping

One–one
mapping

Internal level
(Database)

Figure 1–3 Architecture of a
database.

structure) can be changed without altering the conceptual level. Application programs using the conceptual level need not be changed at all. The DBMS will
provide the necessary connections to run such programs under the changed environment.

1.6 ILLUSTRATIVE EXAMPLE

In this section we introduce a case study that will be used throughout the book.
Here the example is presented as a business problem oriented toward database
design.

Long Hill University (LHU) is a medium-sized liberal arts institution in
Boston offering undergraduate and graduate programs in arts, science, business,
and engineering. The student enrollment is about 6000 per year and the total
number of faculty members is approximately 450. Bachelor's, master's, and doc-
toral degrees are conferred annually. The following six files contain data related
to the students, instructors, and courses:

1. UNIVERSITY. Each record contains three fields:
    a. *Department Designator* (DNO): two-character-long unique identifier of
       a department (e.g., CS = computer science, MA = mathematics, EN
       = English, etc.)
    b. *Department Name* (DNAME): name of a department, up to 25 characters.
    c. *Department Head* (DHEAD): name of the chairperson of a department,
       up to 20 characters.

2. INSTRUCTOR. Each record contains five fields:
    a. *Instructor Name* (INAME): name of an instructor, up to 20 characters.
       INAME has same format as DHEAD in item 1c.
    b. *Degrees* (IDEG): all degrees held by an instructor from bachelor level,
       up to 10 characters.

   c. *Specialty Code* (SPCODE): two-digit numeric field representing each specialty area of an instructor. Multiple SPCODEs are possible.

   d. *Rank* (RANK): 10-character descriptor of the faculty rank (e.g., Asst Prof, Lecturer, etc.) of an instructor.

   e. *Social Security Number* (SSNO): the nine-digit social security number of an instructor.

3. STUDENT. Each record contains seven fields:

   a. *Student Name* (SNAME): name of a student, up to 20 characters. This has same format as DHEAD (1c) and INAME (2a).

   b. *Social Security Number* (SSNO): nine-digit social security number of a student. This has same format as SSNO in item 2e.

   c. *Major Field of Study* (MAJOR): 15-character-long name of the subject. This is left blank if no major field has been selected yet and has the value 'NDEG' for nondegree students.

   d. *Degree Sought* (DEGREE): 10-character-long name of the degree or diploma for a degree candidate. It has the value 'NONE' for nondegree students.

   e. *Advisor* (ADVSR): name of the faculty advisor for a student. This has same format as INAME in item 2a.

   f. *Department Designator* (DNO): same as item 1a, denoting the department in which the student is enrolled.

   g. *College of Registration* (COLREG): 15-character-long name of the college of enrollment (e.g., Liberal Arts, Science, Business, Architecture, etc.).

4. COURSE. Each record has five fields:

   a. *Course Number* (CNO): five-character-long unique identifier of a course; the first two characters are the same as DNO (1a), indicating the department offering the course.

   b. *Course Name* (CNAME): 20-character-long descriptive name of a course.

   c. *Instructor Name* (INAME): name of the course instructor for each section of the course. This has same format as item 2a.

   d. *Department Designator* (DNO): identifier of the department offering the course. This is same as item 1a.

   e. *Section Number* (SECNO): two-digit-long number of a section of a course. Multiple sections of a course are possible.

5. COURSE-LIST. Each record has five fields:

   a. *Course Number* (CNO): same as item 4a.

   b. *Section Number* (SECNO): same as item 4e.

   c. *Student Identification Number* (SID): same as SSNO in item 3b.

   d. *Grade* (GRADE): two-character-long course grade (e.g., A, B−, I, etc.).

   e. *Offering* (OFRNG): eight-character-long descriptor of the semester (e.g., Fall86, Summer84, etc.).

6. SPECIALIZATION. Each record has two fields:
   a. *Specialty Code* (SPCODE): two-digit numeric code representing a spe-
      cialization area. This is same as SPCODE in item 2c.
   b. *Specialty Name* (SPNAME): 20-character-long name of a specialization
      (e.g., European history, database, group theory, etc.).

Let us now suppose that the six files described above have been implemented
as a database. This process requires some restructuring of the file contents, which
we are ignoring at present. Also, we are not specifying a data model such as a
network or relational model for the implementation. We want to examine the
three levels of this database, called LHUDB (Long Hill University Data Base).

The conceptual level of LHUDB contains all the fields listed above. The
fields are grouped into separate files with some duplicate fields if necessary. Each
file is stored as a separate disk file in auxiliary storage at the internal level. Different users access different external levels of LHUDB. For example, the student
list of a given course can be produced from STUDENT and COURSE-LIST files.
For a given faculty member, a list of his or her advisees can be prepared using
STUDENT. A list of all instructors of a given department can be generated using
the three files UNIVERSITY, INSTRUCTOR, and SPECIALIZATION, and so
on.

It should be noted here that LHUDB has several deficiencies from a database
design principle. For example, one relation may be interpreted as unnormalized
and some of the relations are not in the third normal form. Such inadequacies
have been introduced purposely so that they can be analyzed and modified in
Chapter 6, where we study the normalization principles (see Sections 6.1 and 6.3).

1.7 ENTITIES AND RELATIONSHIPS IN THE
CONCEPTUAL LEVEL

Graphically, the conceptual level of a database is represented as a set of rectangles
connected with one another by means of arrows. Each rectangle, called an *entity*,
represents a person, place, object, event, or concept about which the organization
wants to store data. Each arrow represents a *relationship* between two entities.
It is a logical association between them. A relationship is labeled $1:N$, $M:N$, $N:1$,
or $1:1$, according as it is one–many, many–many, many–one, or one–one, respectively. This diagrammatic representation of the conceptual level of a database
is sometimes called a *Bachman diagram* after its inventor, Charles Bachman. This
concept is more applicable for a network data model, although a modified version
can be used for the relational data model.

Figure 1–4 represents the conceptual model of LHUDB. It consists of six
entities and seven relationships. The six entities are the same as the six files
described in Section 1.6. Each of the seven relationships connects two of the six
entities. For example, the relationship between the entities UNIVERSITY and

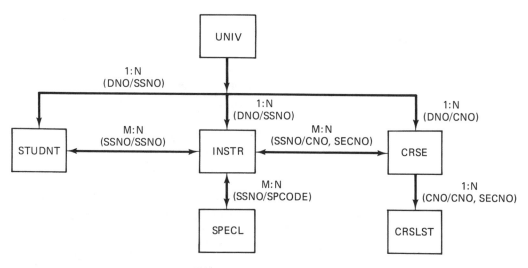

Figure 1–4 Conceptual level of LHUDB.

STUDENT is of the one–many type, because one record in UNIVERSITY corresponding to a given DNO can be associated with multiple records in STUDENT,
each record identified by a single SSNO. This corresponds to the fact that a given
department has many students. Similarly, the relationship between the entities
INSTRUCTOR and COURSE is of the many–many type implemented via the
association of SSNO as the unique identifier of an INSTRUCTOR record and the
pair (CNO, SECNO) as the unique identifier of a COURSE record. This represents
the fact that one instructor teaches many courses, and a single multisection course
has many instructors, one instructor presumably teaching one section of the
course. The remaining relationships have similar interpretations.

1.8 COMPONENTS OF A DBMS

In Section 1.2 we discussed the four functions of a database management system
(DBMS). As a software, the DBMS consists of eight basic components, some of
which are optional. Together they implement the four functions. The eight components of a DBMS are:

1. Data Definition Language (DDL)
2. Data Manipulation Language (DML)
3. Query language
4. Report writer
5. Graphics generator
6. Host Language Interface (HLI)

7. Procedural language

8. Data Dictionary (DD)

Items 5 and 7 are optional. Also, the recent trend is to provide a ninth component, called an application generator. It helps a programmer to generate applications by means of menus and prompts instead of using a formal programming language.

We now restructure the four functions of a DBMS listed in Section 1.2 as a set of seven functions so as to allow us to correlate them with the components of a DBMS in a better way:

1. Create the structure of each record according to data model selected.

2. Create the correspondence between two record types in a hierarchical or network data model.

3. Load data into database.

4. Update (i.e., add, delete, or change) records in the database.

5. Generate reports from the data in the database.

6. Maintain the integrity of data in the database.

7. Maintain data security by means of multilevel passwords. For example, a password can be used to control access to the entire database, to selected records within the database, or to selected data items within a record.

The data definition (or description) language (DDL) of a DBMS handles items 1 and 2. The data manipulation language (DML) is responsible for items 3 through 5. Thus DML handles two types of functions: updating a record and generating a report. The latter can also be done by the *query language, report writer,* or *host language interface.* A query language is a *nonprocedural fourth-generation language* that can be used to generate a report simply by specifying *what* is needed in the report. Once the contents of a report are finalized, its format can be improved by using a report writer. The latter software allows the user to print titles, footnotes, page numbers, dates, and subtotals in the report. If a report is fairly complex, a query language may not be able to produce it. In that case a host language interface can be used. Such an interface works in conjunction with the DBMS and any high-level language, such as FORTRAN, COBOL, and Pascal. The user writes a program in the appropriate language and combines it with host language interface commands to generate the report. In addition to the host language interface, some DBMS packages provide a separate procedural language of its own for producing complex reports. Optionally, a graphics package may also be provided by the DBMS to produce the graphics, such as bar charts, pie charts, and graphs, from the data in the database.

The data dictionary of the DBMS maintains the data integrity in the database and thus supports item 6. It is often called a "database about the database." It contains information on the record format, key data items, owner and member of each set in a hierarchical or network database, access privileges of users, and so on. The password protection scheme of the DBMS is responsible for data security in the database and thus supports item 7.

The query language and the report writer are often regarded as parts of the DML. Also, DDL and DML together are sometimes called the *data sublanguage* or DSL. DSL provides the interface between the external and the conceptual levels.

The discussion above describes a DBMS from a user's viewpoint. We close this section with a description of a DBMS from the system viewpoint. Internally, it consists of a *kernel* and several additional utilities that assist users to access data and allow the database administrators to monitor the use of data and maintain the database. Typical functions performed by the utilities are:

1. Start, stop, and initialize the database system.
2. Describe the shared memory area used by the kernel.
3. Monitor user activities and DBMS processes.
4. Keep a log of data updates to allow for recovery in case of a disk failure.
5. Provide a full backup capability by loading data from the database to ASCII files, and vice versa.

The DBMS takes advantage of both the architecture of the hardware where it is installed and the operating system under which it is run. For example, ORACLE installed on a VAX/VMS system can share the executable code and data among several programs by using the VAX architecture and various VMS features. ORACLE is implemented as a shared image that is mapped on the user's address space at image activation time. Since the ORACLE code is in an installed shared image, only one copy of ORACLE code stays in memory at any time, no matter how many users are running ORACLE. The shared code area is the read-only executable code section of ORACLE.

1.9 SUMMARY

In this chapter we have provided an introduction to general database concepts as a background for studying the relational database systems. We have discussed the relative advantages of a database system over a file processing system, the two most important ones being reduction or elimination of data redundancy and availability of a nonprocedural query language. An operational scenario is presented to describe the user interface with a database.

The database management system (DBMS) is complex software that implements a database and offers data independence. A DBMS uses any one of three available data models: (1) hierarchical, (2) network, and (3) relational. A relational data model is more flexible than the other two, both of which impose a rigid structure on the data format and their interrelationships. Hierarchical and network data models are suitable in a production-type environment with established applications.

The chapter next explains the three levels of a database: (1) external, (2) conceptual, and (3) internal. The DBMS provides the mappings among these levels. A user is concerned with the external level. The conceptual level involves a representation of the entire information content of the database. The internal level deals with the physical storage of data.

To illustrate these concepts, we introduce a case study involving a database for the Long Hill University, a fictitious medium-sized educational institution located in Boston. The database is named LHUDB and contains six files dealing with data on students, teachers, and courses. In the final section of the chapter we have discussed the basic components of a DBMS, such as DDL, DML, query language, host language interface, and data dictionary.

KEY WORDS

access strategy
application program
Bachman diagram
data definition language
  (DDL)
data dictionary (DD)
data independence,
  logical
data independence,
  physical
data manipulation
  language (DML)
data model, entity–
  relationship
data model, hierarchical
data model, network
data model, relational
data redundancy
data sublanguage (DSL)
database architecture
database, conceptual
  level
database, external level
database, internal level

database management
  system (DBMS)
entity
file management system
file processing system
fourth-generation
  language
graphics generator
host language
host language interface
logical record
mapping, conceptual/
  internal level
mapping, external/
  conceptual level
nonprocedural language
operating system
physical record
query language
relationship
report writer
schema
subschema
user interface

REFERENCES AND FURTHER READING

The contents of this chapter are purely introductory in nature and relate to general database concepts. Readers can find additional reading materials in any standard textbook on database systems. The following list includes five such books as suggested reading.

1. S. Atre, *Data Base: Structured Techniques for Design, Performance, and Management,* Wiley, New York, 1980.
2. C. J. Date, *An Introduction to Database Systems,* vol. I, 4th ed., Addison-Wesley, Reading, MA, 1986.
3. D. Kroenke, *Database Processing,* Science Research Associates, Chicago, 1977.
4. F. R. McFadden and J. A. Hoffer, *Data Base Management,* Benjamin-Cummings, Menlo Park, CA, 1985.
5. J. D. Ullman, *Principles of Database Systems,* Computer Science Press, Rockville, MD, 1982.

Chapter 1 of Atre [1] and of Kroenke [3], Chapters 1 and 2 of Date [2] and of McFadden and Hoffer [4], and Chapter 1 of Ullman [5] cover topics related to the present chapter. Atre's discussion of file system versus database system and data independence are quite detailed. Date's treatment of the architecture of a database (i.e., the three levels of a database) is particularly illuminating. McFadden and Hoffer have introduced a business case study in a manufacturing environment to illustrate the basic concepts of entity and relationship in a database. Ullman's treatment is more mathematical and notation oriented than are the other four references. A reader who is less mathematically inclined will have difficulty with this book. Date's book is regarded as almost a classic in database theory.

REVIEW QUESTIONS

1. Explain the difference between a file management system and a database system.
2. List the advantages of a database system to a file management system.
3. Describe the basic functions of a DBMS.
4. Define data independence. Can you enforce data independence in a file management system?
5. Describe the three types of data models used in database systems. Comment on their relative advantages and disadvantages.
6. Discuss with examples the three levels of a database and their interrelations. Also, distinguish between a logical record and a physical record.
7. Define logical data independence and physical data independence. How are these two terms related to the three levels of a database?
8. Discuss the meanings of the terms *entity* and *relationship* as used in a conceptual model.

9. Define and explain the eight components of a DBMS.
10. What is a query language? Why is it desirable that it should be nonprocedural?

EXERCISES

The following exercises relate to the LHUDB discussed in Section 1.6.

1. Suppose that you want to prepare a class list for the course "Introduction to Pascal," which has only one section. The list must contain the name, social security number, and major field of study for each student in the course. Prepare an operational scenario similar to the one in Section 1.2 describing how this list is generated.

2. Design a subschema (external level) that will produce the output of exercise 1.

3. Outline a procedure (using pseudocode or structured English) to generate the output of exercise 1 in a file management system. Assume that all six entities of LHUDB are available as data files in the system.

4. Two of the seven relationships identified in Figure 1–4 are described in Section 1.7. Provide similar explanations of the remaining five relationships in Figure 1–4.

CHAPTER 2

RELATIONAL DATA STRUCTURE

2.1 RELATIONAL DATABASE

In Sections 2.1.1 through 2.1.5 we discuss the concept of a relational database. In 1970, E. F. Codd published his epoch-making paper, "A Relational Model for Large Shared Data Banks," in *Communications of the ACM*, vol. 13, no. 6, in which he laid down the foundation of the relational database system. He introduced the terms *relation*, *attribute*, *tuple*, and *domain*. Here we define and explain each of these terms and illustrate them with examples. We use the relational database LHUDB, introduced in Chapter 1, to illustrate the concepts of this chapter.

Key attributes in a relation play a crucial role in speeding up the data retrieval process in a relational database. B-trees are normally used to implement the indexing of key attributes. These features are unique for relational databases and are explained using the LHUDB database.

2.1.1 Relation, Attribute, Tuple, and Domain

A *relation* is a two-dimensional table, often called a flat file, with the following properties:

1. Entries in the table are single valued; that is, neither repeated groups nor arrays are allowed.
2. Entries in any column are all of the same type.
3. No two rows in the table are identical.
4. Order of rows or columns is immaterial.

(1) <u>UNIV</u>

DNO	CHAR (2)
DNAME	CHAR(25)
DHEAD	CHAR(20)

(2) <u>INSTR</u>

INAME	CHAR(20)
IDEG	CHAR(10)
SPCODE	INT(2)
RANK	CHAR(10)
SSNO	INT(9)
DNO	CHAR(2)

(3) <u>STUDNT</u>

SNAME	CHAR(20)
SSNO	INT(9)
MAJOR	CHAR(15)
DEGREE	CHAR(10)
ADVSR	CHAR(20)
DNO	CHAR(2)
COLREG	CHAR(15)

(4) <u>CRSE</u>

CNO	CHAR(5)
CNAME	CHAR(20)
INAME	CHAR(20)
DNO	CHAR(2)
SECNO	INT(2)

(5) <u>CRSLST</u>

CNO	CHAR(5)
SECNO	INT(2)
SID	INT(9)
GRADE	CHAR(2)
OFRNG	CHAR(8)

(6) <u>SPECL</u>

SPCODE	INT(2)
SPNAME	CHAR(20)

Figure 2–1 Data structure of LHUDB.

Each column of a relation is called an *attribute* and each row is called a *tuple*. If a relation has *n* attributes, each of its rows is an *n*-tuple. Such a relation is called an *n-ary relation* and *n* is said to be the *degree* or *arity* of the relation. Currently, the following synonyms are accepted in the database terminology:

1. *Relation* is synonymous with *table* and *flat file*.
2. *Tuple* is synonymous with *row* and *record*.
3. *Attribute* is synonymous with *column*, *field*, and *data element*.

Finally, a *domain* is a pool of values from which an attribute takes its values. Thus a domain consists of values that are all of the same type—the data type of the attribute. The elementts of a domain are atomic in nature in that they are indecomposable as far as the relation is concerned.

We now illustrate the foregoing concepts using the database LHUDB introduced in Section 1.6. Figure 2–1 contains the data structure of LHUDB. Figure 2–2 shows sample data values in the database.

UNIV

DNO	DNAME	DHEAD
EN	English	Lee Kunkel
CS	Computer Science	Albert Roby
MA	Mathematics	Deb Kumar Roy
HS	History	Cathy Doucette
EE	Electrical Engineering	Raj Chandra Mittra

INSTR (shown in two parts)

INAME	IDEG	SPCODE
Lee Kunkel	BA,MA,PhD	4
Albert Roby	BS,MS,PhD	2
Deb Kumar Roy	BS,MS,PhD	5
Cathy Doucette	MA,PhD	6
Raj Chandra Mittra	BA,MSc,PhD	10
Tom Clark	BA,MA	5
Marcia Brown	BA,BS,MS	2
Susan Woodsmith	MA,MS,PhD	3
Brady Jackson	MA,DLitt	15
Jack Adams	BA,PhD	1

Figure 2–2 Data values in LHUDB.

INSTR (INAME repeated for continuity)

INAME	RANK	SSNO	DNO
Lee Kunkel	Professor	123456789	EN
Albert Roby	Professor	234567891	CS
Deb Kumar Roy	AssocProf	345678912	MA
Cathy Doucette	AssocProf	456789123	HS
Raj Chandra Mittra	Professor	567891234	EE
Tom Clark	AsstProf	678912345	MA
Marcia Brown	Instructor	789123456	CS
Susan Woodsmith	AsstProf	891234567	PH
Brady Jackson	Professor	912345678	RL
Jack Adams	AssocProf	123456798	CS

STUDNT (shown in two parts)

SNAME	SSNO	MAJOR	DEGREE
Roger Brown Smith	556123959	Biology	BS
Cindy Logan	561239595	Computer Science	BS
Benjamin Johnson	612395999	NDEG	NONE
Steve Levin	126939555		BA
Tom Jones	939625155	Mathematics	MS
Beverly Black	512559369	English	PhD

STUDNT (SNAME repeated for continuity)

SNAME	ADVSR	DNO	COLREG
Roger Brown Smith	Jack Adams	BI	Arts & Sci.
Cindy Logan	Deb Kumar Roy	MA	Arts & Sci.
Benjamin Johnson		BA	Business
Steve Levin	Lee Kunkel	EN	Arts & Sci.
Tom Jones	Raj Chandra Mittra	EE	Engineering
Beverly Black	Lee Kunkel	EN	Arts & Sci.

CRSE

CNO	CNAME	INAME	DNO	SECNO
CS225	Assembler Language	Marcia Brown	CS	02
CS547	Discrete Mathematics	Deb Kumar Roy	CS	01
MA423	Differential Geometry	Tom Clark	MA	04

Figure 2–2 (continued)

CNO	CNAME	INAME	DNO	SECNO
EN104	English Composition	Staff	EN	04
RL712	Comparative Religion	Brady Jackson	RL	01
CS761	Expert Systems	Albert Roby	CS	03
EC102	Macroeconomics	Staff	EC	06
EN604	Romanticism	Lee Kunkel	EN	01
HS525	Middle East	Cathy Doucette	HS	02
EE202	Microcomputing	Staff	EE	04
MA611	Algebraic Topology	Tom Clark	MA	01
CS579	Database Systems	Marcia Brown	CS	02
BI104	Biology Concepts	Staff	BI	07

CRSLST

CNO	SECNO	SID	GRADE	OFRNG
CS579	02	561239595	A	Spring 87
CS579	02	612395955	B-	Spring 87
CS579	02	900621515	B+	Spring 87
CS579	02	556123959	I	Spring 87
MA611	01	556123959	C	Fall 86
MA611	01	939625155	A	Fall 86
MA611	01	512559369	C+	Fall 86
MA611	01	612395955	W	Fall 86

SPECL

SPCODE	SPNAME
1	Information Systems
2	Database Systems
3	Kant Doctrine
4	Romantic Literature
5	Differential Geometry
6	Mideast History
7	Topology
8	Automated Reasoning
9	Expert System
10	Microelectronics
11	English Drama
12	Shakespeare
13	Indian History
14	Decision Support Systems
15	Comparative Religion

Figure 2–2   (continued)

The domain of the attribute DNO, for example, is a set of valid department designators such as CS (computer science), EN (English), HS (history), EE (electrical engineering), MA (mathematics), and so on, from which DNO takes its values. This domain may consist of all two-character symbols ($26 \times 26 = 676$ in all) or only a subset of such symbols that are declared as valid department numbers. UNIV, INSTR, STUDENT, CRSE, CRSLST, and SPECL are 3-ary (or ternary), 6-ary, 7-ary, 5-ary, 5-ary, and binary relations, respectively. Finally, a *relational database* is a database in which data are stored as relations. Consequently, we regard LHUDB as a relational database.

From a mathematical standpoint, an n-ary relation R defined on n sets S_1, $S_2, \ldots, S_n$ is described as follows:

R is a subset of the Cartesian product $S_1 \times S_2 \times \cdots \times S_n$.
An n-tuple $(s_1, \ldots, s_n) \in R$ if and only if $s_i \in S_i$, $i = 1, \ldots, n$; and $(s_1, \ldots, s_n)$ is a row in the matrix representation of R.

Thus

$R \subset S_1 \times \cdots \times S_n$, and $S_1, \ldots, S_n$ are called the domains of R.

We can see that the foregoing definition of an n-ary relation indeed matches the definition of a relation as used in the context of a relational database. For example, let us take $n = 3$ and let S_1, S_2, and S_3 be the three distinct sets of admissible values of DNO, DNAME, and DHEAD, respectively. Then S_1, S_2, and S_3 are the domains of the 3-ary relation UNIV.

A row of UNIV represents a 3-tuple of the form (s_1, s_2, s_3), say, where

$s_1 \in$ domain of DNO (i.e., S_1)

$s_2 \in$ domain of DNAME (i.e., S_2)

$s_3 \in$ domain of DHEAD (i.e., S_3)

In other words, as a 3-ary relation UNIV is a subset of the Cartesian product $S_1 \times S_2 \times S_3$.

2.1.2 External and Conceptual Levels

In Chapter 1 we discussed the external and conceptual levels of a database in general. These definitions apply to a relational database in particular. For example, a user can ask the following questions of LHUDB:

1. Print a list of all instructor names, ranks, and their respective departments.
2. Print a list of the names of all students of the mathematics department with their respective advisors and degrees sought.
3. For a given course, print a list of its student names, the instructor name, the section number, and the semester.

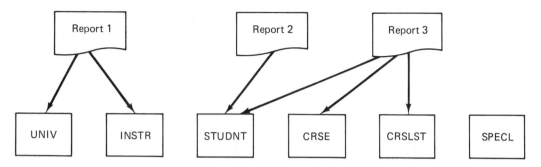

Figure 2–3 External and conceptual levels of LHUDB.

Each of these reports involves an external level of LHUDB. Report 1 uses the relations INSTR and UNIV; report 2 uses the relation STUDNT; and report 3 uses the relations CRSLST, STUDNT, and CRSE. The situation is represented graphically in Figure 2–3. The top row in the diagram represents the three external levels or user views, corresponding to reports 1, 2, and 3.

The bottom row is the conceptual level of LHUDB and corresponds to the data structure of Figure 2–1. The arrows connecting the two levels embody the external/conceptual-level mappings as discussed in Chapter 1. These are many–one mappings since they connect the three external levels (i.e., reports 1, 2, and 3) to the single conceptual level of LHUDB. Theoretically, there can be any number of external levels, one corresponding to each user view of LHUDB.

2.1.3 Internal Level

The internal level involves physical storage of the relations of the relational database, as discussed in Chapter 1. For example, the six relations of LHUDB are stored as six disk files at the internal level, as shown in Figure 2–4. The top row

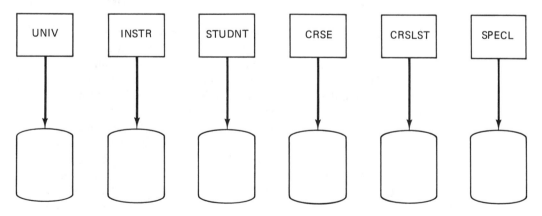

Figure 2–4 Internal level of LHUDB.

represents the six relations of LHUDB at the conceptual level, and the bottom row represents the corresponding six disk files at the internal level. The arrows represent the one–one mapping between the conceptual and internal levels.

The process of database access concerns all three levels (see Section 1.5). In this section we give an overview of how a specific record is accessed and retrieved from the internal level via DBMS. The process takes place as follows (see Figure 2–5):

1. In consequence of a user query the DBMS requests a stored record from the internal level.
2. The file manager receives the request and asks for the stored page containing the record.
3. As a result of the file manager's request, the disk manager determines the physical location of the desired page on the disk and issues the necessary disk I/O operation.
4. Data read from the disk are then returned to the disk manager.
5. The disk manager returns the storage page to the file manager.
6. Finally, the file manager returns the stored record to the DBMS.

The file manager and the disk manager form a part of the operating system that handles the transfer of records from auxiliary storage to the memory. The database access is needed for the two basic data manipulation processes of data retrieval and update. The concepts of key attributes and indexing are crucial in this respect.

2.1.4 Key Attributes and Indexing

One or more attributes in a relation are designated as *key* if they uniquely determine a tuple in the relation. For example, the attribute DNO in the relation UNIV is a key attribute because a given value of DNO uniquely determines a tuple in UNIV.

When an attribute in a relation is declared as a key, a separate *index file* is created at the internal level of the database. This file is separate from the data file that stores the actual data of the relation. Each record in the index file consists of two fields: a data value of the key and a pointer to the record of the data file that contains the actual data values corresponding to the tuple determined by the value of the key. As an example, suppose that DNO is declared as a key in UNIV. Then the index file of DNO consists of five records, corresponding to the five tuples of UNIV. Each record has two fields: the value of DNO (e.g., CS, EE, EN, etc.) and a pointer to the tuple of UNIV that is uniquely identified by the specific value of DNO. In order to retrieve a record in UNIV corresponding to the value DNO = 'CS', say, first a binary search is made of the index file of DNO to obtain the pointer to the tuple in UNIV for which DNO = 'CS', and

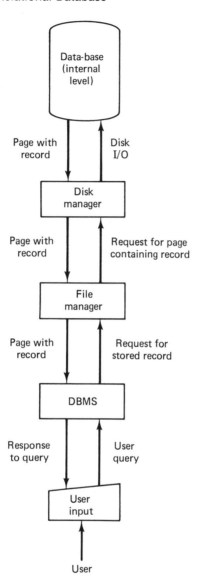

Figure 2–5 Schematic of query processing.

then a direct search is made of the data file of UNIV to retrieve that tuple. The data file for UNIV is said to be *indexed by* the index file for DNO.

The fundamental advantage of an index is that it speeds up retrievals, because a sequential search of the data file for a relation is normally much slower than the two-step search of the index file and the data file for a relation. However, to achieve this efficiency, it is necessary to keep the index file sorted by the index field. Otherwise, the binary search of the index file will fail. Therefore, each time the indexed relation is updated, its index file must be updated and then sorted by the key attribute value. This slows down the update process. Thus when an attribute in a relation is designated as a key, a trade-off issue is involved: What is more important, quicker retrieval based on the value of the key attribute at the cost of an update overhead involved in providing that quicker retrieval, or a slower sequential search without any update overhead? In general, it is better not to declare one or more attributes in a relation as key until it is determined that frequent retrievals will be made using that or those attributes.

2.1.5 B-Trees

The index file for a relation with a very large number of tuples becomes very large when there is a one-to-one correspondence between the records of the index file and those of the data file. To alleviate this problem, multilevel indices are created. Here the index file itself is regarded as a data file, and an index file is built to the first index file. This process can be carried to as many levels as desired, but rarely do we need more than three levels of indexing. This technique is known as building a multilevel or *tree-structured* index. A *B-tree* is a particular type of tree-structured index, where "B" stands for "balanced." This means that in a B-tree the terminal nodes are always at the same distance from the root node of the tree.

As an example, suppose that the relation UNIV in Figure 2–2 contains 100 tuples. Let us design a three-level B-tree for the 100 distinct values of the key attribute DNO as shown in Figure 2–6. The retrieval of a tuple in DEPT for which DNO = 'CS', say, is done as follows. The system starts by searching the top level of the B-tree. Since CS < LI, it follows the leftmost pointer (i.e., the one

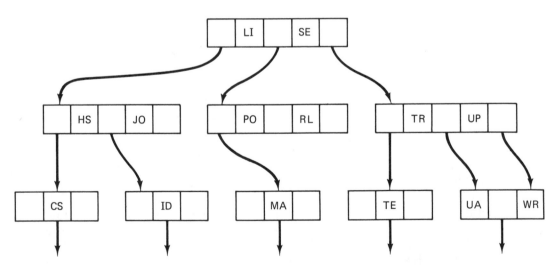

Figure 2–6 B-tree for DNO in UNIV.

originating to the left of LI) and moves to the second level. Here noting that CS < HS, the system follows the pointer to the left of HS and moves to the bottom level. It now finds the pointer pointing to the record for which DNO = 'CS'. The set of arrows originating at the bottom level and pointing downward direct to the actual data values stored in the data files.

In a B-tree all but the terminal nodes represent index sets that are called *nondense* because they are not in a one-to-one correspondence with the data values. The index sets (sometimes called sequence sets) at the terminal nodes are called *dense*. Successive binary searches of the B-tree lead to the exact location of the tuple to be retrieved.

It is true that there is no single storage structure that is optimal for all applications. However, B-trees seem to outperform other mechanisms. As a result, most relational database systems support B-tree as their principal form of storage structure at the internal level, and several support no other.

A problem with a tree-structured index is that insertions and deletions of tuple from relations can cause the tree to become unbalanced. A tree is *unbalanced* when the terminal nodes of the tree are at different distances from the root node. Since searching a tree involves a disk access for every node visited, search times can become very unpredictable in an unbalanced tree. The primary advantage of a B-tree is that the B-tree insertion and deletion algorithms guarantee that the tree will always be balanced. Besides B-trees the techniques of hashing and pointer chains are also used. (See Date [2, pp. 67–75] and Ullman [8, pp. 24–30] for details.)

2.2 RELATIONAL DBMS

In a relational database the data are modeled in the form of relations that are processed by performing logical operations on attributes. These operations are expressed in terms of relational algebra or relational calculus (see Chapters 3 and 4). All such operations result in a collection of rows with selected attributes and values. Some of these collections are new relations created by the relational algebra or calculus commands. Any database management system that can access a relational database, generate responses to ad hoc queries and preformatted reports by using relational algebra or calculus, and perform routine update operations is called a *relational DBMS*. The definition of a relational DBMS is thus a special case of that for a general DBMS. As such it has the standard components, as in the case for a general DBMS (see Section 1.8):

1. Data Definition Language (DDL)
2. Data Manipulation Language (DML)
3. Query language, report writer, and graphics generator
4. Host Language Interface (HLI)
5. Data Dictionary (DD)

Different relational DBMSs have different sets of commands to perform the creation and update of the relational database and to retrieve data from the database. The exact forms of these commands depend on the underlying theory (i.e., relational algebra or relational calculus). Typically, the data retrieval is done by specifying a set of selection criteria that extract the designated set of rows and columns from the relation. These criteria do not involve any specification of how the desired data should be extracted so as to ensure optimization. The relational DBMS determines an optimal way to retrieve data by using its query optimization routines (see Chapter 5).

2.3 SYSTEM R: START OF A RELATIONAL DBMS

In this section we take a glimpse into System R, the first relational DBMS developed during 1974–1979 at the IBM San Jose Research Laboratory. Modeled after the concept introduced by Codd this system was a prototype of the later relational DBMS packages. As developed by IBM, System R runs on IBM 370 under a VM/CMS or MVS operating system. The end-user access language for System R is SQL, *Structured Query Language*. The next three subsections discuss the architecture of System R, an operational scenario to illustrate how this DBMS works to process users' queries, and the public and private segments in System R.

2.3.1 Architecture of System R

System R provides a full set of capabilities for database management. It supports multiple users concurrently accessing data and has complete facilities for transaction backout and system recovery. It can be accessed through either of two interfaces:

1. Stand-alone interface for ad hoc queries implemented via the *user-friendly interface* (UFI).
2. Direct interface by two host languages, PL/I and COBOL, implemented via the *relational data system* (RDS). However, RDS also supports queries entered through UFI.

RDS consists of two distinct subsystems: (1) a precompiler, called XPREP, and (2) an execution system, called XRDI. XPREP is used to precompile host language programs and install them as "canned programs" under System R. XRDI controls the execution of these canned programs and also executes SQL statements entered by ad hoc terminal users. RDS performs four basic functions:

1. Parsing
2. Authorization checking
3. Access path selection
4. Translation from SQL to a System 370 machine language

An ad hoc user of System R is supported by UFI, which controls dialogue management and the formatting of the display terminal for the user. The UFI has an access module of its own, but its access module is not complete because the purpose of UFI is to execute SQL statements that are not known in advance. When a user enters an ad hoc SQL statement, UFI passes the statement to XRDI by means of special 'PREPARE' and 'EXECUTE' calls. The effect of these calls is to cause a new "section" of the access module of UFI to be dynamically generated for the new statement. The dynamically generated part of the access module contains machine-language code and is in every way indistinguishable from the parts that were generated by the precompiler.

Finally, we discuss the *research storage system* (RSS), which is a low-level DBMS providing the underlying support for System R. The RSS supports the *research storage interface* (RSI), which provides simple one-record-at-a-time operators on base tables (i.e., relations). Operators are also supported for data recovery, transaction management, and data definition. Calls to the RSI require explicit use of data areas called segments and access paths called indices and links, along with the use of RSS-generated numeric identifiers for data segments, tables, access paths, and records. The RDS handles the selection of efficient access paths to optimize its operations, and maps symbolic table names to their internal RSS identifiers. The RSI is a navigational interface and supports an object called a *scan* which can move from record to record along a specified access path.

To faciliate gradual database integration and tuning of access paths, the RSS permits new stored tables or new indices to be created at any time, or existing ones destroyed, without quiescing the system and without dumping and relocating the data. One can also add new fields to existing tables, or add or delete pointer chain paths across existing tables. This facility, coupled with the ability to retrieve any subset of fields in a record, provides a degree of data independence at a low level of the system, since existing access modules that execute RSI operations on records will be unaffected by the addition of new fields or access paths.

The hierarchical structure of System R is shown in Figure 2–7. Figure 2–8 correlates the subsystems of System R with the three levels of a DBMS. Finally, Figure 2–9 gives a typical user's view of System R.

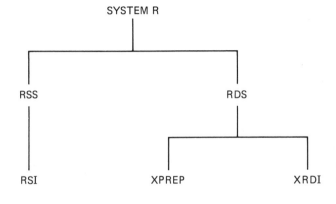

Figure 2–7 Hierarchical structure of System R.

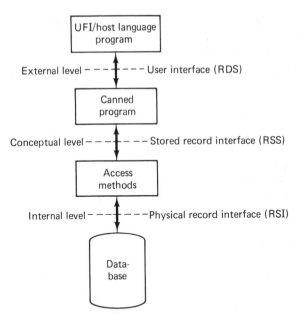

External level $--\dashv---$ User interface (RDS)

Conceptual level $---\dashv---$ Stored record interface (RSS)

Internal level $---\dashv---$ Physical record interface (RSI)

Figure 2–8 Three levels of System R.

Figure 2–8 shows that the external, conceptual, and internal levels of System R are correlated with the subsystems RDS, RSS, and RSI of System R, respectively. Figure 2–9 shows a hypothetical situation where a user requests three queries. The first accesses base table 1 (i.e., relation 1) directly. The second query involves view V1, which uses attributes from base tables 1 and 3. The third query

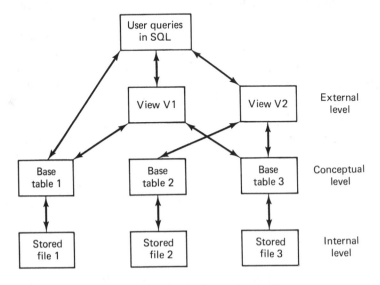

Figure 2–9 User's view of System R.

similarly accesses base tables 2 and 3 via view V2. Each base table is stored separately as a disk file.

2.3.2 Operational Scenario

Let us assume that a user (either an end user or a programmer) has submitted a program P, say, to be processed by System R. The program contains only interactive SQL statements if it is an end-user query, or embedded SQL statements with host language commands if it is an application program. After the user enters P into System R, the following sequence of actions takes place:

1. P requests one or more records to be retrieved from the database.
2. System R invokes the RDS-called precompiler XPREP (see Figure 2–7) to compile the SQL statements.
3. Precompiler scans P and locates the embedded SQL statements.
4. For each SQL statement, the precompiler selects the optimal access path to implement that statement by the process known as optimization. Such access paths are available at RSI.
5. Precompiler generates a System/370 machine language routine, including calls to the RSS to implement the SQL statements. The set of all such routines constitutes the *access module* for P.
6. The precompiler replaces each of the original embedded SQL statements by an ordinary statement like XRDI.
7. The modified program P is now compiled in the normal way to produce the object program P.
8. The Runtime Control System (XRDI) now takes over and executes the object program P. For each CALL XRDI statement it invokes the access module for P and then control passes to RSS.
9. Various RSS and RSI operations perform the actions required by source program P.
10. Finally, System R produces the report at the user's area.

2.3.3 Segments in System R

System R uses segments to store data files and index files at the internal level. The stored database is logically divided into a set of disjoint *segments*. Each segment consists of an integral number of 4096-byte pages (the number of pages in a given segment varies dynamically). The page is the unit of transfer between database and memory. When a page is required from the database, the RSS fetches it into a slot within a memory buffer that is shared among all current users and returns the address of that slot to the component requesting the page. Using a single fixed-size page as the unit for all input/output simplifies buffer management and provides a clean interface for device independence.

Segments provide a mechanism for controlling the allocation of storage and the sharing of data among users. Any given base table is wholly contained within a single segment; any indices on that base table are also contained in that segment. However, a given segment may contain several base tables (plus their indices).

Segments in System R are of three types: public, private, and temporary. A *public segment* contains shared data that can be accessed simultaneously by multiple users. A *private segment* contains data that can be used by only one user at a time or data that are not shared at all. A *temporary segment* contains data that cannot be shared and are not recoverable in the event of system failure. The overhead associated with full support of concurrent sharing, needed for public data, can be avoided for private and temporary data (which do not require such support). Note, however, that the type of segment is fixed at the time of system installation and cannot be changed.

Each segment has a predetermined maximum size (usually very large), but at any given time occupies only as much physical storage as it actually needs for the data objects it currently contains. Pages are allocated to segments as necessary (e.g., when a table grows sufficiently large) and are released when the segment shrinks again (e.g., when an index is dropped). A page map is maintained for each segment, giving the physical location in secondary storage of each page currently allocated to the segment.

At the RSI, segments are identified by a numeric *segment identifier*. Pages are identified by page numbers within segment. At the time of creation of a relation, its contents go into a private segment belonging to the user creating the relation unless the user declares the relation to be available in a public segment.

2.4 DDL AND DML IN RELATIONAL DBMS

In this section we discuss the two primary functions of a relational DBMS:

1. To create the structure of a relation
2. To load data into a relation and to retrieve data therefrom

These two tasks are handled by the data definition language (DDL) and the data manipulation language (DML) of the DBMS, respectively. DDL and DML perform their functions via a set of commands supported by the DBMS. Sections 2.4.1, 2.4.2, and 2.4.3 cover, respectively, the DDL, DML, and built-in group functions. Examples of DDL amd DML commands are given using SQL (Structured Query Language) of ORACLE, a relationall DBMS. In Section 2.4.4 we discuss procedural DMLs offered by some DBMS packages.

2.4.1 Functions and Examples of DDL

A relational DBMS allows a dynamic definition of relations. This means that the user can define the relation structure and later modify it interactively. This is relatively easy to perform because there are no physical links among the relations. A typical DDL command provides the following information on the relation:

1. Name of the relation
2. Name of each attribute of a relation
3. Characteristic and length of each attribute of the relation, such as a two-digit integer or a character string of length 15

Various data types are supported, such as character, integer, real or floating point, date, and so on. In addition, special features such as NOT NULL may be used to indicate that an attribute cannot take null values.

The *data definition language* (DDL) consists of a set of commands that allow the user to define and create relations. The DBMS compiles the DDL commands to generate a set of disk files that are stored in a special file called the *data dictionary*. The latter is often described as "database about the database," since it contains all relevant information about the structure and contents of the database.

The interactive nature of a DDL depends on the individual DBMS. Generally, the user can enter the DDL commands interactively via a terminal. However, System 1022 on DEC-10 and System 1032 on VAX, both inverted file DBMS packages from Software House in Cambridge, require that the structure of each relation be coded and stored in a separate file, called a .DMD file, and then that a LOAD command be used to create the relation using the .DMD file already created with a text editor.

As an example of interactive DDL, we list below the commands from ORACLE, a relational DBMS marketed by Oracle Corporation. Each relation is called a *table* and the following three commands belong to DDL:

1. CREATE TABLE: adds a table to the database
2. ALTER TABLE: modifies an existing attribute or adds a new attribute to an existing table
3. DROP TABLE: removes a table from the database

Data can be of the following types:

1. CHAR: includes digits 0 to 9, letters A to Z (both upper and lower case), and special symbols such as $+$, $-$, %, $, and &
2. NUMBER: includes digits 0 to 9, $+$, $-$, and a decimal point
3. DATE: includes valid dates from January 1, 4712 B.C. to December 31, 4711 A.D.

Optionally, the user may specify a *maximum length* for CHAR and NUMBER columns. Maximum length means the maximum number of characters to be

```
SQL> CREATE TABLE UNIV
  2      (DNO CHAR(2),
  3       DNAME CHAR(25),
  4       DHEAD CHAR(20));

Table created.

SQL> CREATE TABLE INSTR
  2      (INAME CHAR(20),
  3       IDEG CHAR(10),
  4       SPCODE NUMBER(2) NOT NULL,
  5       RANK CHAR(10),
  6       SSNO NUMBER(9) NOT NULL,
  7       DNO CHAR(2));

Table created.
```

Figure 2–10   Example of ORACLE's SQL/DDL commands.

allowed in a field in a CHAR column, or the maximum number of digits allowed in a field in a NUMBER column. For example:

1. CHAR(12): character field with a maximum of 12 characters
2. NUMBER(4): numeric field with a maximum of four digits
3. NUMBER(7,2): numeric field with a maximum of seven digits, two of which are to the right of the decimal point

If the user specifies a maximum length, ORACLE will ensure that no one will put a value in that field that exceeds the specified maximum. If the user does not specify a maximum length for NUMBER fields, ORACLE will assign a default maximum length of 22 digits.

ORACLE uses only the minimum necessary space to hold each data field and does not waste storage by reserving space for the maximum number of characters for each field. For example, if the maximum length of a name field is 12, ORACLE uses five characters of storage space to store a name JONES, say. NULL entries in fields occupy no storage space at all. As an example, the ORACLE DDL statements to create the relations UNIV and INSTR in LHUDB (see Figure 2–1) are given in Figure 2–10.

2.4.2 Functions and Examples of DML

The *data manipulation language* (DML) implements the techniques to process the data in the database. DML performs the following functions:

1. Retrieves data from one or more relations
2. Loads data into relations after they have been created with DDL commands
3. Deletes or changes data currently existing in the relations

Function 1 is called *retrieval*, and functions 2 and 3 are called *update*. The DML enables the user to deal with the data in the relations in logical terms instead of in physical terms. This means that the user need not know how and where the data are stored at the interval level. This preserves the independence of programs from the physical representation of the database.

Ideally, a DML should have the following features:

1. *Simplicity*. Queries can be formulated easily and concisely
2. *Completeness*. Most queries need no program in host language
3. *Nonprocedurality*. User specifies only *what* data are wanted, not *how* to retrieve those data.
4. *Data independence*. User commands provide only *logical* sequence, not the explicit access paths such as indices or physical sequences
5. *Ease of extension*. Retrieval power is extended by built-in group functions (see Section 2.4.3)
6. *Support for high-level language*. Special application programs can be written to generate reports not available via DML.

(a) Retrieval operations.   In a *retrieval operation* the user specifies one or more criteria for selecting the desired data from the database. The selection criteria can involve one or more relations. There are two types of retrieval: (1) simple and (2) qualified. Under *simple retrieval*, the entire contents of a relation are retrieved. Under *qualified retrieval*, only those data are retrieved that match the selection criteria. Qualified retrieval has the following variations:

1. Selection from one relation
2. Result of the selection sorted in ascending or descending order by one or more attributes
3. Selection involving one or more relations linked via common attributes
4. Selection using logical descriptors such as ANY, BETWEEN, CONTAINS, and IN
5. Selection using arithmetic comparison operations, such as $>$, $<$, GT, NE, and $=$
6. Selection using special clauses, such as DISTINCT, GROUP BY, and HAVING

Figure 2–11 gives a few examples of ORACLE's SQL/DML retrieval commands using two relations, UNIV and INSTR, in LHUDB.

```
SQL> SELECT * FROM UNIV;
```

DN DNAME	DHEAD
EN English	Lee Kunkel
CS Computer Science	Albert Roby
MA Mathematics	Deb Kumar Roy
HS History	Cathy Doucette
EE Electrical Engineering	Raj Chandra Mittra

```
SQL> SELECT * FROM INSTR;
```

INAME	IDEG	SPCODE	RANK	SSNO	DN
Lee Kunkel	BA,MA,PhD	4	Professor	123456789	EN
Albert Roby	BS,MS,PhD	2	Professor	234567891	CS
Deb Kumar Roy	BS,MS,PhD	5	AssocProf	345678912	MA
Cathy Doucette	MA,PhD	6	AssocProf	456789123	HS
Raj Chandra Mittra	BA,MSc,PhD	10	Professor	567891234	EE
Tom Clark	BA,MA	5	AsstProf	678912345	MA
Marcia Brown	BA,BS,MS	2	Instructor	789123456	CS
Susan Woodsmith	MA,MS,PhD	3	AsstProf	891234567	PH
Brady Jackson	MA,DLitt	15	Professor	912345678	RL
Jack Adams	BA,PhD	1	AssocProf	123457698	CS

```
10 records selected.


SQL> SELECT DNAME, DHEAD FROM UNIV
  2      WHERE DNO BETWEEN 'A' AND 'K';
```

DNAME	DHEAD
English	Lee Kunkel
Computer Science	Albert Roby
History	Cathy Doucette
Electrical Engineering	Raj Chandra Mittra

```
SQL> SELECT INAME, IDEG, RANK FROM INSTR
  2      WHERE SSNO  < 666666000;
```

Figure 2–11 Example of ORACLE's SQL/DML commands for retrieval.

INAME	IDEG	RANK
Lee Kunkel	BA,MA,PhD	Professor
Albert Roby	BS,MS,PhD	Professor
Deb Kumar Roy	BS,MS,PhD	AssocProf
Cathy Doucette	MA,PhD	AssocProf
Raj Chandra Mittra	BA,MSc,PhD	Professor
Jack Adams	BA,PhD	AssocProf

6 records selected.


```
SQL> SELECT INAME, IDG, DNO FROM INSTR
  2       WHERE RANK IN ('AsstProf', 'Professor');
```

INAME	IDEG	DN
Lee Kunkel	BA,MA,PhD	EN
Albert Roby	BS,MS,PhD	CS
Raj Chandra Mittra	BA,MSc,PhD	EE
Tom Clark	BA,MA	MA
Susan Woodsmith	MA,MS,PhD	PH
Brady Jackson	MA,DLitt	RL

6 records selected.

Figure 2–11 (continued)

(b) Update operations.   An *update operation* inserts a new row or deletes an existing row or changes an existing row in a relation. The relation must already exist before any update operation can take place. The following variations are possible in an update operation:

1. Single-row update
2. Multiple-row update
3. Update with a subquery
4. Multiple-relation update
5. Single-row insertion
6. Multiple-row insertion
7. Single-row deletion
8. Multiple-row deletion
9. Multiple row and multiple relation deletion

As an example, Oracle provides three basic DML commands for update:

1. INSERT: adds a row to a relation
2. UPDATE: changes a value stored in a row
3. DELETE: removes a row from a relation

Figure 2–12 gives ORACLE's INSERT command to store some of the records in UNIV and INSTR, as listed in Figure 2–2. If we want to remove the record of department 'EN', say, we issue the following command:

```
DELETE FROM UNIV WHERE DNO = 'EN';
```

Finally, suppose we want to change the rank of Marcia Brown from instructor to assistant professor. The following command performs that function:

```
UPDATE INSTR SET RANK = 'AsstProf'
        WHERE SSNO = 789123456;
```

```
SQL> insert into univ values
   2      ('CS','Computer Science','Albert Roby');
commit complete

1 record created.

SQL> insert into univ values
   2      ('MA','Mathematics','Deb Kumar Roy');
commit complete

1 record created.

SQL> insert into instr values
   2      ('Deb Kumar Roy','BS,MS,PhD',5,'AssocProf',345678912,'Ma');
commit complete

1 record created.

SQL> insert into instr values
   2      ('Cathy Doucette','MA,PhD',6,'AssocProf',456789123,'HS');
commit complete

1 record created.
```

Figure 2–12 Example of ORACLE's SQL/DML INSERT command.

2.4.3 Built-in Group Functions

A *built-in group function* is a command available in the DBMS to perform some limited arithmetic or statistical functions on a group of rows. For instance, an AVG function computes the average value of a numeric attribute over an entire relation or over a set of selected rows in the relation. Since such functions work on a group of rows rather than a single row, they are often called *group functions*.

Some of the standard built-in arithmetic group functions supported by ORACLE DML are:

1. AVG: computes the average value
2. SUM: computes the total value
3. MIN: finds the minimum value
4. MAX: finds the maximum value
5. COUNT: counts the number of values.

Two standard statistical functions supported by some DBMSs are:

1. MEAN: computes the arithmetic mean of a numeric attribute's values; same as AVG function mentioned earlier
2. STDEV: computes the standard deviation of a numeric attribute's values

For example, System 1022 on DEC-10 and System 1032 on VAX-11 support MEAN and STDEV. An example of ORACLE's built-in COUNT function is

```
SELECT COUNT(INAME) FROM INSTR WHERE DNO = 'CS';
```

This command returns the total number of instructors in the computer science department.

2.4.4 Procedural DML

Sometimes the DML includes a procedural programming language in order to generate more complex reports that cannot be produced by the nonprocedural DML commands. A procedural DML supports the three standard features of any high-level programming language:

1. *Assignment:* implemented via LET or its equivalent and used for initializing or declaring variables or defining formulas
2. *Decision:* implemented via IF-THEN-ELSE commands and used for testing some decision criteria
3. *Repetition:* implemented via DO WHILE commands and used for executing loops

To use the procedural DML, the user prepares a command file, similar to a program file, containing the procedural DML commands, compiles it, and then executes it to produce the reports. Once created, the command file can be stored for use at any later time.

For example, System 1022 on DEC-10 and System 1032 on VAX-11 support DPL (Data Programming Language) as procedural DMLs. UNIFY offers ACCELL IDS as a procedural DML, although the vendor of UNIFY claims that ACCELL IDS is nonprocedural in nature. It is difficult to accept the latter claim since ACCELL IDS uses all three features of a procedural language mentioned above. ORACLE provides in version 6.0 PL/SQL, a procedural DML that includes SQL commands.

2.5 QUERY LANGUAGE, REPORT WRITER, AND GRAPHICS GENERATOR

In this section we discuss an important subset of the DML, called the *query language*. Its primary use is to handle ad hoc queries from end users. The report writer and the graphics generator provide additional capabilities to produce decent-looking reports and to generate business graphics such as bar charts, pie charts, and line graphs. In Sections 2.5.1, 2.5.2, and 2.5.3 we discuss query language, report writer, and graphics generator, respectively.

2.5.1 Query Language

In this section we provide only an overview of the query language. This topic is discussed more thoroughly in Chapter 5. The DDL and DML together are often called the *data sublanguage* or DSL. The query language is a subset of the DSL. Technically, a query language should be used to handle ad hoc queries only. However, conventionally it includes both DDL and DML commands. SQL has been declared as the industry standard for nonprocedural query languages. ORACLE was the first commercially available relational DBMS supporting SQL. Due to the widespread use of SQL, more and more non-SQL relational DBMSs are now supporting SQL. System R developed by IBM (see Section 2.3) was the first relational DBMS supporting SQL.

The user of a query language, which is nonprocedural by definition, provides selection criteria to define the query. These criteria contain three basic information:

1. Name(s) of attribute(s) to be selected
2. Name(s) of relation(s) containing the(se) attribute(s)
3. Condition(s) of selection

```
SQL> SELECT INAME, RANK FROM INSTR
  2      WHERE INAME IN
  3          (SELECT DHEAD FROM UNIV);
```

INAME   RANK
_____

Albert Roby   Professor
Cathy Doucette   AssocProf
Deb Kumar Roy   AssocProf
Lee Kunkel   Professor
Raj Chandra Mittra   Professor

Figure 2–13   Example of nested subquery in ORACLE's SQL.

The standard form of a query in SQL is

```
SELECT attribute(s) FROM relation(s) WHERE condition(s)
```

Figure 2–11 contains several examples of SQL queries.

A query may contain more than one selection expression. Such queries are said to contain nested subqueries, where an attribute in one level of nesting is described in the next level, and so on. The execution of the nested subquery starts with the innermost selection criterion and expands outward until the entire query is processed. Any level of nesting is allowed. Figure 2–13 gives an example of a nested subquery using ORACLE's SQL.

The query language can be used in two interfaces:

1. *Interactive*. The user enters the query language statement, it is processed interactively, and the result is displayed or printed at the terminal.

2. *Host language*. The user writes an application program that contains one or more statements from the interactive interface of the language. When the program is compiled and executed, the DBMS processes the query language statements embedded in the program. This issue is discussed in more detail in Section 2.6.

2.5.2 Report Writer

The result of an ad hoc query appears in the form of a display or printout containing the requisite information. Any two consecutive columns in the display are separated by a blank space for readability. Thus the output does not look like a formal report in which titles, page numbers, date, and so on, can be included. The *report writer* of a DBMS is a software component that supports the production of a well-formatted reports. In general, the report writer provides the following features:

1. *Column title:* descriptive heading for each attribute listed in the report.
2. *Report title, page, and date:* descriptive heading for the report, page number

starting with 1 and increasing by 1 thereafter, and the date when the report is generated. In a multipage report these items are printed on the top of each page.

3. *Footnote:* descriptive comment or title printed at the bottom of each page.

4. *Subtotals and control breaks:* decomposition of the report into separate groups of rows with subtotals printed at the end of each group, if appropriate.

5. *Page size:* number of rows to be printed on each page.

```
SQL> TTITLE 'I N S T R U C T O R   L I S T' 'WITH RESPECTIVE DEPARTMENTS'
SQL> COLUMN INAME HEADING 'INSTRUCTOR NAME'
SQL> COLUMN IDEG HEADING 'DEGREE'
SQL> COLUMN DNAME HEADING 'DEPARTMENT NAME'
SQL> BTITLE 'FOR   GENERAL   DISTRIBUTION'
SQL> RUN
  1   SELECT INAME, IDEG, RANK, DNAME FROM UNIV, INSTR
  2*      WHERE INSTR.DNO = UNIV.DNO
```

```
Tue Jul  7                                                    page   1
                       I N S T R U C T O R   L I S T

                       WITH RESPECTIVE DEPARTMENTS

INSTRUCTOR NAME        DEGREE        RANK        DEPARTMENT NAME
_____

Albert Roby           BS,MS,PhD     Professor   Computer Science
Marcia Brown          BA,BS,MS      Instructor  Computer Science
Jack Adams            BA,PhD        AssocProf   Computer Science
Raj Chandra Mittra    BA,MSc,PhD    Professor   Electrical Engineering
Lee Kunkel            BA,MA,PhD     Professor   English
                       FOR   GENERAL   DISTRIBUTION

Tue Jul  7                                                    page   2
                       I N S T R U C T O R   L I S T

                       WITH RESPECTIVE DEPARTMENTS

INSTRUCTOR NAME        DEGREE        RANK        DEPARTMENT NAME
_____

Cathy Doucette        MA,PhD        AssocProf   History
Deb Kumar Roy         BS,MS,PhD     AssocProf   Mathematics
Tom Clark             BA,MA         AsstProf    Mathematics

                       FOR   GENERAL   DISTRIBUTION

8 records selected.
```

Figure 2–14 Example of ORACLE's report writer.

We now illustrate some of these features using ORACLE's report writer. ORACLE provides four commands to produce formatted reports:

1. **COLUMN**: formats a column's heading and data
2. **TTITLE**: puts a title on the top of the page
3. **BTITLE**: puts a title on the bottom of the page
4. **COMPUTE**: computes subtotals and totals

Let us prepare a report listing each instructor's name, degree, rank, and department name. The title of the report is "INSTRUCTOR LIST WITH RE-SPECTIVE DEPARTMENTS," split into two lines. Each column has a separate heading and there is a footnote at the bottom reading "FOR GENERAL DIS-TRIBUTION." Figure 2–14 contains the SQL commands and the report. The report is printed as two pages with five rows on each page.

2.5.3 Graphics Generator

The graphics generator allows the user to produce business graphics from the data in the database. It is analogous to a report writer except that here the "report" consists of a picture instead of a table of rows and columns with some headings and possible subtitles. For many kinds of data a graph is a much more effective means of communication than is a conventional report. Standard examples of graphics include bar charts, pie charts, scatter graphs, and line graphs. Two examples are given in Figures 2–15 and 2–16 using the graphics generator of DATATRIEVE, a relational DBMS from Digital Equipment Corporation.

FREQUENCY OF CARD_TYPE

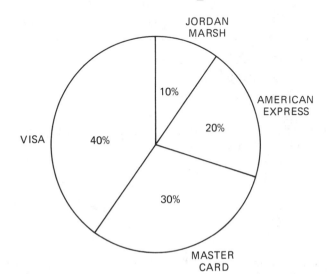

Figure 2–15 Pie chart using DATATRIEVE.

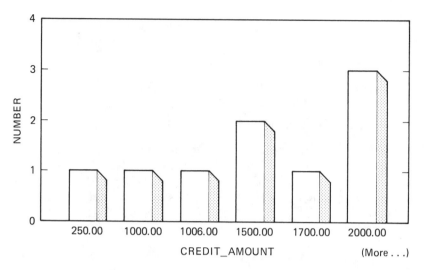

Figure 2–16 Bar graph using DATATRIEVE.

A relation called CUST (Customer) consists of the 10 records listed below.

| | CREDIT | | |
CARD TYPE	AMOUNT	LAST NAME	FIRST NAME
AMERICAN EXPRESS	2000.00	KLINE	MICHELLE
AMERICAN EXPRESS	2000.00	SMITH	MARYLEE
JORDAN MARSH	1000.00	HAYES	MIKE
MASTER CARD	1500.00	YCHORSKI	JANUS
MASTER CARD	1700.00	JONES	ROBERT
MASTER CARD	2000.00	MITTRA	SITANSU
VISA	250.00	NUTILE	DONNA
VISA	1006.00	BROWN	CATALINA
VISA	1500.00	FORD	JAMES
VISA	2500.00	GOUSS	FRED

To generate a pie chart (see Figure 2–15) of the frequency of card types on a percentage basis, use the following commands:

```
DTR> SET PLOTS CDD$TOP.DTR$LIB.VT125
DTR> FIND CUST
[10 records found]
DTR> PLOT PIE CT OF CUST
DTR> PLOT HARDCOPY
```

Note that DTR> is the system prompt for DATATRIEVE. To generate a bar graph (see Figure 2–16) of credit amount frequency, use the following commands:

```
DTR> FIND CUST
[10 records found]
DTR> PLOT HISTO CAMT OF CUST SORTED BY CAMT
DTR> PLOT HARDCOPY
```

2.6 HOST LANGUAGE INTERFACE

A *host language interface* (HLI) is a group of subroutines that perform functions more comprehensive than those provided by the interactive query language. The HLI uses the syntax of a specific host language, which can be any procedural language, such as FORTRAN, COBOL, Pascal, or PL/I. An application program written in a host language using the HLI typically includes some query language commands in the interactive mode and some commands from the host language. An application program is required when the query language is not able to generate the required reports. Recall that a query language is best suited for responding to ad hoc requests in an interactive mode. An application program using HLI, on the other hand, generates more complex reports needed by the users.

The HLI uses DDL and DML commands along with the host language commands to produce the reports, because it is usually necessary for an application program to do more than just create or manipulate the relations in a database. For example, it may have to perform a variety of computational tasks. The latter are done by the host language commands. The DDL and DML commands are invoked by calls to procedures provided by the DBMS. These procedures access the definitions of the external and conceptual levels required by the program. Necessary linkages may be provided by the underlying operating system. Figure 2–17 shows how the data are seen by an application program.

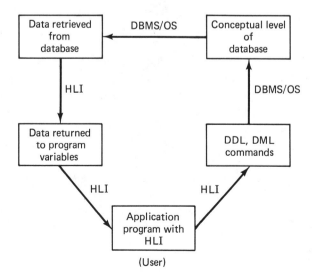

Figure 2–17 Role of HLI in application program.

```
DCL GVNDNO   CHAR(2);

DCL NAME     CHAR(25)  VAR;

DCL HEAD     CHAR(20)  VAR;

EXEC SQL DECLARE UNIV TABLE
         (DNO   CHAR(2),
          DNAME CHAR(25),
          DHEAD CHAR(20));

EXEC SQL INCLUDE SQLCA;

EXEC SQL SELECT DNAME, DHEAD
         INTO   :NAME, :HEAD
         FROM   UNIV
         WHERE  DNO = :GVNDNO;

PUT SKIP LIST (NAME, HEAD);
```

Figure 2–18   Fragment of a PL/I program with SQL interfaces.

As an example of HLI we now make some comments on the PL/I interface of SQL. Figure 2–18 contains a fragment of a PL/I program using SQL interface and relating to the database LHUDB. The program prints a list of department names and their chairpersons in response to given DNOs.

We note the following features of the HLI of SQL:

1. SQL statements are identified by the EXEC SQL command so that they can be distinguished from the statements of the host language.
2. SQL statements can include references to host language variables. Such references are identified by a colon (:) to separate them from SQL attribute names.
3. The INTO clause provides the names of host language variables that receive the variables used in the relations.
4. Any table used in a host language program is always declared by the statement EXEC SQL DECLARE. This allows the precompiler to perform certain syntax checks on the DML statements referring to the table.
5. After any SQL statement has been executed, feedback information is returned to the program in an area called the SQL Communication Area (SQLCA). In particular, a numeric status indicator is returned in a field of the SQLCA called SQLCODE. A SQLCODE value of zero means that the statement was executed successfully; a positive value means that the statement did execute, but constitutes a warning that some exceptional condition occurred (e.g., a value of $+100$ indicates that no data were found to satisfy

the request); and a negative value means that an error occurred and the statement did not complete successfully. In principle, therefore, every SQL statement in the program should be followed by a test on SQLCODE and appropriate action taken if the value is not what was expected. The SQL Communication Area is included in the program by means of an EXEC SQL INCLUDE SQLCA statement.

6. The data type (e.g., character, numeric, etc.) of a host language variable must be compatible with the SQL data type of the attribute with which it is compared or to which it is assigned.

7. Host language variables can have the same names as the attributes in relations.

A significant difference between the operation of a programming language and that of a database query language such as SQL is that the former works on one record at a time while the latter handles sets of records (i.e., tuples or rows) belonging to a relation. Hence a mechanism is needed to present the result of a query to a host language program one record at a time. Different DBMSs implement this mechanism in different ways. For example, a SQL interface uses a variable called CURSOR to perform this function. The operation of CURSOR and its affiliates is summarized below:

1. A call is made to a procedure that causes the SQL query to be executed.

2. A CURSOR is opened via a command

```
EXEC SQL DECLARE cursor-name CURSOR FOR
```

on the selection resulting from execution of the query. This CURSOR is used to process tuples of the referred selection one at a time.

3. A FETCH call is made to retrieve the next tuple. This call retrieves the first tuple of a selection associated with a newly opened CURSOR. Subsequent FETCH calls advance the CURSOR to the next tuple of the selection and then retrieve the tuple to which the CURSOR points. The retrieved tuple is placed in a host language record that is manipulated by the host language program.

4. FETCH calls are repeated until all tuples have been processed. A special code returned by the FETCH call allows the host language program to determine when all the tuples have been processed.

5. Three executable statements are provided to operate on each cursor:

```
EXEC SQL OPEN (cursor-name)
EXEC SQL FETCH (cursor-name) INTO (host-var.)
EXEC SQL CLOSE (cursor-name)
```

The host language interface for SQL uses the interactive SQL commands for fetching data from the database. Consequently, the programmer can test and debug the SQL part of the program interactively. This means that he or she can create some sample tables, load data into them, and then perform the required data retrieval or update using the SQL commands. Once this part runs error free, he or she can start to write the host language code using a 3GL such as FORTRAN, COBOL and so on. Thus, the interactive interface provides a very convenient debugging method for the programmer.

2.7 INTEGRITY RULES

The data values stored in a database must be consistent and should allow the user both retrieval and update capabilities without corrupting the database. The goal of the integrity rules is to enforce these requirements. These rules handle two categories of integrity maintenance:

1. Entity integrity and referential integrity
2. Relational integrity among data values stored in the database

In Sections 2.7.1 through 2.7.4 we discuss these topics with examples. Entity and referential integrity rules deal with key attributes (see Section 2.1.4), both primary and foreign, that are discussed in Section 2.7.1. In Sections 2.7.2 and 2.7.3 we discuss these two integrity rules with examples. Finally, in Section 2.7.4 we treat the relational integrity that maintains consistency of data values. Examples are given to show that this is done either directly by DBMS commands or indirectly through application programs.

2.7.1 Primary and Foreign Keys

As indicated in Section 2.1.4, keys identify unique tuples in a relation and speed up the data retrieval process. There are three types of keys: candidate, primary, and foreign.

A *candidate key* is basically just a unique identifier. It consists of one or more attributes. For example, DNO is a candidate key in UNIV and so is DNAME, because either of them uniquely defines a tuple for a given value of the attribute. Similarly, SSNO is a candidate key in INSTR and so is INAME if we can assume that no two instructors have the same name. Since no two tuples in a relation can be identical, every relation has at least one candidate key: the set of all attributes of the relation. Normally, a relation has only one candidate key.

If there are two or more candidate keys, any one of them is labeled the *primary key* and the rest are called *alternate keys*. A primary key must have *minimality*. This means that if attributes $(a_1, a_2, \ldots, a_n)$ form a candidate key, no proper subset of them can, in general, determine a unique tuple from the relation. Primary keys provide the only tuple-level addressing mechanism within a relational database. DNO can be regarded as a primary key for UNIV, and DNAME, an alternate key.

Finally, a *foreign key* in a relation R is an attribute or a combination of attributes of R whose values must match those of the primary key of some relation R', where R and R' need not be distinct. Also, a foreign key in a relation need not be a part or whole of the primary key of that relation. For example, DNO is a foreign key in the relation INSTR, because DNO is a primary key of the relation UNIV. However, DNO does not form a part of SSNO, which is the primary key of INSTR.

The matching of foreign and primary keys among relations provides linkages among these relations in a database. Since the relations are otherwise disjoint in that no user-visible pointers exist among them as in a hierarchical or network database, this matching feature represents certain relationships or references in a relational database.

2.7.2 Entity and Referential Integrity Rules

We state these two rules below:

1. *Entity integrity*. An attribute forming a part or whole of the primary key of a relation must not accept null values.
2. *Referential integrity*. If a relation R has a foreign key FK, say, that matches the primary key PK, say, of another relation R', then every value of FK must equal the value of PK in some tuple of R'.

The *entity integrity* rule merely enforces the commonsense dictum that a tuple in a relation cannot exist if its unique identifier is null. The *referential integrity* rule has two implications pertaining to update operations:

1. A new tuple can be inserted or an existing tuple can be modified only when the value of the foreign key in the tuple matches a value of the primary key of an existing tuple.
2. An existing tuple cannot be deleted if the value of its primary key matches that of a foreign key in another tuple.

2.7.3 Enforcement of Integrity Rules

Most SQL-based products support the entity integrity rule but not the referential integrity rule. In 1984 the American National Standards Database Committee proposed a number of suggestions for the improvement of SQL. One of their recommendations was to include an optional PRIMARY KEY clause with the CREATE TABLE command so that each relation would identify its primary key at the time of creation. Then, to enforce the referential integrity, this primary key would be matched with a corresponding foreign key.

Since a primary key is a unique identifier of tuples, it is necessary that no two tuples in a relation have the same value of the primary key. ORACLE enforces this requirement by means of the CREATE UNIQUE INDEX command.

The enforcement of referential integrity is more difficult because it involves tuples in different relations. As an example, suppose that a database contains two relations R1 and R2 such that the foreign key R2.FK matches the primary key R1.PK. The operations that can potentially violate the referential integrity are:

1. An INSERT on R2 or an UPDATE on the attribute R2.FK introduces a nonnull value for R2.FK that does not already exist as a value for R1.PK.
2. A DELETE on R1 or an UPDATE on attribute R1.PK leaves "dangling references" in R2 (i.e., there exist tuples in R2 that do not reference any tuple in R1).

The simplest way to alleviate such conditions is to reject both operations 1 and 2, whenever they are attempted. Date [4, pp. 49–57] has given a language proposal for enforcing the integrity rules.

A DBMS that implements referential integrity requires an internal representation of all referential constraints. The *reference graph* is such a representation. It consists of two new relations, REFGRAPH1 and REFGRAPH2, say, with following structures:

1. *REFGRAPH1 with attributes*

LABEL	(label of a referential constraint)
R2	(name of referencing relation)
A1, . . . , AN	(attributes of the foreign key in R2)
COUNT	(number of referenced relations in the constraint)

2. *REFGRAPH2 with attributes*

LABEL	(same as in REFGRAPH1)
R1	(name of referenced relation)
B1, . . . , BN	(attributes of the primary key in R1 that must match A1, . . . , AN, respectively)
SEQNO	(tuple identifier; e.g., if COUNT has value n, there will be n tuples identified by values 1, . . . , n of SEQNO)

```
[instr]           UNIFY RELEASE 3.2           24 AUG 1987 - 14:22

[A]DD

Instructor Name : Susan Woodsmith
Degree          : MA,MS,PhD
Specialty Code  : 3
Rank            : AsstProf
Soc.Security No : 891234567
Dept. Number    : PH

→ → no matching value in univ
```

Figure 2–19 Referential integrity for ADD in UNIFY.

Together REFGRAPH1 and REFGRAPH2 keep track of all the foreign keys in the database.

Despite its importance, relational DBMSs do not, in general, implement the referential integrity rule. To my knowledge, UNIFY, marketed by UNIFY Corporation in Sacramento, CA, is the only relational DBMS that supports the referential integrity completely. As an example, let us implement UNIV and INSTR using UNIFY. We note that DNO is a foreign key in INSTR which must match the primary key DNO of UNIV. Let us insert a new tuple in INSTR for which DNO = 'PH', a value that does not exist in UNIV (see Figure 2–11). UNIFY does not allow this operation (see Figure 2–19). Next, let us delete the tuple with DNO = 'CS' from UNIV (see Figure 2–11). Since INSTR already has tuples with DNO = 'CS', UNIFY does not allow this deletion (see Figure 2–20).

A final clarifying comment is in order. In Figure 2–11, INSTR contains tuples with DNO values not currently existing in UNIV (e.g., DNO = 'PH', DNO = 'RL'). This is permissible because ORACLE does not support referential integrity. A similar situation will not be allowed under UNIFY.

2.7.4 Relational Integrity

Relational integrity involves the issue of data consistency and as such is related to data validation. For example, in a relation containing data on customers' credit

```
[univ]            UNIFY Release 3.2           24 AUG 1987 - 15:03
[D]ELETE]
Dept. Number : CS
Dept. Name   :
Dept. Head   :

→ → value exists in instr
```

Figure 2–20 Referential integrity for DELETE in UNIFY.

limits and their respective amounts outstanding, the latter cannot exceed the former, because a customer cannot charge an amount on credit that exceeds his or her credit limit. As another example, suppose that a relation provides data on sources of grant money which can come from three possible areas: federal, state, or private funds. Then, for any grant, the sum of the percentages of funds from these three sources must equal 100.

A relational integrity constraint can involve a single relation or multiple relations. The two examples given above involve a single relation each. For an example using multiple relational integrity, suppose that a database contains two relations: GRANT and FUNDSOURCE. For a given grant, its identifying number, total amount, and amount coming from each source (e.g., federal, state, and private) appear in GRANT. In FUNDSOURCE, the amount of each source type (e.g., federal, state, or private) appears with the grant number and grant amount. Then it is necessary that for a given grant number, the amount received from a specific source (e.g., federal) must be the same in both GRANT and FUND-SOURCE. Therefore, if different values are entered accidentally, the system should be able to detect and prevent that as a part of the enforcement of relational integrity in the database.

Relational integrity is normally implemented through application programs, because it is regarded as a part of the data validation process. However, some DBMSs offer a limited form of relational integrity. Three examples are given below.

(a) RIM.   Relational Information Management (RIM), a relational DBMS marketed by Boeing Commercial Airplane Company of Seattle, offers relational integrity as a part of its data definition language (DDL). After defining the attributes of each relation and creating their structures, the user can invoke an optional command called RULES, which belongs to the DDL. If this feature is used, the correspondingly defined constraints are used at the time of loading data into the relations or during the update of the relations. Those tuples in a relation that violate any one or more of the constraints cannot be loaded. For each relation at most 10 rules can be specified. Each rule dictates that the value of an attribute in one relation must be related to a constant or to the value of an attribute in the same or a different relation by means of one of six comparison operators:

$$EQ = equal$$

$$NE = not\ equal$$

$$GT = greater\ than$$

$$GE = greater\ than\ or\ equal\ to$$

$$LT = less\ than$$

$$LE = less\ than\ or\ equal\ to$$

These operators apply to numbers and character strings. RIM thus supports relational integrity for both single and multiple relations.

(b) QBE.   Query By Example (QBE) is supported by IBM as one of the two user interfaces to its query product called Query Management Facility (QMF), the other interface being SQL. (See Section 5.9.3 for more details on QBE.) In QBE the user enters a query by essentially filling in blanks in a form displayed on the screen.

The QBE system maintains a constraint table for each relation. To create a constraint on relation *R* we call for a *table skeleton* for *R*. We enter one or more rows representing the constraints into the skeleton. Below the relation name we enter

```
I. CONSTR(<condition list>).I.
```

The first I. refers to the entry itself and the second I. to the constraint in the portion of the row that follows. The ⟨condition list⟩ can consist of any or all of I. (insert), D. (delete), and U. (update), and identifiers that represent user-defined conditions. The terms in the ⟨condition list⟩ indicate when the integrity constraint is to be tested; for example, CONSTR(I.,U.). tells us to test the constraint whenever an insertion or modification occurs in the relevent relation. CONSTR. is short for CONSTR(I.,U.,D.).

What follows in the rows are entries for some or all of the attributes. An entry may be a constant, which says that the tuple being inserted, deleted, or modified must have that constant value for that attribute. An entry can be of the form θc, where c is a constant and θ an arithmetic comparison which says that the tuple must stand in relation θ to c in that attribute. An entry can be blank or have a variable name beginning with underscore, which means that the tuple can be arbitrary in that attribute. Moreover, there can be additional rows entered in the skeleton for *R* or in another skeleton; these rows place additional constraints on the values that may appear in the tuple being inserted, deleted, or modified, according to the semantics of the QBE language.

As an example, suppose that we have a relation CUSTOMER with the attributes NAME, CRLIMIT, and BALANCE. The following skeleton represents the constraint that no customer can have a credit limit exceeding 5000 and that this constraint be invoked at the time of inserting or updating a tuple.

CUSTOMER	NAME	CRLIMIT	BALANCE
I.CONSTR(I.,U.).I.		< 5000	

(c) SQL.   The version of SQL implemented in ORACLE does not support relational integrity. However, the original proposal for SQL includes a general-purpose command called ASSERT that can implement relational integrity. An *assertion* pertaining to a single relation takes the form

```
ASSERT <assertion-name> ON <relation-name> <predicate>
```

For example, if we wish to define an integrity constraint that no account balance is negative, we write

```
ASSERT balance-constraint ON deposit
          balance >= 0
```

In most general form, the ASSERT statement takes the form

```
ASSERT <assertion-name> : <predicate>
```

When an assertion is made, the system tests it for validity. If the assertion is valid, any future modification to the database is allowed only if it does not cause an assertion to be violated. This testing may introduce a significant amount of overhead if complex assertions have been made.

Because of the high overhead of the assertion testing, an alternative scheme called *triggering* is sometimes used for integrity preservation. A *trigger* is a statement that is executed automatically by the system as a side effect of a modification to the database. To design a trigger mechanism, we must:

1. Specify the conditions under which the trigger is to be executed.
2. Specify the actions to be taken when the trigger executes.

Assertions and triggers are created and destroyed via ASSERT, DEFINE TRIGGER, DROP ASSERTION, and DROP TRIGGER statements. SQL∗ Forms from Oracle Corporation supports the trigger mechanism.

2.8 VIEWS

A relation defined at the conceptual level of a database is stored as a disk file at the internal level; that is, for every relation there exists a file that directly stores the contents of the relation. A view, by contrast, is often described as a *virtual* relation in that no corresponding data file exists at the internal level.

In Sections 2.8.1 through 2.8.5 we discuss the concept of a view and its role in database operations. In Section 2.8.1 we define a view with examples. Retrieval and update operations using views are discussed in Sections 2.8.2 and 2.8.3. In Section 2.8.4 we deal with the relationship of views and logical data independence. Some of the basic advantages of views are summarized in Section 2.8.5.

2.8.1 Definition of Views

Views belong to the external level of a database. When a user retrieves information involving some of the attributes from one or more relations in the conceptual level, the resulting structure is regarded as a *view*. The external level then consists of views and individual relations of the database. A user can operate on a view if it were a single relation. Accordingly, a view is normally described as a virtual relation. The definition of the view is stored in the data dictionary of the system. This definition shows how the view is derived from existing relations by using appropriate selection criteria.

A view provides a "window" on the real data, although it does not contain a copy of those data values. The window is dynamic in the sense that any changes made to the underlying relation(s) defining the view will be visible through the window automatically and instantaneously. Individual attributes in a view inherit their data types from the underlying relations. We can define one view in terms of other views and carry on that process up to any number of levels.

If a view is removed, its underlying relations are not affected. But if any other views are defined in terms of this view, they will be dropped automatically. Similarly, if a relation is removed, all views defined in terms of that relation are also dropped.

In SQL a view is created by the CREATE VIEW command, whose syntax is

```
CREATE VIEW view-name(attribute-1, . . . , attribute-n) AS
subquery;
```

Here the subquery involves selection criteria defining the view. As such it contains the structure

```
SELECT.......FROM.........WHERE
```

and may include nested levels of subqeries. In principle, any information that can be derived via a SELECT command can be defined as a view. However, the definition cannot include an ORDER BY clause, which is used for storing the retrieved information by one or more attributes. The reason for this restriction is quite simple. The clause ORDER BY in a view definition is meaningless, because the object being defined (i.e., the view) is a relation, albeit virtual, and a relation does not have an inherent ordering. It is, of course, possible to impose an ordering dynamically when data are retrieved from the view by including an ORDER BY clause in the SELECT statement that performs the retrieval from the view (see Section 2.8.2).

A view can be removed from the database by the command

```
DROP VIEW view-name;
```

As a result, the definition of the specified view is removed from the data dictionary of the system.

Figure 2–21 gives an example of view creation using UNIV and INSTR relations. Figure 2–22 shows that the clause ORDER BY is not allowed while creating a view.

```
SQL> CREATE VIEW FACULTY  (NAME, RANK, DEPT)
   2    AS
   3    SELECT INAME, RANK, DNAME
   4      FROM UNIV, INSTR WHERE
   5      UNIV.DNO = INSTR.DNO;

View created.
```

Figure 2-21   Example of CREATE VIEW command.

2.8.2 Retrieval Operations on Views

Externally, for a user the retrieval of information from a database through views appears the same as that using relations. Internally, however, the retrieval operations on a view are translated into equivalent operations on the underlying relations. Barring a few exceptions noted below, the translation process is quite straightforward and works perfectly well. When a user issues a SELECT command on a view, the translation is done by merging that SELECT operation with the SELECT operation that is saved in the data dictionary containing the definition of the view. In effect, all references to the view are replaced by the view definition.

As an example, suppose that a user issues the command

```
SELECT NAME, DEPT FROM FACULTY;
```

In executing this query, the definition of FACULTY (see Figure 2–21) is retrieved by the system and the replacement of NAME by INAME from INSTR and the replacement of DEPT by DNAME from UNIV occur and then the two relations are combined on the basis of the common value of DNO. The result of the query appears in Figure 2–23.

Retrieval operations can lead to problems when grouped views are involved. A view whose definitions includes a GROUP BY or a HAVING clause in SQL is called a *grouped view*. A view whose definition directly contains a FROM clause that refers to another grouped view is also considered to be a grouped view, and

```
SQL> CREATE VIEW DEPT
   2    AS
   3    SELECT DNAME, DHEAD FROM UNIV
   4      ORDER BY DNAME;
     ORDER BY DNAME
     *
ERROR at line 4: ORA-0933:  SQL command not properly ended
```

Figure 2-22   ORDER BY clause not allowed in CREATE VIEW command.

```
SQL> SELECT NAME, DEPT FROM FACULTY;

NAME                    DEPT
```

```
Albert Roby             Computer Science
Marcia Brown            Computer Science
Jack Adams              Computer Science
Raj Chandra Mittra      Electrical Engineering
Lee Kunkel              English
Cathy Doucette          History
Deb Kumar Roy           Mathematics
Tom Clark               Mathematics


8 records selected.
```

Figure 2–23 Example of a query from a view.

so on, to any number of levels. Grouped views are subject to two main restrictions:

1. A grouped view cannot be combined with any other relation or view via the join operation.
2. A FROM clause that references a grouped view cannot have an associated WHERE clause, or GROUPED BY clause, or HAVING clause.

The general principle pertaining to the retrieval operations with views is that the translated form of the original query must always be a legal SELECT expression in SQL.

2.8.3 Update Operations on Views

An update operation involves insertion, deletion, and modification of data. Since operations on views are converted into equivalent operations on the underlying relations, a view can be updated if and only if the corresponding tuples in the underlying relations can be uniquely identified. In the absence of such unique identification update anomalies may arise, resulting in errors. Thus not all views can be updated. Some views are inherently *updatable* whereas others are not.

A view can contain some or all of the attributes of its parent relation(s). In case not all of the attributes are included in the view, the primary key(s) of the parent relation(s) must be included in the view to make it inherently updatable. The reasoning behind this requirement is that when primary key values are given, the corresponding tuples are uniquely identified and hence no update anomalies arise. However, even in this case, since some of the attributes of the parent relation(s) are missing from the view, these attribute values will be updated with NULL values. This may lead to bad side effects since any comparison using

NULL is false by definition. Also, built-in arithmetic functions such as SUM or AVG do not operate on NULL values.

Let us take an example to illustrate the foregoing situation. We define a view INSTR-SPECL from INSTR as follows:

```
CREATE VIEW INSTR-SPECL
AS
SELECT SSNO, INAME, IDEG, SPCODE
FROM INSTR;
```

Assuming that SSNO is the primary key of INSTR, this view is inherently updatable. Let us update the view with the values

```
(695715596, 'JILL MARCUS', 'MA, PHD', 10).
```

This will insert a new tuple in the parent relation INSTR with NULL values for the attributes RANK and DNO. Figure 2–24 contains the ORACLE SQL commands to create and update the view INSTR-SPECL. Note that the last row at the end of Figure 2–24 has blanks for RANK and DNO in the parent relation INSTR. Consequently, no join can be performed with UNIV via DNO. A query against INSTR with the criterion

```
RANK = 'AsstProf'
```

say, will ignore this new tuple, and so on. As a result, it is desirable that the following restrictions be made for view updates:

1. An update will apply *only* to the actual relations.
2. A view can be updated *only when* its definition includes all of the attributes of its parent relation.

In System R (see Section 2.3 and following), a view can be updated if it satisfies the following conditions:

1. It is derived from a single relation.
2. Each distinct row (column) of the view corresponds to a uniquely identifiable row (column) of the relation.

It should be clear that if a view satisfies these conditions, any update against it can easily be mapped into an update on the corresponding relation; in other words, such views are updatable.

In SQL, a view is updatable if and only if all of the following six conditions

```
SQL> CREATE VIEW INSTR_SPECL
  2     AS
  3     SELECT SSNO, INAME, IDEG, SPCODE FROM INSTR;

View created.

SQL> INSERT INTO INSTR_SPECL
  2     VALUES
  3     (695715596,'JILL MARCUS','MA,PHD',10);

1 record created.

SQL> SELECT * FROM INSTR_SPECL;
```

SSNO	INAME	IDEG	SPCODE
123456789	Lee Kunkel	BA,MA,PhD	4
234567891	Albert Roby	BS,MS,PhD	2
345678912	Deb Kumar Roy	BS,MS,PhD	5
456789123	Cathy Doucette	MA,PhD	6
567891234	Raj Chandra Mittra	BA,MSc,PhD	10
678912345	Tom Clark	BA,MA	5
789123456	Marcia Brown	BA,BS,MS	2
891234567	Susan Woodsmith	MA,MS,PhD	3
912345678	Brady Jackson	MA,DLitt	15
123457698	Jack Adams	BA,PhD	1
695715596	JILL MARCUS	MA,PHD	10

```
11 records selected.

SQL> SELECT * FROM INSTR;
```

INAME	IDEG	SPCODE	RANK	SSNO	DN
Lee Kunkel	BA,MA,PhD	4	Professor	123456789	EN
Albert Roby	BS,MS,PhD	2	Professor	234567891	CS
Deb Kumar Roy	BS,MS,PhD	5	AssocProf	345678912	MA
Cathy Doucette	MA,PhD	6	AssocProf	456789123	HS
Raj Chandra Mittra	BA,MSc,PhD	10	Professor	567891234	EE
Tom Clark	BA,MA	5	AsstProf	678912345	MA
Marcia Brown	BA,BS,MS	2	Instructor	789123456	CS
Susan Woodsmith	MA,MS,PhD	3	AsstProf	891234567	PH
Brady Jackson	MA,DLitt	15	Professor	912345678	RL
Jack Adams	BA,PhD	1	AssocProf	123457698	CS
JILL MARCUS	MA,PHD	10		695715596	

```
11 records selected.
```

Figure 2–24 ORACLE SQL commands for view update.

apply to the view definition, that is, to the SELECT expression that defines the view (Date [5, pp. 80–81]):

1. It does not include the key word DISTINCT.
2. Every item in the SELECT clause consists of a simple reference to a column of the underlying table (i.e., it is not a constant, nor an operational expression such as C + 1, nor a reference to a built-in function such as AVG).
3. The FROM clause identifies exactly one table, and that table in turn is updatable.
4. The WHERE clause does not include a subquery.
5. There is no GROUP BY clause.
6. There is no HAVING clause.

2.8.4 Views and Logical Data Independence

In Section 1.5 we discussed the logical data independence in a database as a mapping between the external and the conceptual levels. A database offers logical data independence if user operations (i.e., queries and application programs) are independent of the logical structure of the database. Views can provide logical data independence since they are defined by users in terms of the conceptual level.

Views are not affected as long as the conceptual level remains unchanged. The latter can change under two conditions:

1. Restructing of the database
2. Reorganization of the database

A *restructuring* of the database is needed under the following circumstances:

1. The expansion of an existing relation to include a new field (corresponding to the addition of new information concerning an existing type of entity)
2. The inclusion of a new relation (corresponding to the addition of a new type of entity)

Neither of these changes should have any effect on existing views, since, by definition, those views can contain no reference to the new attributes or relations. Thus the view mechanism can insulate users from the effects of growth in the database. We refer to this insulation as *immunity to growth*.

A *reorganization* of the database is needed when the conceptual level is changed in such a way that the placement of information within the conceptual level is altered. For example, an existing relation is broken into two or more new relations with additional attributes introduced. Consequently, the allocation of existing attributes to new relations may change as well. In this case the existing view definitions do not hold in general and hence must be modified. This issue is closely related to the update operation for views, as discussed in Section 2.8.3.

2.8.5 Advantages of Views

Views offer the following advantages:

1. Logical data independence.
2. Retrieval and formatting of data according to user needs.
3. Convenient facility for data protection. For example, if certain users are not authorized to access some information, their access privilege may be limited to those views that do not include the restricted information.

2.9 DATED RELATIONS

A *dated relation* is one that carries its history around. Specifically, the file that holds the relation contains an entry indicating the date and time at which each item was inserted into the relation, and when, if ever, the item was deleted. Retaining this information makes it possible to access a dated relation "as of" any specified time in its past; it also makes it possible to roll back the relation to an earlier state. Dated relations provide a storage-efficient mechanism for maintaining several versions of a relation, as well as suggesting a recovery mechanism. Normally, this concept is implemented through application programs. However, if a DBMS supports dated relations, the user can use this feature through a non-procedural query language. Dated relations allow the user to establish an audit trail for all database updates.

LOGIX, a relational DBMS marketed by Venturcom Inc. of Cambridge, Massachusetts, is the only DBMS known to me that supports dated relations. At the time of creation and initial data loading of a relation, LOGIX creates two additional attributes, TIME-IN and TIME-OUT, that contain, respectively, the date and time when each data value was entered (i.e., inserted or modified) into the relation and the date and time when that value was deleted, if at all. Consequently, each tuple appears once for each update of that tuple. The most current value of a tuple is characterized by the condition that the TIME-OUT column is blank. LOGIX uses four basic commands for maintaining dated relations:

1. ASOF. When a user issues a command

```
DISPLAY relation ASOF time-date
```

LOGIX displays the contents of the relation as they were on the designated "time-date." In particular, a command

```
DISPLAY relation
```

displays the current contents of the relation.

2. HISTOF. When a user issues a command

```
DISPLAY HISTOF relation
```

LOGIX displays a complete history of that relation, consisting of all the updates made since the creation of the relation up to the current instant.

3. FLASH. When a user issues a command

```
FLASH TO time-date
```

LOGIX allows the user to flashback to the designated "time-date." All operations performed subsequent to this command assumes that all contents of all relations in the database have values as of the user-specified "time-date." To bring the operations to current relation contents, the user has to replace "time-date" in the FLASH command by the current time and date.

4. ROLLBACK. This command allows the user to roll the system back to any specified time and date. For example, the command

```
ROLLBACK TO time-date relation
```

hides, but does not erase, the update history of the relation since the designated "time-date." The current version of the relation is the same as that on the specified "time-date."

Note that FLASH works on *all* the relations in the database, while ROLLBACK operates on the specified relation. As an example, let us consider the

UNIV ASOF 10:21 MAY 17

DNO	DNAME	DHEAD
EN	English	Lee Kunkel
CS	Computer Science	Albert Roby
MA	Mathematics	Deb Kumar Roy
HS	History	Phyllis Braun
EE	Electrical Engineering	Raj Chandra Mittra
PH	Philosophy	Roger Lebowitz

Figure 2–25 Output of ASOF command in LOGIX.

HISTOF   UNIV

DNO	DNAME	DHEAD	TIME-IN	TIME-OUT
EN	English	Lee Kunkel	01 09 16:45	
CS	Computer Science	Albert Roby	01 09 16:45	
MA	Mathematics	Deb Kumar Roy	01 09 16:45	06 21 12:25
MA	Mathematics & Statistics	Deb Kumar Roy		
HS	History	Cathy Doucette	01 09 16:45	04 16 09:11
HS	History	Phyllis Braun	04 16 09:11	
EE	Electrical Engineering	Raj Chandra Mittra	01 09 16:45	
PH	Philosophy	Roger Lebowitz	02 05 17:48	

Figure 2–26   Output of HISTOF command in LOGIX.

relation UNIV in LHUDB. Assume that the first five records (see Figure 2–11) were entered on January 9, 1987 at time 16:45 (i.e., 4:45 P.M.). Subsequently, the following three updates were made as follows:

1. April 16, 1987; 09:11; DHEAD of History was changed to Phyllis Braun.
2. June 21, 1987; 12:25; DNAME of Mathematics was changed to Mathematics and Statistics.
3. February 5, 1987; 17:48; a new tuple was entered with values

   PH, Philosophy, Roger Lebowitz

Then the command

   DISPLAY UNIV ASOF "10:21 May 17"

will produce the output given in Figure 2–25, and the command

   DISPLAY HISTOF UNIV

will produce the output given in Figure 2–26.

2.10 SUMMARY

We began the chapter with the basic concepts of a relational database and a relational DBMS. A relation is defined as a table whose rows are called tuples or records and whose columns are called attributes. An attribute takes values from its domain. A relational database consists of several relations. This collection of relations constitutes the conceptual level of the database. A user accesses this level via his or her own external level that provides a partial view of the conceptual level. Retrieval of information is speeded up if an attribute is declared as a key. The implementation of this feature is done through index files and B-trees, which belong to the internal level of the database. The example of LHUDB is used for illustrating all of these concepts.

A relational DBMS is a software that allows the creation and manipulation of data in a relational database. Its main components are (1) data definition language (DDL); (2) data manipulation language (DML); (3) query language, report writer, and graphics generator; (4) host language interface (HLI); and (5) data dictionary. As an example of a relational DBMS, System R, developed by IBM during 1974–1979, is discussed in this chapter. System R consists of a hierarchy of subsystems, each of which performs a specific function in order to process the user request. An operational scenario describes how System R would handle a "program" that can consist of a single command from an end user or be an application program written in a procedural language, including some SQL statements.

The data definition language (DML) allows the user to create interactively the structure of a relation and to modify it later, if needed. This information is entered into the data dictionary for future response. The data manipulation language performs two major functions: information retrieval from the database and update of the data in the database. Normally, a set of built-in arithmetic group functions such as SUM, AVG, and COUNT are included in the data manipulation language. A query language is defined as a nonprocedural language used for both retrieval and update operations. Some DBMSs also offer a procedural DML for the use of application programmers. A report writer may be described as a subset of the query language used for generating nicely formatted reports. A graphics generator produces business graphics such as bar graphs and pie charts using the information resulting from a query.

The relational DBMS ORACLE is used to illustrate the DDL and DML commands of SQL, a query language inherited from System R and now regarded as an industry standard of nonprocedural query languages. The examples use two of the relations, UNIV and INSTR, from LHUDB.

A host language interface (HLI) is used to perform more complex functions that cannot be handled by a nonprocedural query language. An application program using HLI contains both DML commands and commands from a procedural host language such as COBOL or FORTRAN. An HLI is not needed if the DBMS provides a procedural DML, as in System 1032 on VAX, for example.

The integrity of data in a database is maintained through three integrity rules: (1) entity integrity, (2) referential integrity, and (3) relational integrity. The first two involve primary and foreign keys in a relation. The last one ensures the consistency of data in the database and is normally implemented through application programs. Several examples of all three types of integrity rules are given.

A view or a virtual relation belongs to the external level of the database. It differs from a relation in the sense that no data values are stored at the internal level for a view. Only the definition of the view is kept in the data dictionary. However, a user retrieves information from a view in exactly the same way as from a relation. A view is no longer available if its defining relations are deleted from the database. To avoid possible update anomalies, a view should be declared as not updatable if its definition does not include the primary key(s) of its defining relation(s). SQL provides a set of six conditions all of which must be satisfied by a view definition in order to make it updatable. Otherwise, a view is updated whenever its defining relation(s) are updated.

Finally, a dated relation is a relation that carries its update history with itself. By including two new attributes, TIME-IN and TIME-OUT, a dated relation keeps tracks of all the updates made to it since its creation. A user can retrieve data from a dated relation as of any specified date, current or past. The current value of an attribute is characterized by the condition that the TIME-OUT attribute is blank.

KEY WORDS

access module
access path
alternate key
arity of a relation
assignment
attribute
B-tree
built-in function
candidate key
column
conceptual level
cursor mechanism
data definition language
  (DDL)
data dictionary
data element
data manipulation
  language (DML)
data sublanguage (DSL)
database, reorganization
  of
database, restructuring
  of

DATATRIEVE
dated relation
decision
degree of a relation
domain
entity integrity
external level
field
flat file
foreign key
graphics generator
group function
grouped view
host language interface
  (HLI)
immunity to growth
index file
index set, dense
index set, nondense
indexing
interactive interface
internal level

key attribute
logical data
  independence
LOGIX
maximum length
minimality
ORACLE SQL
primary key
procedural DML
qualified retrieval
query language
record
reference graph
referential integrity
relation
relational database
relational DBMS
relational integrity
repetition
report writer
retrieval operation,
  relation
retrieval operation, view
row
segment identifier

segments in System R
simple retrieval
System R
System R, architecture
System R, execution
  system
System R, precompiler
System R, relational
  data system (RDS)
System R, research
  storage interface (RSI)
System R, research
  storage system (RSS)
System R, user friendly
  interface (UFI)
table
table skeleton
tree-structured index
tuple
unbalanced tree
updatable view
update operation,
  relation
update operation, view
view
virtual relation

REFERENCES AND FURTHER READING

The following references contain additional materials related to the topics covered in this chapter.

1. M. W. BLASGEN et al., System R: An Architectural Overview, *IBM Systems Journal*, vol. 20, no. 1, 1981, pp. 41–62.

2. C. J. DATE, *Introduction to Database Systems*, vol. I, 4th ed., Addison-Wesley, Reading, MA, 1986.

3. C. J. DATE, *Introduction to Database Systems*, vol. II, 3rd ed., Addison-Wesley, Reading, MA, 1983.

4. C. J. DATE, *Relational Database Selected Writings*, Addison-Wesley, Reading, MA, 1986.

5. C. J. DATE, *The SQL Standard*, Addison-Wesley, Reading, MA, 1987.

6. H. F. KORTH and A. SILBERSCHATZ, *Database System Concepts*, McGraw-Hill, New York, 1986.

7. F. R. McFADDEN and J. A. HOFFER, *Data Base Management*, Benjamin-Cummings, Menlo Park, CA, 1985.

8. J. D. ULLMAN, *Principles of Database Systems*, Computer Science Press, Rockville, MD, 1982.

The paper by Blasgen et al. [1] is a good and comprehensive description of System R that includes query optimization, data independence, view updates, transaction management, compilation of programs, execution of precompiled programs, and concurrency control. Date [2], Korth and Silberschatz [6], and McFadden and Hoffer [7] contain additional information on DDL and DML for general database systems that are applicable, in particular, to relational databases. Date [5] contains ANSI SQL commands to enforce view mechanism and integrity rules. However, many of these commands are optional and not commercially available. Date [3] and Korth and Silberschatz [6] discuss a pseudolanguage to enforce relational integrity. Date [4] is a collection of articles dealing with various aspects of the relational databases. Date's Chapters 3, 4, 17 and 18 contain materials related to the present chapter; most specifically, in Chapter 18, Date discusses an extension of the CURSOR mechanism (see Section 2.6) to handle a tree-structured relation. The extended cursor is called a reopenable cursor. Ullman [8] discusses relational integrity concepts and illustrates them with examples from Query By Forms (QBF).

REVIEW QUESTIONS

1. Define the terms *relation*, *attribute*, and *domain*. Why is a relation often called a flat file? What does *flat* signify in this context?

2. Explain the mathematical meaning of the term *relation*. What is the degree of a relation?

3. Describe how a specific record in a relation is accessed and retrieved from the internal level.

4. What is a key attribute? What are the advantages and disadvantages of declaring one or more attributes in a relation as key?

5. Describe the usage of a B-tree. What are dense and nondense index sets?

6. Discuss the architecture of System R.

7. Suppose that you want to generate a list of instructor names, ranks, and degrees using System R. Describe an operational scenario to perform that task.

8. Describe the function of segments in System R.

9. List the functions of DDL and DML in a relational DBMS.

10. Why is a built-in function of DML sometimes called a group function?

11. Do you think that a query language must be nonprocedural? Justify your answer.

12. What is a report writer? Describe its usage.

13. What is the difference between a procedural DML and a host language interface? Explain your answer with examples.

14. Under what circumstances do you need a graphics generator in addition to a report writer?

15. Explain the operation of CURSOR in the SQL host language interface.
16. Discuss the two categories of integrity rules. Why are they needed?
17. How can you enforce entity integrity rule using SQL commands?
18. Explain the difference between a primary key and a foreign key.
19. What does referential integrity mean? How does it help to maintain data integrity in the database?
20. Explain the concept of reference graph. How is it related to referential integrity?
21. Discuss the concept of relational integrity. How can it be implemented in a database? How is it related to data validation in a database?
22. Describe the difference between a view and a relation.
23. What is a grouped view? Why can a grouped view lead to problems in retrieval operations on views?
24. Describe the anomalies that can occur while updating a view.
25. List the conditions under which a view is updatable.
26. Define a dated relation with an example.
27. How does a dated relation keep track of all its updates?
28. How can a dated relation help in database recovery procedure?

EXERCISES

The following exercises relate to the LHUDB described in Section 1.6. You need a relational DBMS to do them.

1. Create the relations STUDNT, CRSE, and CRSLST of Figure 2–1. Then load the data described in Figure 2–2 into these three relations.
2. Declare a primary key in each of the three relations in Exercise 1. Are there any foreign keys in these relations? Give reasons for your answer.
3. Formulate a set of relational integrity rules to ensure data integrity among these three relations. Can you formulate similar rules for UNIV and INSTR?
4. Create views to generate the following lists.
   (a) Student name, major, advisor name, advisor rank, department name.
   (b) Course name, instructor name, department name.
   (c) Course name, section number, student name, instructor name.
5. Using a report writer, prepare nicely formatted reports for each of the three views in Exercise 4.
6. Formulate a set of entity integrity and referential integrity rules for LHUDB consisting of five relations: UNIV, INSTR, STUDNT, CRSE, and CRSLST.

CHAPTER 3

RELATIONAL ALGEBRA

3.1 CONCEPT OF RELATIONAL ALGEBRA

The SQL type of query language is based on a set of n-ary set-theoretic operations on relations. Codd [1] introduced eight such operations to develop the query language of a relational database system. These operations constitute the relational algebra. The DML part of the query language performs two functions:

1. Data retrieval from relations
2. Update of relations

The first function involves the capability of writing an expression using the relational algebra formalisms. Accordingly, the discussion of relational algebra provides the mathematical foundation of the data manipulation component of SQL-type languages.

In Sections 3.1.1., 3.1.2, and 3.1.3 we discuss the mathematical background needed to understand the relational algebra commands, the notion of a nonprocedural language, and the capability of relational algebra to implement nonprocedural languages.

3.1.1 Mathematical Prerequisites for Relational Algebra

A *set* is defined as a collection of entities having a common property. The entities are called the *elements* of the set. For example, the set of all employees of a company, the set of all real numbers between 0 and 1 inclusive, the set of all points on a line, and so on, are all sets, by this definition. A set can be described in two possible ways:

1. A complete enumeration of its elements
2. Specifying the defining property of the set

Let S be the set of all integers between 1 and 10 inclusive. Then we can write S in either of two ways.

$$S = \{1, 2, 3, 4, 5, 6, 7, 8, 9, 10\}$$

$$S = \{n \mid n \text{ is a positive integer, } 1 \leqslant n \leqslant 10\}$$

The order in which the elements of a set are listed is not important. A set is *finite* or *infinite* according as the number of its elements is finite or infinite. If an element x belongs to a set S, we write $x \in S$.

If every element of a set A is also an element of a set B, we say that A is a *subset* of B, and we write $A \subset B$. Two sets A and B are *equal* if $A \subset B$ and $B \subset A$.

Given two sets A and B, their *union* is defined as the set of all elements that belong to A or B or both, and is written as $A \cup B$. Thus

$$A \cup B = \{x \mid x \in A \qquad \text{or} \qquad x \in B\}$$

Given two sets A and B, their *intersection* is defined as the set of all elements that belong to both A and B, and is written $A \cap B$. Thus

$$A \cap B = \{x \mid x \in A \qquad \text{and} \qquad x \in B\}$$

If $A \cap B$ is empty, A and B are called *disjoint* sets.

More generally, given n sets $A_1, \ldots, A_n$, their union and intersection are written, respectively, as

$$\bigcup_{i=1}^{n} A_i = A_1 \cup \cdots \cup A_n = \{x \mid x \in A_i, \text{ for at least one } i, 1 \leqslant i \leqslant n\}$$

$$\bigcap_{i=1}^{n} A_i = A_1 \cap \cdots \cap A_n = \{x \mid x \in A_i, \text{ for all } i, 1 \leqslant i \leqslant n\}$$

The *difference* of two sets A and B is defined as the set of all elements that belong to A but not to B, and is written as $A - B$. Thus

$$A - B = \{x \mid x \in A, x \notin B\}$$

The *Cartesian product* of two sets A and B is written as $A \times B$ and consists of all ordered pairs of elements of which the first element is in A and the second element is in B. Thus

$$A \times B = \{(a, b) \mid a \in A, b \in B\}$$

More generally, the Cartesian product of n sets $A_1, \ldots, A_n$, is written as

$$\underset{i=1}{\overset{n}{\times}} A_i = A_1 \times \cdots \times A_n = \{(a_1, \ldots, a_n) \mid a_i \in A_i, 1 \le i \le n\}$$

Note that union and intersection are both associative and commutative, that is,

$$(A \cup B) \cup C = A \cup (B \cup C)$$

$$(A \cap B) \cap C = A \cap (B \cap C)$$

$$A \cup B = B \cup A$$

$$A \cap B = B \cap A$$

However, difference is neither associative nor commutative, while Cartesian product is associative but not commutative. Figure 3–1 shows graphically the union, intersection, and difference of two sets A and B. The shaded area in each diagram represents the resulting sets $A \cup B$, $A \cap B$, and $A - B$.

Given a set S and an n-ary operation f on S with range T, S is said to be *closed* with respect to f if $T = S$. By definition, f is a mapping

$$f \colon \underbrace{S \times \cdots \times S}_{n \text{ times}} \to T$$

so that

$$f(x_1, \ldots, x_n) \in T \qquad \text{for all } x_1, \ldots, x_n \in S$$

Hence S is closed with respect to f if we have

$$f(x_1, \ldots, x_n) \in S \qquad \text{for all } x_1, \ldots, x_n \in S$$

For example, the set of all positive integers is closed with respect to addition and multiplication, but not with respect to subtraction, because the difference of two positive integers can be negative: for example, $7 - 12 = -5$, which is not a positive integer. If S is closed with respect to f, we say that f has the property of *closure* in S.

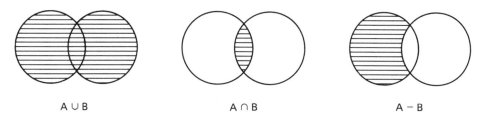

AᵁB   A∩B   A − B

Figure 3–1 Union, intersection, and difference of two sets.

Two relations R_1 and R_2, say, in a relational database are said to be *union compatible* if R_1 and R_2 have the same degree, say n, and if the kth attribute of R_1 has the same domain as the kth attribute of R_2, where $k = 1, \ldots, n$. These corresponding attributes need not have the same name.

Let $f_1, \ldots, f_n$ be n different operations on a set S. Let $f_{i_1}, \ldots, f_{i_k}$, $k < n$, be a subset of these n operations. If each of the remaining $n - k$ operations of the total set of n operations $f_1, \ldots, f_n$ can be written in terms of $f_{i_1}, \ldots, f_{i_k}$, then $f_{i_1}, \ldots, f_{i_k}$ are said to be *primitive* operations, while the remaining $n - k$ operations are said to be *derived* operations. For example, given the three binary operations of addition, multiplication, and exponentiation on the set of all positive integers, addition is a primitive operation, whereas multiplication and exponentiation are derived operations, because we can write as follows:

$$m \times n = m + m + \cdots + m \qquad \text{addition repeated } n \text{ times}$$

$$m^n = m \times m \times \cdots \times m \qquad \text{multiplication repeated } n \text{ times and each multiplication expressible in terms of additions}$$

Two sets A and B are said to be *isomorphic* if there exists a one-to-one and onto correspondence between their elements. Two finite sets with the same number of elements are always isomorphic. Isomorphic sets are abstractly equivalent.

3.1.2 Nonprocedural Languages

In Section 2.5.1 we characterized a query language as nonprocedural without giving a precise definition of the latter. Intuitively, we think of a nonprocedural language as one where the user specifies what data are needed but does not describe how to get them. A more formal definition follows.

A *nonprocedural language* is one in which the program does not follow the actual steps a computer follows in executing a program. For a normal data processing application, these steps and their general sequence are:

1. Perform Housekeeping: clear memory, initialize counters and work areas, etc.
2. Open files and check labels.
3. Read input records.
4. Perform arithmetic and logic functions on the input records.
5. Produce output records.
6. Repeat steps 3 through 5 until all records are processed.
7. Print any final output records; close files.
8. End program or return control to supervisor or monitor.

These steps are typically followed when preparing programs for procedural languages, because the source program with procedural languages tends to be translated in a more direct manner into the object (machine language) program.

For nonprocedural languages, there is very little relationship necessary between the sequence of the source language statements and the sequence of the resulting machine language instructions. Thus the source program language is freed from the eight-step process listed above and can be more closely related to the following aspects of the program:

1. Description of the files and records to be read
2. Arithmetic and logic operations to be performed on the input data
3. Format of the output

Nonprocedural languages tend to be more problem oriented than do procedural languages. This is particularly true for the programming of commercial (business) applications. The major purpose (and value) of nonprocedural languages is to permit the programming activity to focus more strongly on the problem being solved rather than on the computer resources (hardware, software) being used. Nonprocedural languages have numerous benefits and some limitations when compared to procedural languages.

The key advantage of nonprocedural languages is the lower amount of programming effort required to produce a working program compared to most procedural languages. The reason for this is that much of the internal logic of the object program is provided by the "generator program," which translates the source program into the object program. The basic disadvantage of nonprocedural languages is their flexibility: for example, the loss of programmer control over the input/output functions of the computer and the inability to minimize the use of memory or of execution time through more direct control of hardware operations. The latter functions are better performed with a procedural language having a close relationship between the source language and the machine language so that control over the machine functions is increased.

3.1.3 Relational Algebra: Vehicle for Nonprocedurality

Any query formulation expression in a query language describes the objective of the query, that is, what data are to be read, processed, and displayed or printed in terms of a set of relational algebraic expressions. These expressions implement the nonprocedurality of the query language. They trigger the data access mechanism of the DBMS, which is totally transparent to the user. The process of navigating around the internal level of the database to locate the desired data is done automatically by the system, not manually by the user.

Nonprocedurality is really relative rather than absolute. The query languages based on relational calculus are more nonprocedural in nature than those based on relational algebra (see Chapter 4). The main difference between procedural and nonprocedural languages is that the latter offers a higher level of abstraction in being more remote from the processing logic of the program than the former.

3.2 BASIC RELATIONAL ALGEBRAIC OPERATIONS

As mentioned in Section 3.1, in 1972 Codd [1] introduced eight basic relational algebra operations for query languages. Each operation is either *unary* or *binary*, according as it takes one relation or two relations, respectively, as input and produces a new relation as output. These eight operations are divided into two groups of four each:

1. The traditional set-theoretic operations of union, intersection, difference, and Cartesian product (all modified slightly to take account of the fact that their operands are relations, as opposed to arbitrary sets)
2. The special relational operations of select, project, join, and divide

Numerous variations on the original relational algebra have been proposed since the publication of Codd's paper in 1972. The descriptions of these operations in Sections 3.2.1 and 3.2.2 are fairly close to Codd's original versions.

3.2.1 Traditional Set-Theoretic Operations

Four relations belong to this category: (1) union, (2) intersection, (3) difference, and (4) Cartesian product.

(1) Union.   Let R_1 and R_2 be two union-compatible relations of degree n. Then R_1 UNION R_2 is the relation of degree n whose tuples belong to R_1 or R_2 or both. It is called the *union of R_1 and R_2*.

Using the relation INSTR in LHUDB, we define R_1 and R_2 as follows:

R_1 = set of all tuples for which RANK is 'AssocProf' or 'Professor'

R_2 = set of all tuples for which DNO is 'CS' or 'MA'

Then R_1 consists of seven tuples with

> INAME = Lee Kunkel, Albert Roby, Deb Kumar Roy, Cathy Doucette, Raj Chandra Mittra, Brady Jackson, Jack Adams

Also, R_2 consists of five tuples with

> INAME = Albert Roby, Deb Kumar Roy, Tom Clark, Marcia Brown, Jack Adams

Therefore, R_1 UNION R_2 consists of nine tuples with

INAME = Lee Kunkel, Albert Roby, Deb Kumar Roy, Cathy Doucette, Raj Chandra Mittra, Brady Jackson, Jack Adams, Tom Clark, Marcia Brown

Figure 3–2 gives the SQL implementation of the UNION operation.

The union operation is both commutative and associative. Also, if as sets $R_1 \subset R_2$, then R_1 UNION $R_2 = R_2$. Although defined as a binary operation, UNION can be extended to a k-ary operation. Thus given k union-compatible relations $R_1, \ldots, R_k$, we define

$$R_1 \text{ UNION } R_2 \text{ UNION } \cdots \text{ UNION } R_k$$

to be a relation whose tuples belong to at least one R_i, $i = 1, \ldots, k$.

(2) Intersection.   The *intersection* of two union-compatible relations R_1 and R_2, each of degree n, is the relation of degree n that consists of tuples belonging to both R_1 and R_2. The new relation is written as R_1 INTERSECT R_2.

Using R_1 and R_2 as defined in Section 3.2.1(1), we find that R_1 INTERSECT R_2 consists of three tuples of INSTR for which

INAME = Albert Roby, Deb Kumar Roy, Jack Adams

```
SQL> SELECT * FROM INSTR WHERE INAME IN
  2     (SELECT INAME FROM INSTR WHERE RANK = 'AssocProf'
  3     UNION
  4     SELECT INAME FROM INSTR WHERE RANK = 'Professor'
  5     UNION
  6     SELECT INAME FROM INSTR WHERE DNO = 'CS'
  7     UNION
  8     SELECT INAME FROM INSTR WHERE DNO = 'MA');
```

INAME	IDEG	SPCODE	RANK	SSNO	DN
Albert Roby	BS,MS,PhD	2	Professor	234567891	CS
Brady Jackson	MA,DLitt	15	Professor	912345678	RL
Cathy Doucette	MA,PhD	6	AssocProf	456789123	HS
Deb Kumar Roy	BS,MS,PhD	5	AssocProf	345678912	MA
Jack Adams	BA,PhD	1	AssocProf	123456798	CS
Lee Kunkel	BA,MA,PhD	4	Professor	123456789	EN
Marcia Brown	BA,BS,MS	2	Instructor	789123456	CS
Raj Chandra Mittra	BA,MSc,PhD	10	Professor	567891234	EE
Tom Clark	BA,MA	5	AsstProf	678912345	MA

9 records selected.

Figure 3–2   SQL implementation of UNION.

Figure 3–3 gives the SQL implementation of the INTERSECT operation. Like the union operation, intersection is both commutative and associative. It can be extended to a k-ary operation.

(3) Difference. Given two union-compatible relations R_1 and R_2 of degree n each, their *difference* is the relation of degree n that consists of tuples belonging to R_1 but not belonging R_2. This relation is written as R_1 DIFF R_2.

Using R_1 and R_2 as defined above, R_1 DIFF R_2 consists of four tuples of INSTR with

> INAME = Lee Kunkel, Cathy Doucette, Raj Chandra Mittra, Brady Jackson

Figure 3–4 gives the SQL implementation of R_1 DIFF R_2.

The difference operation is neither commutative nor associative. It is a binary operation and cannot be extended to a k-ary operation. Difference and intersection are connected by the equation

$$R_1 \text{ INTERSECT } R_2 = R_1 \text{ DIFF } (R_1 \text{ DIFF } R_2)$$

The result can be proved mathematically by using set-theoretic definitions of intersection and difference.

(4) Cartesian product. The *Cartesian product* of any two relations R_1 and R_2 of degree m and n, respectively, is a relation of degree $m + n$ that consists of all tuples t such that t is the concatenation of a tuple t_1 in R_1 and a tuple t_2 in R_2. Thus if we take

$$t_1 = (a_1, \ldots, a_m)$$

$$t_2 = (b_1, \ldots, b_n)$$

```
SQL> SELECT * FROM INSTR WHERE INAME IN
   2    ((SELECT INAME FROM INSTR WHERE RANK = 'AssocProf'
   3     UNION
   4     SELECT INAME FROM INSTR WHERE RANK = 'Professor')
   5    INTERSECT
   6    (SELECT INAME FROM INSTR WHERE DNO = 'CS'
   7     UNION
   8     SELECT INAME FROM INSTR WHERE DNO = 'MA'));

INAME              IDEG           SPCODE RANK             SSNO DN
```
INAME	IDEG	SPCODE	RANK	SSNO	DN
Albert Roby	BS,MS,PhD	2	Professor	234567891	CS
Deb Kumar Roy	BS,MS,PhD	5	AssocProf	345678912	MA
Jack Adams	BA,PhD	1	AssocProf	123456798	CS

Figure 3–3 SQL implementation of INTERSECT.

```
SQL> SELECT * FROM INSTR WHERE INAME IN
  2     ((SELECT INAME FROM INSTR WHERE RANK = 'AssocProf'
  3      UNION
  4      SELECT INAME FROM INSTR WHERE RANK = 'Professor')
  5      MINUS
  6     (SELECT INAME FROM INSTR WHERE DNO = 'CS'
  7      UNION
  8      SELECT INAME FROM INSTR WHERE DNO = 'MA'));
```

INAME	IDEG	SPCODE	RANK	SSNO	DN
Brady Jackson	MA,DLitt	15	Professor	912345678	RL
Cathy Doucette	MA,PhD	6	AssocProf	456789123	HS
Lee Kunkel	BA,MA,PhD	4	Professor	123456789	EN
Raj Chandra Mittra	BA,MSc,PhD	10	Professor	567891234	EE

Figure 3–4 SQL implementation of DIFF.

the concatenation of t_1 and t_2 is the tuple

$$t = (a_1, \ldots, a_m, b_1, \ldots, b_n)$$

Thus t consists of $m + n$ elements so that the Cartesian product is of degree $m + n$. This product is written as R_1 MULT R_2. If R_1 has p tuples and R_2 has q tuples, R_1 MULT R_2 has $p \times q$ tuples.

For example, define R_1 and R_2 as follows by using UNIV and INSTR:

> R_1 = set of all tuples in UNIV consisting of the attributes DNAME and DHEAD

> R_2 = set of all tuples in INSTR consisting of the attributes RANK, SSNO, and IDEG

Hence R_1 is a binary and R_2 is a ternary relation. Then R_1 MULT R_2 is a 5-ary relation consisting of 50 tuples, since R_1 has two attributes and five tuples, while R_2 has three attributes and 10 tuples. Figure 3–5 gives the SQL implementation of R_1 MULT R_2.

The Cartesian product is associative but not commutative. It can be extended to a k-ary operation from a binary operation.

3.2.2 Special Relational Operations

Four relations belong to this category: (1) selection, (2) projection, (3) join, and (4) division.

(1) Selection.   Let R be a relation of degree n and let θ represent any valid arithmetical comparison operator, such as $=$, $>$, $<=$, $=$, and so on. The

```
SQL> SELECT DNAME, DHEAD, RANK, SSNO, IDEG FROM UNIV, INSTR;
```

DNAME	DHEAD	RANK	SSNO	IDEG
English	Lee Kunkel	Professor	123456789	BA,MA,PhD
Computer Science	Albert Roby	Professor	123456789	BA,MA,PhD
Mathematics	Deb Kumar Roy	Professor	123456789	BA,MA,PhD
History	Cathy Doucette	Professor	123456789	BA,MA,PhD
Electrical Engineering	Raj Chandra Mittra	Professor	123456789	BA,MA,PhD
English	Lee Kunkel	Professor	234567891	BS,MS,PhD
Computer Science	Albert Roby	Professor	234567891	BS,MS,PhD
Mathematics	Deb Kumar Roy	Professor	234567891	BS,MS,PhD
History	Cathy Doucette	Professor	234567891	BS,MS,PhD
Electrical Engineering	Raj Chandra Mittra	Professor	234567891	BS,MS,PhD
English	Lee Kunkel	AssocProf	345678912	BS,MS,PhD

DNAME	DHEAD	RANK	SSNO	IDEG
Computer Science	Albert Roby	AssocProf	345678912	BS,MS,PhD
Mathematics	Deb Kumr Roy	AssocProf	345678912	BS,MS,PhD
History	Cathy Doucette	AssocProf	345678912	BS,MS,PhD
Electrical Engineering	Raj Chandra Mittra	AssocProf	345678912	BS,MS,PhD
English	Lee Kunkel	AssocProf	456789123	MA,PhD
Computer Science	Albert Roby	AssocProf	456789123	MA,PhD
Mathematics	Deb Kumar Roy	AssocProf	456789123	MA,PhD
History	Cathy Doucette	AssocProf	456789123	MA,PhD
Electrical Engineering	Raj Chandra Mittra	AssocProf	456789123	MA,PhD
English	Lee Kunkel	Professor	567891234	BA,MSc,PhD
Computer Science	Albert Roby	Professor	567891234	BA,MSc,PhD

Figure 3-5 SQL implementation of MULT. (Only 22 tuples of a total of 50 are shown.)

θ-*selection of R* on attributes a_1 and a_2 is defined to be the following set of tuples t:

$$\{t \mid t \in R, \qquad \text{and} \qquad t.a_1 \; \theta \; t.a_2 \text{ holds}\}$$

where $t.a$ means the value of the attribute a for the tuple t. In particular, $t.a_2$ may be replaced by a constant. Thus the θ-selection of R may be defined as

$$\{t \mid t \in R, \qquad \text{and} \qquad t.a_1 \; \theta \; c \text{ holds}\}$$

where c is a constant. The θ-selection operation is unary and yields a horizontal subset of the relation R (i.e., the subset of all tuples of R that satisfy the given comparison operator θ). Consequently, the θ-selection is often written using the WHERE clause as follows:

$$R \text{ WHERE } R.a_1 \; \theta \; R.a_2$$

The expression $R.a_1 \; \theta \; R.a_2$ is called the *predicate* of the θ-selection.

We can extend the predicate of a θ-selection from a simple comparison operator θ to an arbitrary Boolean combination of such simple comparisons by using the three basic Boolean operations of conjunction ($\wedge$), disjunction ($\vee$), and negation ($\sim$) (see Section 4.2). The extended definitions are formulated below in terms of the θ-selection and three set-theoretic operations discussed in Section 3.2.1:

1. R WHERE $p \wedge q$ is equivalent to

$$(R \text{ WHERE } p) \text{ INTERSECT } (R \text{ WHERE } q)$$

2. R WHERE $p \vee q$ is equivalent to

$$(R \text{ WHERE } p) \text{ UNION } (R \text{ WHERE } q)$$

3. R WHERE $\sim p$ is equivalent to

$$R \text{ DIFF } (R \text{ WHERE } p)$$

Note that p and q are simple comparison operators of the form $R.a_1 \; \theta \; R.a_2$. Also, the binary operations $p \wedge q$ and $p \vee q$ can be extended to k-ary operations $p_1 \wedge \cdots \wedge p_k$ and $p_1 \vee \cdots \vee p_k$, because INTERSECT and UNION can be so extended.

The θ-selection is often abbreviated to selection alone. However, the algebraic selection operation is not the same as the SELECT operation of SQL. The latter operation is much more powerful and can be used to implement the set-theoretic operations of relational algebra. R_1 and R_2 of Section 3.2.1(1) are examples of selection operation (see Figure 3–6).

Date [3, Chapter 18] has proposed an extended SELECT operation in SQL in order to handle a *tree-structured relation*. Such a relation represents a many–

```
SQL> CREATE VIEW R1 (INAME,IDEG,SPCODE,RANK,SSNO,DNO)
   2 AS
   3 SELECT * FROM INSTR WHERE
   4      RANK = 'AssocProf' OR RANK = 'Professor' ;

View created.

SQL> SELECT * FROM R1;
```

INAME	IDEG	SPCODE	RANK	SSNO	DN
Lee Kunkel	BA,MA,PhD	4	Professor	123456789	EN
Albert Roby	BS,MS,PhD	2	Professor	234567891	CS
Deb Kumar Roy	BS,MS,PhD	5	AssocProf	345678912	MA
Cathy Doucette	MA,PhD	6	AssocProf	456789123	HS
Raj Chandra Mittra	BA,MSc,PhD	10	Professor	567891234	EE
Brady Jackson	MA,DLitt	15	Professor	912345678	RL
Jack Adams	BA,PhD	1	AssocProf	123456789	CS

```
7 records selected.

SQL> CREATE VIEW R2 (INAME,IDEG,SPCODE,RANK,SSNO,DNO)
   2 AS
   3 SELECT * FROM INSTR WHERE
   4      DNO = 'CS' OR DNO = 'MA' ;

View created.

SQL> SELECT * FROM R2;
```

INAME	IDEG	SPCODE	RANK	SSNO	DN
Albert Roby	BS,MS,PhD	2	Professor	234567891	CS
Deb Kumar Roy	BS,MS,PhD	5	AssocProf	345678912	MA
Tom Clark	BA,MA	5	AsstProf	678912345	MA
Marcia Brown	BA,BS,MS	2	Instructor	789123456	CS
Jack Adams	BA,PhD	1	AssocProf	123456798	CS

Figure 3–6 SQL implementation of selection.

many relationship among its attribute values. As an example, suppose that a given database contains a parts inventory relation

        PARTS (P#, PNAME, QTY-ON-HAND, . . .)

and another relation,

        PP (MAJORP#, MINORP#)

that shows which parts contain which other parts as its immediate components. Thus some sample values are

PP:	MAJORP#	MINORP#
	P1	P2
	P1	P3
	P1	P5
	P1	P6
	P2	P4
	P2	P6
	P3	P5
	P3	P6
	P3	P7
	P4	P3
	P4	P6

A complete listing of all the components of a given part, say P1, can be determined by constructing and traversing the parts tree of Figure 3–7. However, the SELECT command is incapable of extracting that information from the database. Date [3, pp. 407–412] has outlined a 10-step procedure to extend the SELECT command for handling such a "parts explosion problem."

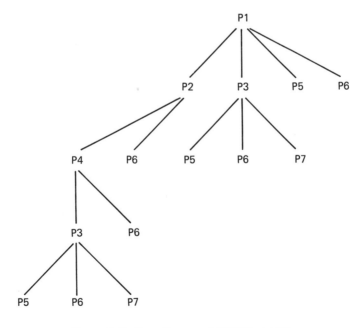

Figure 3–7 Tree diagram of PARTS and PP.

(2) Projection.   Let R be a relation of degree n with attributes $a_1, \ldots,$ a_n. Let $a_{i_1}, \ldots, a_{i_k}, k < n$, be a subset of these n attributes. The *projection* of R on attributes $a_{i_1}, \ldots, a_{i_k}$ is the set of all tuples $t = (t_1, \ldots, t_k)$ such that t appears in R with values $t_1, \ldots, t_k$ for the attributes $a_{i_1}, \ldots, a_{i_k}$, respectively.

The projection is written as $R[a_{i_1}, \ldots, a_{i_k}]$. It yields a vertical subset of a given relation, namely, a subset obtained by selecting specified attributes in a specified left-to-right order, and then eliminating redundant duplicate tuples within the attributes selected, if necessary. Since the order of attributes within a relation is important in projection, we can permute the attributes of a given relation in this way, if needed. Projection is a unary operation.

As an example, INSTR [INAME, SSNO, RANK, DNO] is a projection of the relation INSTR onto the four attributes INAME, SSNO, RANK, and DNO. Figure 3–8 gives the SQL implementation of this projection.

(3) Join.   Let R_1 and R_2 be two relations of degrees m and n, respectively, and let θ be any valid arithmetic comparison operation, as used in Section 3.2.2(1). The θ-*join* of the relation R_1 on attribute a and the relation R_2 on attribute b is the set of all tuples t such that t is the concatenation of a tuple $t_1 \in R_1$ and a tuple $t_2 \in R_2$ and the condition $t_1.a \; \theta \; t_2.b$ holds. Clearly, θ-join can be expressed in terms of Cartesian product and selection as follows:

1. Perform R_1 MULT R_2 and call it relation R.
2. Perform R WHERE $R.a \; \theta \; R.b$.

The θ-join of R_1 and R_2 has $m + n$ attributes since it involves the Cartesian product operation. The total number of its tuples is less than $p \times q$, since the θ-

```
SQL> SELECT INAME, SSNO, RANK, DNO FROM INSTR;

INAME                      SSNO RANK          DN

Lee Kunkel             123456789 Professor    EN
Albert Roby            234567891 Professor    CS
Deb Kumar Roy          345678912 AssocProf    MA
Cathy Doucette         456789123 AssocProf    HS
Raj Chandra Mittra     567891234 Professor    EE
Tom Clark              678912345 AsstProf     MA
Marcia Brown           789123456 Instructor   CS
Susan Woodsmith        891234567 AsstProf     PH
Brady Jackson          912345678 Professor    RL
Jack Adams             123456798 AssocProf    CS

10 records selected.
```

Figure 3–8   SQL implementation of projection.

selection will eliminate some of the tuples from the total number, $p \times q$, of the tuples of the Cartesian product, where R_1 and R_2 have degree p and q.

For example, let θ represent the operator "not equal," abbreviated NE. Define the NE-join of UNIV and INSTR to consist of all tuples from the Cartesian product UNIV MULT INSTR for which the condition

```
UNIV.DNO NE INSTR.DNO
```

holds. The NE-join selects 42 tuples by means of the defining condition. Figure 3–9 gives the SQL implementation of this join.

If θ represents the equality operation, $=$, the θ-join is called an *equijoin*. Hence an equijoin of the relation R_1 on attribute a and the relation R_2 on attribute b consists of all tuples t such that t is a concentration of a tuple t_1 in R_1 with a tuple t_2 in R_2, where $t_1.a = t_2.b$. Therefore, the equijoin always has two identical attribute values, $t_1.a$ and $t_2.b$. If we eliminate one of them by taking a projection of the equijoin, the result is called a *natural join,* or simply a *join*. The algorithm for the join of R_1 on a with R_2 on b can be written as follows:

1. Perform R_1 MULT R_2 and call it relation R.
2. Perform R WHERE $R.a = R.b$ and call it relation S.
3. Perform a projection of S on all its attributes except the attribute $R.a$ (or $R.b$).

We observe that if R_1 is of degree m and R_2 of degree n, the join of R_1 and R_2 is of degree $m + n - 1$. It is written R_1 JOIN R_2. Since the join is defined in terms of Cartesian product, selection, and projection, and since the Cartesian product is an associative binary operation whereas selection and projection are both unary operations, it follows that the join operation is also associative. Consequently, it can be extended to a k-ary operation. Thus

$$(\cdots ((R_1 \text{ JOIN } R_2) \text{ JOIN } R_3) \cdots \text{ JOIN } R_k)$$

can be unambiguously written as

$$R_1 \text{ JOIN } R_2 \text{ JOIN } R_3 \cdots \text{ JOIN } R_k$$

We also note that if R_1 and R_2 have no common attributes, then R_1 JOIN R_2 is the same as R_1 MULT R_2.

We now illustrate the join operation by using UNIV and INSTR, which have a common attribute DNO. Hence the join of UNIV and INSTR via the attribute DNO is a relation consisting of eight attributes: DNO, DNAME, DHEAD, INAME, IDEG, SPCODE, RANK, and SSNO. Of course, the order of these attributes can be changed by the projection operation. The new relation UNIV JOIN INSTR consists of those tuples for which we have UNIV.DNO =

```
SQL> SELECT UNIV.DNO, DNAME, DHEAD, INAME, IDEG, SPCODE, RANK, SSNO
  2  FROM UNIV, INSTR WHERE
  3    UNIV.DNO != INSTR.DNO ;
```

DN DNAME	DHEAD	INAME
IDEG	SPCODE RANK	SSNO
CS Computer Science	Albert Roby	Lee Kunkel
BA,MA,PhD	4 Professor 123456789	
MA Mathematics	Deb Kumar Roy	Lee Kunkel
BA,MA,PhD	4 Professor 123456789	
HS History	Cathy Doucette	Lee Kunkel
BA,MA,PhD	4 Professor 123456789	

DN DNAME	DHEAD	INAME
IDEG	SPCODE RANK	SSNO
EE Electrical Engineering	Raj Chandra Mittra	Lee Kunkel
BA,MA,PhD	4 Professor 123456789	
EN English	Lee Kunkel	Albert Roby
BS,MS,PhD	2 Professor 234567891	
MA Mathematics	Deb Kumar Roy	Albert Roby
BS,MS,PhD	2 Professor 234567891	

DN DNAME	DHEAD	INAME
IDEG	SPCODE RANK	SSNO
HS History	Cathy Doucette	Albert Roby
BS,MS,PhD	2 Professor 234567891	
EE Electrical Engineering	Raj Chandra Mittra	Albert Roby
BS,MS,PhD	2 Professor 234567891	
EN English	Lee Kunkel	Deb Kumar Roy
BS,MS,PhD	5 AssocProf 345678912	

Figure 3–9 SQL implementation of NE-join. (Only 9 tuples of a total of 42 are shown.)

INSTR.DNO. Figure 3–10 gives the SQL implementation of this relation. The join selects eight tuples.

In performing the join operation on two relations R_1 and R_2 we face one problem. If a tuple in R_1 does not match any tuple in R_2 under the joining condition,

```
SQL> SELECT UNIV.DNO, DNAME, DHEAD, INAME, IDEG, RANK, SPCODE, SSNO
   2  FROM UNIV, INSTR WHERE
   3    UNIV.DNO = INSTR.DNO ;
```

DN DNAME	DHEAD	INAME
IDEG RANK	**SPCODE SSNO**	
CS Computer Science	Albert Roby	Albert Roby
BS,MS,PhD Professor	2 234567891	
CS Computer Science	Albert Roby	Marcia Brown
BA,BS,MS Instructor	2 789123456	
CS Computer Science	Albert Roby	Jack Adams
BA,PhD AssocProf	1 123456798	
DN DNAME	DHEAD	INAME
IDEG RANK	**SPCODE SSNO**	
EE Electrical Engineering	Raj Chandra Mittra	Raj Chandra Mittra
BA,MSc,PhD Professor	10 567891234	
EN English	Lee Kunkel	Lee Kunkel
BA,MA,PhD Professor	4 123456789	
HS History	Cathy Doucette	Cathy Doucette
MA,PhD AssocProf	6 456789123	
DN DNAME	DHEAD	INAME
IDEG RANK	**SPCODE SSNO**	
MA Mathematics	Deb Kumar Roy	Deb Kumar Roy
BS,MS,PhD AssocProf	5 345678912	
MA Mathematics	Deb Kumar Roy	Tom Clark
BA,MA AsstProf	5 678912345	

8 records selected.

Figure 3–10 SQL implementation of natural join.

that tuple in R_1 will not appear as a part of the concatenated tuple in the relation produced by R_1 JOIN R_2. In this sense it is often said that the join operation can lose information. To remedy this problem, the operation of *outer join* was proposed by I. J. Heath in 1971 (see Date [3, p. 337]) and was formally defined by M. Lacroix and A. Pirotte in 1976. Later in 1979 Codd extended the definition to capture more meaning. The join is sometimes called *inner join,* to distinguish it from the outer join.

An outer join is obtained by appending certain additional tuples to the result of the corresponding inner join. There is one such additional tuple for each unmatched tuple in each of the original relations. Each such additional tuple consists of a copy of the unmatched tuple extended with null values in other attribute positions. The null values are interpreted as missing or unknown information. More formally, we can define the outer join as follows:

Let R and S be two relations of degree m and n, respectively; let R have attributes $r_1, \ldots, r_m$, and S have attributes $s_1, \ldots, s_n$. Suppose that $r_i = s_j$, for some fixed i and j, so that the inner join, R JOIN S, yields a new relation T of degree $m + n - 1$ and with attributes

$$r_1, \ldots, r_m, s_1, \ldots, s_{j-1}, s_{j+1}, \ldots, s_n$$

Define two new relations R^* and S^* of degrees m and n, respectively, as follows:

$$R^* = R \text{ DIFF } T[r_1, \ldots, r_m]$$

$$S^* = S \text{ DIFF } T[s_1, \ldots, s_{j-1}, r_i, s_{j+1}, \ldots, s_n]$$

where $T[r_1, \ldots, r_m]$ is the projection of T on the attributes $r_1, \ldots, r_m$ alone, and a similar definition applies to $T[s_1, \ldots, s_{j-1}, r_i, s_{j+1}, \ldots, s_n]$.

Then the outer join of R on r_i with S on s_j produces the new relation X given by

$$T \text{ UNION } (R^* \text{ MULT } \underbrace{(?, \ldots, ?)}_{n-1 \text{ times}}) \text{ UNION } (\underbrace{(?, \ldots, ?)}_{m-1 \text{ times}} \text{ MULT } S^*)$$

We observe that R^* consists of the set of tuples in R that do not appear as subsets of tuples in T (i.e., the set of unmatched tuples of R with respect to the inner join T). Similarly, S^* consists of the set of unmatched tuples in S with respect to the inner join T. Each "?" represents a null value of an attribute. As a result,

$$R^* \text{ MULT } \underbrace{(?, \ldots, ?)}_{n-1 \text{ times}}$$

represents a relation of degree $m + n - 1$ obtained by forming the Cartesian product of the set of unmatched m-tuples in R with the set of $(n - 1)$-tuples of null values representing the $n - 1$ unmatched attributes in T. A similar interpretation holds for the relation

$$\underbrace{(?, \ldots, ?)}_{m \, - \, 1 \text{ times}} \text{ MULT } S*$$

Finally, the two union operations together produce all possible tuples, matched and unmatched, with strings of null values.

Let us now illustrate this concept by means of a small example adapted from Date [3, pp. 340–342]. Let S ($S\#$, CITY) and P ($P\#$, CITY) be two relations of degree 2 each with the following data:

S:	S#	City
	S1	London
	S2	Paris
	S3	?
	S4	New York
	S5	Chicago

P:	P#	CITY
	P1	London
	P2	Oslo
	P3	?
	P4	New York
	P5	Boston

The inner join T of S and P on the common attribute CITY is given by

T:	S#	CITY	P#
	S1	London	P1
	S4	New York	P4

We note that $m = n = 2$, so that T has degree $m + n - 1 = 3$. Now $S*$ and $P*$ are given by

$$S* = S \text{ DIFF } T[S\#, \text{ CITY}]$$

$$P* = P \text{ DIFF } T[P\#, \text{ CITY}]$$

Hence $S*$ and $P*$ have the following data:

$S*$:	S#	CITY
	S2	Paris
	S3	?
	S5	Chicago

$P*$:	P#	CITY
	P2	Oslo
	P3	?
	P5	Boston

Finally, the outer join X of S and P is given by

$$T \text{ UNION } (S* \text{ MULT } (?)) \text{ UNION } ((?) \text{ MULT } P*)$$

Hence X has the following data:

X:	S#	CITY	P#
	S1	London	P1
	S2	Paris	?
	S3	?	?
	S4	New York	P4
	S5	Chicago	?
	?	Oslo	P2
	?	?	P3
	?	Boston	P5

Similar to the outer join operation which extends the inner join, it is possible to define outer equijoin and outer θ-join as extensions of equijoin and θ-join, respectively.

(4) Division. The division operation divides a dividend relation A of degree $m + n$ by a divisor relation B of degree n and produces a *quotient relation* of degree m. The $(m + i)$th attribute of A and the ith attribute of B ($i = 1, 2, \ldots, n$) should be defined on the same domain. Consider the first m attributes of A as a single composite attribute X, and the last n as another composite attribute Y; relation A can then be thought of as a set of pairs of values (x, y). Similarly, relation B can be thought of as a set of single values (y). Then the result of dividing A by B is the relation C, with sole (composite) attribute X, such that every value x of $C.X$ appears as a value of $A.X$, and the pair of values (x, y) appears in A for all values y appearing in B. The relation C is written A DIVIDE B. Division is a binary operation and is neither associative nor commutative.

Let us write the dividend relation A as

$$A(a_1, \ldots, a_m, a_{m+1}, \ldots, a_{m+n}) = \{(x, y) \mid x \in X, y \in Y\}$$

and the divisor relation B as

$$B(b_1, \ldots, b_n) = \{y \mid y \in Y\}$$

Then x is an m-tuple $(a_1, \ldots, a_m)$ and y is an n-tuple $(a_{m+1}, \ldots, a_{m+n})$. The quotient relation C (i.e., A DIVIDE B) consists of all m-tuples $(c_1, \ldots, c_m)$ defined by the following condition:

$$(c_1, \ldots, c_m) = x \text{ such that } x \in A.X, (x, y) \in A \qquad \text{for all } y \in B.Y$$

The division operation is helpful for queries that include the phrase "for all." As an example, let A(INAME, CNO) be a relation of degree 2 with the following data:

A:	INAME	CNO
	Lee Kunkel	EN101
	Lee Kunkel	EN435
	Lee Kunkel	EN693
	Lee Kunkel	MG682
	Lee Kunkel	EN764
	Lee Kunkel	EN579
	Ed Brown	EN101
	Ed Brown	EN435
	Ed Brown	MG682
	Tom Clark	MA425
	Tom Clark	MG682
	Tom Clark	MA235
	Marcia Brown	CS682
	Marcia Brown	CS579
	Susan Woodsmith	EN693

Let B(CNO) be a relation of degree 1 with the following data:

B:	CNO
	EN435
	MG682

Then *A* DIVIDE *B* is a relation *C*, say, of degree 1 with the data

C:	INAME
	Ed Brown
	Lee Kunkel

We note that *C* contains the INAMEs for the instructors of both EN435 and MG682.

3.3 PRIMITIVE ALGEBRAIC OPERATIONS

The eight relational algebraic operations discussed in Section 3.2 are not mutually independent. The following five are regarded as *primitive operations* since the remaining three can be defined in terms of these primitives:

1. Union
2. Difference
3. Cartesian product
4. Selection
5. Projection

To show that these five operations are primitive, we need to show that no one of them can be derived as a logical consequence of the other four. Date [2, pp. 279–280] has given a plausibility argument to establish this fact. Ullman [5, p. 172] has outlined a method to prove the mutual independence of the five primitives in a rigorous mathematical way. The latter task is a significant job.

We next show that the remaining three operations—join, intersection, and division—can be expressed in terms of the five primitives. As shown in Section 3.2.2(3), join, equijoin, and natural join are all expressible in terms of Cartesian product, selection, and projection. All forms of outer joins can be defined in terms of inner join or join (which is expressible in terms of Cartesian product, selection, and projection, as noted above), union, and difference. The intersection operation can be expressed in terms of the difference operation as follows:

$$A \text{ INTERSECT } B = A \text{ DIFF } (A \text{ DIFF } B)$$

$$= B \text{ DIFF } (B \text{ DIFF } A)$$

as shown in Section 3.2.1(3). Finally, division can be expressed in terms of projection, difference, and Cartesian product as follows: Let A have composite attributes X and Y and B have the composite attribute Z as in Section 3.2.2(4). Then A DIVIDE B can be written in the following equivalent form:

$$A \text{ DIVIDE } B = A[X] \text{ DIFF } ((A[X] \text{ MULT } B) \text{ DIFF } A) [X]$$

where $A[X]$ denotes the projection of A on its (composite) attribute X.

3.4 CLOSURE PROPERTY OF RELATIONAL ALGEBRA OPERATIONS

If we perform any one or more of the eight relational algebra operations on the relations of a database, we *always* get another relation in the same database. For example, if we take a projection of a union, or a join of two selections, or the difference of a join and an intersection, and so on, we still get another relation. Thus we can write *nested relational expressions,* expressions in which the operands themselves are represented by other expressions instead of just attribute names. Conceptually, we can regard a relational database as a collection of relations of degree n, for different values of n, that is *closed* with respect to the eight relational algebra operations. The *closure property* ensures that the result of any relational algebra operation, simple or composite, is another relation. We now examine the theoretical basis of the foregoing assertion.

Let a relational database consist of n relations $R_1, \ldots, R_n$ of degrees $d_1, \ldots, d_n$, respectively. Then, mathematically, R_i is a subset of a Cartesian product set of degree d_i, that is, a product set having d_i distinct factor sets (see Section 2.1.1). Since this holds for $i = 1, \ldots, n$, we find that the relations of the database are isomorphic to the subsets of a Cartesian product set C of order $d_1 + d_2 + \cdots + d_n$. For example, R_1 is isomorphic to the subset of C consisting of all those tuples that have the first d_1 elements identical with the elements of tuples in R_1 and have zero everywhere else; and similarly for $R_2, \ldots, R_n$. Consequently, each relation R_i, $i = 1, \ldots, n$, is essentially a subset of C. Now, a set is closed with respect to the operations of union and difference performed on its subsets. Also, any Cartesian product performed on some or all of $R_1, \ldots, R_n$ can produce a subset that is a Cartesian product of order at most $d_1 + \cdots + d_n$, and therefore such a set is still isomorphic to a subset of C. Finally, a selection or a projection performed on any one of $R_1, \ldots, R_n$ yields a horizontal or a vertical subset of the original relation and hence is still a subset of C. Thus the results of all five primitive operations produce subsets of C and as such belong to the relational database, which is, therefore, closed with respect to the five primitive operations. Hence the database is also closed with respect to the remaining three derived operations, each of which is expressible in terms of the five primitives.

3.5 SUMMARY

In this chapter we have discussed relational algebra, which forms the basis of the query languages like SQL. There are eight operations belonging to the relational algebra. Four of them—union, intersection, difference, and Cartesian product—are traditional set-theoretic operations. The first three apply only to union-compatible relations, relations that are of the same degree and for which the kth attributes, $k = 1, \ldots, n$, have the same domains. Union, intersection, and Cartesian product, although initially defined as binary operations can be extended to k-ary operations. Difference, however, is binary and cannot be so extended.

The remaining four operations are termed special relational operations and include selection, projection, join, and division. The first two operations are unary and return, respectively, a horizontal and a vertical subset of a relation. The join operation has different versions: θ-join, equijoin, natural join or simple join, and outer join. To contrast with outer join, natural join is often called inner join. The basic distinction between the inner join and outer join is that the former returns only those tuples that match the values of the common attribute, whereas the latter return all tuples, both matched and unmatched, by using null values for the unmatched tuples. All tuples of joins can be extended to k-ary operations. Finally, the operation of division is strictly binary.

Five of the eight operations above are primitive, that is, they are mutually independent and the remaining three operations can be expressed in terms of them. These five primitive operations are union, difference, Cartesian product, selection, and projection.

The chapter closes with a discussion of the closure property of the relational algebra operations. It is shown mathematically that by performing any number of these operations on the relations in a database we always get another relation; that is, the database is closed with respect to the eight relational algebra operations.

Since the chapter uses some mathematical concepts, these are summarized at the beginning. Also, a brief discussion of nonprocedural languages appears there.

KEY WORDS

binary operation

Cartesian product of relations

Cartesian product of sets

closed set

closure property

derived operations

difference of relations

difference of sets

disjoint sets

dividend relation

division

divisor relation

element

equal set

equijoin

inner join

intersection of relations

intersection of sets

isomorphic sets

join

k-ary operation

level of abastraction

natural join

nested relational expression

nonprocedural language

null value

order of a Cartesian product

outer join

predicate

primitive operations

projection

query language

quotient relation

SELECT command in SQL

selection

set

subset

theta-join (θ-join)

theta-selection (θ-selection)

tree-structured relation

unary operation

union of relations

union of sets

union-compatible relations

REFERENCES AND FURTHER READING

The following references contain additional materials related to the topics covered in this chapter.

1. E. F. Codd, *Relational Completeness of Data Base Sublanguages,* Data Base Systems, Courant Computer Science Symposia Series, vol. 6, Prentice-Hall, Englewood Cliffs, NJ, 1972.
2. C. J. Date, *Introduction to Database Systems,* vol. I, 4th ed., Addison-Wesley, Reading, MA, 1986.
3. C. J. Date, *Relational Database Selected Writings,* Addison-Wesley, Reading, MA, 1986.
4. H. F. Korth and A. Silberschatz, *Database System Concepts,* McGraw-Hill, New York, 1986.
5. J. D. Ullman, *Principles of Database Systems,* Computer Science Press, Rockville, MD, 1982.

Codd's paper [1] gives a comprehensive discussion with examples of the eight relational algebra operations. Date's treatment [2, Chapter 13] follows Codd's rather closely. Date [3, Chapters 16 and 18] discusses outer joins and extended SELECT operation to handle tree-structured relations. In Chapter 16, Date has given a very detailed proposal to implement various types of outer joins. Korth and Silberschatz [4] contains some good examples of the division operation. Ullman [5] gives an outline of the proof that the five primitive operations are mutually independent. Date's [2, pp. 279–280] intuitive "proof" that the five primitive operations are truly primitive is quite inadequate.

The topics on mathematical prerequisites discussed in Section 3.1.1 can be found in any text on discrete mathematics for computer science. For example, the following is a good source:

R. SKVARCIOUS and W. ROBINSON. *Discrete Mathematics for Computer Science,* Benjamin-Cummings, Menlo Park, CA, 1985.

REVIEW QUESTIONS

1. Define a nonprocedural language. Why is a query language regarded as nonprocedural?
2. Explain the meaning of the statement "SQL is at a higher level of abstraction than COBOL."
3. Define the following terms and provide an example of the use of each.
   (a) Union.
   (b) Intersection.
   (c) Difference.
   (d) Cartesian product.

4. How does the union of two relations resemble the union of two sets?

5. Union, intersection, and Cartesian product are associative and can be extended to k-ary operations. What role does associativity play in this extendability to k-ary feature?

6. Define θ-selection of a relation. How does this operation compare with the SELECT . . . FROM . . . WHERE construct of SQL?

7. How do you define θ-selections with composite predicates?

8. Define a tree-structured relation. Why is the SELECT command in SQL incapable of retrieving information from such a relation?

9. Define projection of relation. Why is it said that the θ-selection returns a horizontal subset of a relation whereas the projection returns a vertical subset?

10. Define the following terms.
    (a) θ-join.
    (b) Equijoin.
    (c) Natural join.
    (d) Inner join.
    (e) Outer join.

11. What additional information is provided by an outer join that is not available from an inner join?

12. Explain the operation of outer join with an example.

13. Define division of two relations with examples. Why can the division not be extended to a k-ary operation?

14. Define the five primitive operations. Why are they called primitive?

15. Explain the closure property of the relational algebra operations.

EXERCISES

1. What are the special cases of the operation R_1 JOIN R_2 for the following cases?
   (a) R_1 and R_2 have no attributes in common.
   (b) R_1 and R_2 have all attributes in common.
   Give reasons for your answer.

2. State the primary key of each of the following operations.
   (a) R_1 MULT R_2.
   (b) R_1 UNION R_2.
   (c) R_1 DIFF R_2.
   (d) R_1 JOIN R_2.
   Assume that R_1 and R_2 are such that all four operations are defined.

3. Perform the outer join of UNIV and INSTR using DNO as the common attribute. (*Hint:* You have to augment the tuples of UNIV with null values of some of the attributes.)

4. Perform a θ-join of UNIV and INSTR where θ is "greater than." Then perform the equijoin and the join of these two relations.

5. Give relational algebra versions of the queries in Figure 2–11.

CHAPTER 4

RELATIONAL CALCULUS

4.1 DISTINCTION BETWEEN RELATIONAL ALGEBRA AND RELATIONAL CALCULUS

The relational calculus represents an alternative to the relational algebra as a basis for the formulation of data manipulation languages. Relational calculus differs from relational algebra in its level of abstraction for formulating the query. The algebra based query describes what is needed from the database and also the order in which the data are to be retrieved. But the calculus based query merely describes what is to be retrieved without specifying the order of the operations. The calculus notations provide the power to employ such abstractions.

As an example, consider the following query:

List the department name and department head for each instructor whose rank is associate professor or professor.

Using relational algebra operations, we can formulate this query as follows:

1. Perform UNIV JOIN INSTR using DNO as the common attribute.

2. Perform a θ-selection of the join where θ is equality (=) and the predicate of the selection is (RANK = 'AssocProf') UNION (RANK = 'Professor').

3. Perform a projection of this θ-selection on the attributes DNAME and DHEAD.

The SQL version of this query is given in Figure 4–1. Note that SQL is not based strictly on relational algebra (see Section 4.4.2). The query above can be written as follows in relational calculus formalism:

Find DNAME and DHEAD from UNIV such that there exists an INSTR tuple with the corresponding DNO for which RANK has the value 'AssocProf' or 'Professor'.

Comparing the relational algebra version with the relational calculus version, we note that the former provides a set of operations to be performed in a specific order, whereas the latter merely describes the defining characteristics of the desired result and the system has to determine what operations (e.g., join, projection, etc.) are to be performed in what order to derive the result. For this reason, relational algebra–based languages are called *prescriptive,* whereas relational calculus–based languages are called *descriptive.* On this basis some authors (e.g., Korth and Silberschatz [5, p. 63]) even claim that relational algebra–based languages are procedural, whereas relational calculus–based languages are nonprocedural. We disagree with this contention because relational algebra–based languages do not include procedural constructs such as DO-WHILE or IF-THEN-ELSE. The most that can be said is that algebraic languages have a lower degree of nonprocedurality than that of the calculus-based languages. This issue is treated in more detail in Sections 4.4.1 and 4.4.2, after we have discussed the features of relational calculus.

A word on the terminology: Relational calculus is based on first-order predicate logic (often called predicate calculus) and has nothing to do with differential or integral calculus of mathematics. The term is a carryover from past usage and is indeed misleading.

```
SQL> SELECT DISTINCT DNAME, DHEAD FROM UNIV, INSTR WHERE
   2    (RANK = 'AssocProf' OR RANK = 'Professor')
   3    AND UNIV.DNO = INSTR.DNO;

DNAME                        DHEAD
_____

Computer Science             Albert Roby
Electrical Engineering        Raj Chandra Mittra
English                      Lee Kunkel
History                      Cathy Doucette
Mathematics                  Deb Kumar Roy

SQL> SPOOL OFF
```

Figure 4–1 SQL version of query.

4.2 MATHEMATICAL PREREQUISITES FOR RELATIONAL CALCULUS

Relational calculus is founded on a branch of mathematical logic called predicate calculus. The idea of using predicate calculus as the basis for a data manipulation language was first suggested by J. L. Kuhns in 1967. Later in 1972, E. F. Codd formulated the basics of relational calculus as an applied predicate calculus specifically tailored to relational databases. (See Codd [1] for details.)

We now provide a brief overview of the fundamentals of predicate calculus or predicate logic. Predicate calculus uses a *predicate* as the basic element and three operations as basic operations:

1. A unary operation of negation, written as NOT or $\sim$
2. A binary operation of conjunction, written as AND or $\wedge$
3. Another binary operation of disjunction, written as OR or $\vee$

In terms of these we define two additional operations and two quantifiers:

4. IF . . . THEN or $\rightarrow$ (implication)
5. IFF $\leftrightarrow$ (equivalence)
6. FORALL x or $\forall x$ (universal quantifier)
7. EXISTS x or $\exists x$ (existential quantifier)

These five operations are governed by their respective truth tables, given below.

1. NOT, $\sim$ negation

p	$\sim p$
T	F
F	T

2. AND, $\wedge$ conjunction

p	q	$p \wedge q$
T	T	T
T	F	F
F	T	F
F	F	F

3. OR, $\vee$ disjunction

p	q	$p \vee q$
T	T	T
T	F	T
F	T	T
F	F	F

4. IF . . . THEN, → implication

p	q	$p \rightarrow q$
T	T	T
T	F	F
F	T	T
F	F	T

Implication is defined in terms of negation and conjunction as

$$p \rightarrow q \quad \text{means} \quad \sim p \vee q$$

Its truth table is derived by using this definition.

5. IFF, ↔ equivalence

p	q	$p \leftrightarrow q$
T	T	T
T	F	F
F	T	F
F	F	T

Equivalence is defined in terms of implication by

$$p \leftrightarrow q \quad \text{means} \quad (p \rightarrow q) \wedge (q \rightarrow p)$$

Its truth table is derived by using this definition.

In all of the truth tables above, p and q represent symbolic predicates and T and F stand for truth values of "true" and "false," respectively. The two quantifiers are described below with examples.

6. FORALL, ∀ universal quantifier

A property is true for all values of a variable.

Example 1. Binary relation ">" is defined by

$$> = \{(x, y) \mid \forall x, y \in \mathbb{R}, x > y\}$$

Example 2. If $x > y$ and $y > z$, then $x > z$.

$$(\forall x, y, z)((x > y) \wedge (y > z)) \rightarrow (x > z)$$

7. EXISTS, ∃ existential quantifier

A property is true for at least one value of a variable.

Example 3. Given any two numbers x and y, there is always at least one number between them.

$$(\forall x, y)(\exists z)((x > z) \wedge (z > y))$$

Example 4. Every relation has at least one key attribute.

$$(\forall R)(\exists a) \quad (a \text{ is a key attribute in } R)$$

We now state the following results without proof:

1. $\sim(p \wedge q)$ means $\sim\!p \vee \sim\!q$ ⎱
     $\sim(p \vee q)$ means $\sim\!p \wedge \sim\!q$ ⎰   De Morgan's law

2. $\sim(\forall x\ P(x))$ means $\exists y(\sim\!P(y))$

3. $\sim(\exists x\ P(x))$ means $\forall y(\sim\!P(y))$

4.3 TWO TYPES OF RELATIONAL CALCULUS

There are two types of relational calculus: (1) tuple relational calculus and (2) domain relational calculus. In tuple relational calculus the tuple variable (i.e., row of a relation) is used as the basic entity, whereas in domain relational calculus the domain variable is used as the basic entity. The domain variables represent the components of a tuple variable. However, both types use predicate calculus for the manipulation of operations. Essentially, a domain variable is an attribute and a tuple variable is a row.

4.3.1 Tuple Relational Calculus

The basic entity of a tuple relational calculus is the *tuple variable* or *range variable*. A tuple variable t ranges over a relation R in the sense that the only admissible values of t are the tuples in R. *Tuple relational calculus expressions* are of the form $\{t \mid \psi(t) \text{ holds}\}$, where t is the only free tuple variable in ψ, and $\psi(t)$ is a formula built from atoms and a collection of operators in relational calculus.

The *atoms* of the expressions $\psi(t)$ are of three types:

1. $R(s)$, where R is a relation and s is a tuple variable. The atom $R(s)$ signifies that s is a tuple of R.

2. $s(i)\ \theta\ u(j)$, where s and u are tuple variables and θ is an arithmetic comparison operator ($<$, $=$, etc.). This atom stands for the assertion that the ith component of s stands in relation θ to the jth component of u. For example, $s(1) < u(2)$ means that the first component of s is less than the second component of u.

3. $s(i)\ \theta\ a$ and $a\ \theta\ s(i)$, where θ and $s(i)$ are as in type 2, and a is a constant. The first of these atoms asserts that the ith component of s stands in relation θ to the constant a, and the second has an analogous meaning. For example, $s(1) = 3$ means that the value of the first component of s is 3.

We next define the terms: free variable, bound variable, and formula. Conceptually, we can say that an occurrence of a variable in a formula is *bound* if that variable has been introduced by a "for all" or "there exists" quantifier, and we say that the variable is *free*, if not.

The notion of a free variable is analogous to that of a global variable in a programming language, that is, a variable defined outside the current procedure. A bound variable is like a local variable, one that is defined in the procedure at hand. In effect, the quantifiers of relational calculus play the role of declarations in a programming language.

Finally, a *formula* is defined recursively as follows:

1. Every atom is a formula. All occurrences of tuple variables mentioned in the atom are free in this formula.

2. If ψ_1 and ψ_2 are formulas, then $\psi_1 \wedge \psi_2$, $\psi_1 \vee \psi_2$, and $\sim\psi_1$ are formulas asserting that ψ_1 and ψ_2 are both true; that ψ_1 or ψ_2, or both, are true; and that ψ_1 is not true, respectively. Occurrences of tuple variables are free or bound in $\psi_1 \wedge \psi_2$, $\psi_1 \vee \psi_2$, and $\sim\psi_1$ if they are free or bound in ψ_1 or ψ_2, depending on where they occur. Note that an occurrence of a variable s could be bound in ψ_1 while another occurrence of s is free in ψ_2, for example.

3. If ψ is a formula, then $(\exists s \mid \psi(s))$ is also a formula, where $\exists$ is the existential quantifier. The formula means that there exists a value of s such that when we substitute this value for all free occurrences of s in ψ, the formula ψ becomes true. Occurrences of s that are free in ψ are bound to $\exists s$ in $(\exists s \mid \psi(s))$. Other occurrences of tuple variables in ψ, including possible occurrences of s that are bound in ψ, are free or bound in $(\exists s \mid \psi(s))$ according as they are free or bound in ψ.

4. If ψ is a formula, then $(\forall s \mid \psi(s))$ is also a formula. Free occurrences of s in ψ are bound to $\forall s$ in $(\forall s)(\psi)$, and other occurrences of variables in ψ are treated as in condition 3. The formula $(\forall s)(\psi)$ asserts that whatever value of the appropriate degree we substitute for free occurrences of s in ψ, the formula ψ becomes true.

5. Parentheses may be placed around formulas as needed. We assume the order of precedence is: arithmetic comparison operators highest, then the quantifiers $\exists$ and $\forall$, then $\sim$, $\wedge$, and $\vee$, in that order.

6. Nothing else is a formula.

4.3.2 Safe Tuple Relational Calculus Expression

Let R be a relation of degree n with attributes $a_1, \ldots, a_n$ that have the respective domains $D_1, \ldots, D_n$. Then each tuple of R belongs to the Cartesian product $D_1 \times \cdots \times D_n$. Now the tuple relational calculus expression $\{t \mid \sim R(t)\}$ returns all those tuples t that belong to $D_1 \times \cdots \times D_n$ but are not in R. If one or more of the domains D_i are infinite sets, the expression above returns an infinite set of tuples, which is meaningless to deal with. For instance, we cannot store or print them. Consequently, it is necessary to restrict the calculus to yield only finite relations. This leads us to the concept of safe tuple relational calculus expressions.

Given a formula ψ, we define a set $DOM(\psi)$ to consist of all symbols that either appear explicitly in ψ or are components of a tuple in some relation R mentioned in ψ. We call DOM(ψ) the *domain* of the formula ψ. DOM(ψ) is a function of the actual relations to be substituted for the relation variables in ψ. Since each relation has only a finite number of tuples, DOM(ψ) is a finite set. As an example, suppose that $\psi(t) = c \vee R(t)$, where c is a constant and $R(t)$ is an n-ary relation. Then DOM(ψ) is given by

$$\mathrm{DOM}(\psi) = \{c\} \cup R_1 \cup R_2 \cup \cdots \cup R_n$$

where R_i is the set of all values of the ith attribute appearing in R, $i = 1, 2, \ldots,$ n.

A tuple relational calculus expression $\{t \mid \psi(t)\}$ is defined to be *safe* if the following three conditions hold:

1. Each component of t belongs to DOM(ψ).
2. For each existentially quantified subformula of ψ of the form

$$(\exists s)(\psi_1(s))$$

the subformula is true if and only if there is a tuple s with values from DOM(ψ_1) such that $\psi_1(s)$ holds.

3. For each universally quantified subformula of ψ of the form

$$(\forall s)(\psi_1(s))$$

the subformula is true if and only if $\psi_1(s)$ is true for all tuples s with values from DOM(ψ_1).

The purpose of the notion of safety is to ensure that only values from DOM(ψ) appear in the result and to ensure that we can test for existentially quantified and universally quantified subformulas without having to test infinitely many possibilities.

Consider rule 2. For $(\exists s)(\psi_1(s))$ to be true, we need to find only one s for which $\psi_1(s)$ is true. In general, there would be infinitely many tuples to test. However, rule 2 tells us that we may restrict our attention to tuples with values from DOM(ψ_1). This reduces to a finite number the number of tuples we must consider. The situation for rule 3 is similar. To assert that $(\forall s)(\psi_1(s))$ is true, we must, in general, test all possible tuples. This requires us to examine infinitely many tuples. However, due to rule 3, it is sufficient for us to test $\psi_1(s)$ for those tuples s whose values are taken from DOM(ψ_1), which is finite.

4.3.3 Domain Relational Calculus

The domain relational calculus is built from the same operators as the tuple relational calculus. The essential differences are listed below.

1. There are no tuple variables in the domain calculus, but there are *domain variables* to represent components of tuples, instead.

2. An atom is either of the form
   a. $R(x_1 x_2 \cdots x_n)$, where R is an n-ary relation and every x_i is a constant or domain variable, or
   b. $x \, \theta \, y$, where x and y are constants or domain variables and θ is an arithmetic relational operator such as $=$ or $>$.

   $R(x_1 x_2 \cdots x_n)$ asserts that the values of those x_i's that are variables must be chosen so that $x_1 x_2 \cdots x_n$ is a tuple in R. The meaning of the atom $x \, \theta \, y$ is that x and y must have values that make $x \, \theta \, y$ true.

3. Formulas in the domain relational calculus use the connectives $\wedge$, $\vee$, and $\sim$, as in the tuple calculus. We also use $\exists x$ and $\forall x$ to form expressions of the domain calculus, but x is a domain variable instead of a tuple variable.

The notion of free and bound domain variables and the scope of a bound variable are defined in the domain relational calculus exactly as in the tuple relational calculus. A domain relational calculus expression is of the form $\{x_1 x_2 \cdots x_n \mid \psi(x_1, x_2, \ldots, x_n)\}$, where ψ is a formula whose only free domain variables are the distinct variables $x_1, x_2, \ldots, x_n$.

In analogy with tuple calculus, we define a domain calculus expression $\{x_1 x_2 \cdots x_n \mid (x_1, x_2, \ldots, x_n)\}$ to be *safe* if

1. $\psi(x_1, x_2, \ldots, x_n)$ true implies that x_i is in $\text{DOM}(\psi)$.
2. If $(\exists s)(\psi_1(s))$ is a subformula of ψ, then $\psi_1(s)$ true implies that $s \in \text{DOM}(\psi_1)$.
3. If $(\forall s)(\psi_1(s))$ is a subformula of ψ, then $\psi_1(s)$ true implies that $s \in \text{DOM}(\psi_1)$.

4.4 COMPARISON OF ALGEBRA-BASED AND CALCULUS-BASED LANGUAGES

Three alternative mathematical foundations of DML used for retrieval operations are (1) relational algebra, (2) tuple relational calculus, and (3) domain relational calculus. In the next three sections we compare their respective features. In Section 4.4.1 we discuss the distinction between descriptive and prescriptive query languages with examples and specify the corresponding differences in query processing. A classification scheme of query languages is provided in Section 4.4.2. Finally, in Section 4.4.3 we address some additional features of DML beyond those that are handled by relational algebra and relational calculus.

4.4.1 Descriptive versus Prescriptive Query Languages

We saw in Section 4.1 that a DML based on relational algebra is prescriptive, whereas that based on relational calculus is descriptive. The latter is at a higher level than the former. This fact is reflected in the way that a query is processed when formulated in terms of relational algebra or relational calculus. We now illustrate this point by using the example of Section 4.1.

The English formulation of the query is as follows (repeated for the sake of reference):

List the department name and department head for each instructor whose rank is associate professor or professor.

We now give three alternative formulations, F1, F2, and F3, based on relational algebra, tuple relational calculus, and domain relational calculus, respectively:

```
(F1)   ((UNIV JOIN INSTR TO TEMP1)
        (TEMP1 WHERE
                RANK = 'AssocProf'
                UNION
                RANK = 'Professor'
                TO TEMP2)
        (TEMP2 [DNAME, DHEAD]))
```

(F2) $\{t^{(2)} \mid (\exists u^{(3)})(\exists v^{(6)})(\text{UNIV}(u) \wedge \text{INSTR}(v) \wedge u(1) = v(6) \wedge (v(4)$

$= \text{'AssocProf'}) \vee (v(4) = \text{'Professor'}) \wedge t(1) = u(2) \wedge t(2) = u(3))\}$

Here the notation $r^{(n)}$ means that r is an n-tuple. Also, from the implementations of UNIV and INSTR we know that

$$u(1) = \text{DNO}$$

$$u(2) = \text{DNAME}$$

$$u(3) = \text{DHEAD}$$

$$v(1) = \text{INAME}$$

$$v(2) = \text{IDEG}$$

$$v(3) = \text{SPCODE}$$

$$v(4) = \text{RANK}$$

$$v(5) = \text{SSNO}$$

$$v(6) = \text{DNO}$$

(F3) $\{t_1 t_2 \mid (\exists u_1)(\exists u_2)(\exists u_3)(\exists v_1)(\exists v_2) (\exists v_3)(\exists v_4)(\exists v_5)(\exists v_6) (\text{UNIV}(u_1 u_2 u_3)$

$\wedge \text{INSTR}(v_1 v_2 v_3 v_4 v_5 v_6) \wedge u_1 = v_6 \wedge (v_4 = \text{'AssocProf'} \vee v_4$

$= \text{'Professor'}) \wedge t_1 = u_2 \wedge t_2 = u_3)\}$

We observe that F2 and F3 merely express the target tuple variable $t^{(2)}$ or the target domain variables (t_1, t_2) in terms of UNIV and INSTR written in tuple or domain notations. But F1 consists of three distinct steps that must be executed in that order to derive the target binary relation TEMP2[DNAME, DHEAD].

4.4.2 Classification of Query Languages

Query languages are classified into three categories according as they are based on relational algebra, tuple relation calculus, or domain relational calculus. For example, QQL (Quick Query Langue) of LOGIX is based on relational algebra, QUEL (QUEry Language) of INGRES is based on tuple relational calculus, and QBE (Query By Example) developed by IBM at Yorktown Heights, New York, is based on domain relational calculus. These languages are all discussed in Chapter 5. SQL is a hybrid between relational algebra and tuple relational calculus, although it leans toward the relational algebra formalism. We now clarify this issue.

SQL supports the two relational algebra commands, UNION and INTERSECT. Its SELECT statements use WHERE clauses with predicates using the relational algebra syntax. But SQL also offers the existential quantifier EXISTS of relational calculus. SQL queries using compound predicates (see Section 3.2.2) can be formulated using the Boolean operations of conjunction (AND), disjunction (OR), and negation (NOT), all of which belong to relational calculus.

4.4.3 Additional Features of Data Manipulation Languages

Data manipulation languages perform two types of functions: retrieval and update. All commands based on relational algebra or relational calculus pertain to the retrieval operations only. Thus, DML commands provide some additional features listed below:

1. *Update*. These commands allow insertion, deletion, or modification of data.
2. *Arithmetic capability*. Often, atoms in calculus expressions or selections in algebraic expressions can involve arithmetic computation as well as comparisons, such as $A < B + 3$. Note that $+$ and other arithmetic operators do not appear in either relational algebra or relational calculus.
3. *Assignment and print command*. DML generally allows the printing of the relation constructed by an algebraic or calculus expression or the assignment of a computed relation to be the value of a relation name.
4. *Built-in group functions*. Operations such as average, sum, min, max, and count can often be applied to columns of a relation to obtain a single quantity.

4.5 EQUIVALENCE THEOREMS ON EXPRESSIVE POWER

Query languages based on relational algebra, tuple relational calculus, or domain relational calculus are equivalent to one another in terms of expressive power. Historically, Codd [1, pp. 78–85] first proposed the tuple relational calculus in a formulation slightly different from that used in Sections 4.3.1 and 4.3.2. Codd's objective was to use the calculus as a benchmark for evaluating data manipulation languages for relational data models. He introduced a query language named ALPHA, which was never implemented commercially, as an example of a tuple relational calculus–based language. Codd's main contention was that a query language that does not at least have the expressive power of the safe formulas of relational calculus, or equivalently of the eight operations of relational algebra, is inadequate. In fact, almost all of the currently available query languages utilize one of the three alternative mathematical bases. Some, like SQL, even use a combination of them.

In this section we prove mathematically that the three formalisms are equivalent. This involves proving the following three theorems:

Theorem 1.   If E is a relational algebra expression, there is a safe expression E' in tuple relational calculus such that E is equivalent to E'.

Proof. The proof proceeds by mathematical induction on the number n of relational algebra operations used in E.

(a) *Basis step:* Let $n = 0$ so that E has no algebra operations. Then E is either a relation variable R, say, or E is a row or a subset thereof in a relation. In the first case, E is equivalent to $\{t \mid R(t)\}$, which is a safe expression in tuple relational calculus. In the second case, we can write

$$E = \{t_1, t_2, \ldots, t_k\}$$
$$= \{t \mid (t = t_1) \vee (t = t_2) \vee \cdots \vee (t = t_k)\}$$

where $t = t_i$ is shorthand for the expression

$$(t(1) = t_i(1)) \wedge (t(2) = t_i(2)) \wedge \cdots \wedge (t(m) = t_i(m))$$

and t is assumed to be an m-tuple. This means that $t(i)$ is one of the finite set of symbols appearing explicitly as the ith component of a constant tuple t_j.

(b) *Induction step:* Let the theorem be true for $n \leqslant p$, where $p > 1$ is an integer. We show that the result holds for $n = p + 1$. Since E is a relational algebraic expression, it can be expressed in terms of one or more of the five primitive operations: union, difference, Cartesian product, projection, and selection (see Section 3.3). Hence we need to consider only these five primitive operations and show that the result holds in each case. We assume that E contains $p + 1$ algebraic operations.

(i) *Union:* Let $E = E_1$ UNION E_2, where E_i, $i = 1, 2$, contains p or fewer operations. By the induction hypothesis, we can write

$$E_i = \{t \mid \psi_i(t)\}, \quad i = 1, 2$$

where ψ_i is a safe tuple calculus expression. Hence E can be written as

$$E = \{t \mid \psi_1(t) \vee \psi_2(t)\}$$

The tuple variable t in E belongs to

$$\text{DOM}(\psi_1(t) \vee \psi_2(t)) = \text{DOM}(\psi_1) \cup \text{DOM}(\psi_2)$$

which is finite, so that E is a safe expression.

(ii) *Difference:* Let $E = E_1 \text{ DIFF } E_2$, where E_1 and E_2 are defined as in (i) above. Then E can be written in the equivalent form

$$E = \{t \mid \psi_1(t) \wedge (\sim\psi_2(t))\}$$

Also,

$$\text{DOM}(\psi_1(t) \wedge (\sim\psi_2(t))) \subset \text{DOM}(\psi_1) \cup \text{DOM}(\psi_2)$$

which is finite. Hence E is a safe expression.

(iii) *Cartesian product:* Let $E = E_1 \text{ MULT } E_2$, where E_1 and E_2 are defined as in part (i), and let E_1 and E_2 have respective degrees k and m. Then we can write E as

$$E = \{t^{(k+m)} \mid (\exists u)(\exists v)(\psi_1(u) \wedge \psi_2(v) \wedge t(1) = u(1) \wedge \cdots \wedge t(k)$$
$$= u(k) \wedge t(k+1) = v(1) \wedge \cdots \wedge t(k+m) = v(m)\}$$

By assumption, $\text{DOM}(\psi_1)$ and $\text{DOM}(\psi_2)$ are finite. Also, we note that

$$t(i) = \begin{cases} u(i), & i \leq k \\ v(i-k), & k < i \leq k+m \end{cases}$$

so that t can take values only from $\text{DOM}(\psi_1)$ or $\text{DOM}(\psi_2)$. Hence E is a safe expression.

(iv) *Projection:* Let R be a relation of degree m with attributes $a_1, \ldots, a_m$ and let E be a projection of R given by

$$E = R[a_{i_1}, \ldots, a_{i_k}], \qquad k \leq m$$

Then we can write

$$E = \{t^{(k)} \mid (\exists u)(\psi(u) \wedge (t(1) = u(i_1)) \wedge \cdots \wedge (t(k) = u(i_k)))\}$$

where R is equivalent to a safe expression $\{t \mid \psi(t)\}$ and $\text{DOM}(\psi)$ is finite. Since t takes values only from $\text{DOM}(\psi)$, it follows that the expression for E is safe.

(v) *Selection:* Let R be a relation as in part (iv) and let E be defined by

$$E = R \text{ WHERE } q$$

where q represents the predicate defining the selection. Then E is equivalent to the expression

$$\{t \mid \psi(t) \wedge q'\}$$

where $\psi(t)$ is defined as in part (iv) and q' is derived from q by replacing each operand that denotes component i by $t(i)$. This expression is safe because t can take values belonging to $\text{DOM}(\psi)$.

We have proved that the result holds for $n = p + 1$. By the principle of mathematical induction, the result holds for all values of n.

Theorem 2.   If E is a tuple relational calculus expression, there is a safe domain relational calculus expression E' equivalent to E.

Proof. Let $E = \{t^{(k)} \mid \psi(t)\}$ be a safe tuple calculus expression so that $\text{DOM}(\psi)$ is finite and t has components $t(i)$, $i = 1, \ldots, k$. Let us introduce new k domain variables $t_1, \ldots, t_k$ and replace E with E' given by

$$E' = \{t_1, \ldots, t_k \mid \psi'(t_1, \ldots, t_k)\}$$

where ψ' is the value of ψ with any atom $R(t)$ in ψ being replaced by $R(t_1 \cdots t_k)$ and each free occurrence of $t(i)$ in ψ being replaced by t_i, where $i = 1, \ldots, k$.

Next, we consider the appearance of quantifiers $(\exists u)$ and $(\forall u)$ in E, where u is an m-tuple. Let us introduce m domain variables $u_1, \ldots, u_m$. Within the scope of this quantification of u, we make the following replacements in ψ:

$$u(i) \text{ by } u_i, \quad i = 1, \ldots, m$$

$$R(u) \text{ by } R(u_1 \cdots u_m)$$

$$(\exists u) \text{ by } (\exists u_1) \cdots (\exists u_m)$$

$$(\forall u) \text{ by } (\forall u_1) \cdots (\forall u_m)$$

The resulting expression E is a safe domain relational calculus expression that is equivalent to E.

Theorem 3.   If E is a safe domain relational calculus expression, there is a relational algebra expression E equivalent to E.

Proof. Using the three results listed at the end of Section 4.2, we can write E in the form

$$E = \{(x_1, \ldots, x_k) \mid \psi(x_1, \ldots, x_k)\}$$

where ψ involves only the operations $\vee$, $\sim$, and $\wedge$. Since E is safe, $\text{DOM}(\psi)$ is finite. We now define recursively an algebraic expression φ' for each domain calculus subexpression φ appearing in ψ. Here $\text{DOM}(\varphi) \subset \text{DOM}(\psi)$ is finite. We consider the following possible cases:

(a) φ is an atom of the form $x_1 \theta x_2$, $x_1 \theta a$, or $a \theta x_1$, where x_1 and x_2 are domain variables, not necessarily distinct, and a is a constant. The equivalent algebraic expressions φ' are given by

$$x_1 \theta x_2 = (\text{DOM}(\varphi) \text{ MULT DOM}(\varphi))$$

$$\text{WHERE } x_1 \theta x_2$$

$$x_1 \ \theta \ a \ = \ \text{DOM}(\varphi) \ \text{WHERE} \ x_1 \ \theta \ a$$

$$a \ \theta \ x_1 \ = \ \text{DOM}(\varphi) \ \text{WHERE} \ a \ \theta \ x_1$$

(b) φ is an atom of the form $R(a_1, \ldots, a_m)$, where each a_i, $i = 1, \ldots, m$, is either a constant or a domain variable. Then its equivalent algebraic expression φ' is given by

$$\varphi' \ = \ S[a_{j_1} \cdots a_{j_k}]$$

where S is a shorthand for the expression R WHERE F; F is a selection predicate that has the term $u = v$ whenever a_{i_u} and a_{i_v} are the same variable, and $u < v$; and the list $j_1, \ldots, j_k$ is any list for which $a_{j_1} = a_1, \ldots, a_{j_k} = a_k$, and $k \leq m$.

(c) $\varphi = \sim\lambda$, where λ is an atom. Then, by cases (a) and (b), there exists an algebraic expression λ' equivalent to λ. We define φ' by the expression (DOM(φ) MULT DOM(φ) MULT $\cdots$ MULT DOM(φ)) DIFF λ' where the Cartesian product within parentheses has m terms and λ has m components.

(d) Assume that

$$\varphi(y_1, \ldots, y_m)$$

$$= \lambda_1(u_1, \ldots, u_k, v_1, \ldots, v_p) \lor \lambda_2(u_1, \ldots, u_k, w_1, \ldots, w_q)$$

where v_i's and w_j's are mutually distinct for $1 \leq i \leq p$, $1 \leq j \leq q$. By cases (a) and (b), there exist algebraic expressions λ'_1 and λ'_2 for λ_1 and λ_2, respectively. Let φ_1 be the relational algebraic expression consisting of λ'_1 with columns added for all attributes in λ'_2 DIFF λ'_1. Also, let φ_2 be the algebraic expression consisting of λ'_2 with columns added for all attributes in λ'_1 DIFF λ'_2. Then the algebraic expression for φ is φ_1 INTERSECT φ_2.

(e) Assume that

$$\varphi(y_1, \ldots, y_m) \ = \ (\exists y_{m+1})(\varphi(y_1, \ldots, y_{m+1}))$$

By cases (a) through (d), there exists a relational algebraic expression φ' that is equivalent to $\varphi(y_1, \ldots, y_{m+1})$. The algebraic expression for $\varphi(y_1, \ldots, y_m)$ is given by the projection of φ' on the attributes of the relation φ' DIFF y_{m+1}.

Cases (a) through (e) exhaust all the possibilities arising out of the operators $\lor$ and $\sim$ and the quantifier $\exists$. This completes the proof.

4.6 RELATIONAL COMPLETENESS OF QUERY LANGUAGES

We have already seen that algebra- and calculus-based languages are equivalent in their expressive power. A language is said to be *relationally complete* if it is at least as powerful as the tuple relational calculus, that is, if its expressions permit

Relational Algebra	SQL
(a) *R* UNION *S*	SELECT * FROM R UNION SELECT * FROM S
(b) *R* DIFF *S*	SELECT * FROM R WHERE NOT EXISTS (SELECT * FROM S WHERE all-attributes-of-R = all-attributes-of-S
(c) *R* MULT *S*	SELECT * FROM R, S
(d) *R* WHERE *p*	SELECT * FROM R WHERE p
(e) *R*[*a, b, ..., k*]	SELECT DISTINCT a, b, ..., k FROM R

Figure 4-2   SQL implementation of relational algebra operations.

the definition of any relation definable by tuple relational calculus, and hence by relational algebra or domain relational calculus. Relational completeness is a basic measure of selective or expressive power for query languages in general.

To show that a query language is relationally complete, we need to show that it can emulate the relational algebra operations or the relational calculus expressions, tuple or domain. It is usually easier to show that a given language can emulate the relational algebra operations than to show that it can emulate the relational calculus expressions. Indeed, to establish its relational completeness, it is sufficient to show that the language can emulate the five primitive relational algebra operations (see Section 3.3).

We finally show that SQL is relationally complete by writing a SQL expression for each of the five primitive relational algebra operations shown in Figure 4-2. It should be noted that similar expressions were given in Sections 3.2.1 and 3.2.2 for the special case of the relations UNIV and INSTR of LHUDB.

4.7 CLASSIFICATION OF RELATIONAL DATABASE SYSTEMS

A relational database system has three components related to three characteristics of data:

1. *Data structure:* all the relations in the database and their respective domains
2. *Data integrity:* two integrity rules: entity integrity and referential integrity
3. *Data manipulation:* a set of relational algebra operations or their equivalent relational calculus expressions to handle both retrieval and update functions

The Relational Task Group (RTG) of the American National Standards Institute (ANSI) has developed a characterization of relational database systems. According to RTG, a DBMS can be called relational if, as a minimum, it satisfies the following four conditions:

1. All information in the database is represented as values in tables which are called relations.
2. No user-visible navigation links exist among these tables.
3. The system supports at least the selection, projection, and equijoin operations of the relational algebra, or their equivalent expressions in relational calculus.
4. Data manipulation is possible without resorting to commands for iteration or recursion, and with the provision that none of the operations cited in condition 3 is restricted by whatever access paths have been predefined.

Depending on whether a system satisfies some or all of these criteria, or whether it satisfies any additional criteria, we can define an entire spectrum of database systems. Using this approach, Codd has proposed one scheme of classifying the relational database systems. According to this scheme, there are four types of relational systems: tabular, minimally relational, relationally complete, and fully relational (see Codd [2, pp. 112–113]). According to the other scheme based on the mode of data sublanguage used, there are two types of relational database systems: uniform relational and nonuniform relational (see Codd [2, pp. 113–114] and Schmidt and Brodie [6, pp. VI–VII, Foreword]). Next, we discuss these schemes.

A system that satisfies only condition 1 is called *tabular* because it stores the information as tables. Codd earlier used the term *semirelational* instead of tabular. But in his later paper [2, p. 112] he commented that the term *tabular* was more appropriate, because it implied that the system does not provide automatic navigation through the schema. On the other hand, a semirelational system provides automatic navigation for the user. From the data characteristics viewpoint, the tabular system supports only the data structure, but neither the data integrity nor the data manipulation features.

A system that satisfies all of the conditions 1 through 4 is called *minimally relational*. Such a system supports the data structure and the data manipulation features but does not have data integrity.

A system that satisfies conditions 1, 2, and 4 and provides all eight relational algebra operations instead of only the subset specified in condition 3 is called *relationally complete*. Relational completeness has been discussed in details in Section 4.6.

Finally, a system that is relationally complete and satisfies the two integrity rules is called *fully relational*. A fully relational database system supports all three data characteristics mentioned above: data structure, data integrity, and data manipulation.

Most of the existing relational database systems fall somewhere between being minially relational and fully relational. UNIFY is the only fully relational database management system, up to my knowledge. ORACLE and INGRES, for example, are relationally complete but not fully relational. Date [3, pp. 322–325] has outlined a procedure to enforce the two integrity rules in a relationally complete system. His methodology is described in terms of SQL, but can be extended to any other relational query language.

Codd has described the other classification scheme of relational databases as follows [6, p. VI]: Some relational systems support a data sublanguage that is usable in two modes: (1) interactively at a terminal and (2) embedded in an application program written in a host language. There are strong arguments for such a *double-mode* data sublanguage:

1. Using such a language, application programmers can separately debug at a terminal the database statements they wish to incorporate into their application programs.
2. Such a language significantly enhances communication among programmers, analysts, end users, database administration staff, and so on.
3. Frivolous distinctions between the languages used in these two modes place an unnecessary learning and memory burden on those users who have to work in both modes.

The importance of this feature in productivity suggests that relational DBMSs be classified according to whether or not they possess this feature. Accordingly, we call relational DBMSs that support a double-mode data sublanguage *uniform relational*. Thus a uniform relational DBMS supports relational processing at both an end-user interface and at an application programming interface using a data sublanguage common to both interfaces. The natural term for all other relational DBMSs is *nonuniform relational*.

4.8 SUMMARY

In this chapter we have discussed the relational calculus that forms the basis of one class of query languages. There are two types of relational calculus: tuple and domain. Since both of them use the concepts and formalism of predicate logic, the chapter starts with an overview of the same. It then describes the difference between algebra-based query languages and calculus-based query languages.

A tuple variable is the basic entity of tuple relational calculus. A tuple relational calculus expression is of the form $\{t \mid \psi(t) \text{ holds}\}$, where $\psi(t)$ is a formula built from atoms and a collection of operators. An atom can represent a tuple of a relation or two tuple variables connected by an arithmetic comparison operator. A formula is defined recursively in terms of atoms, quantifiers, and the three predicate logic operations: conjunction, disjunction, and negation. The tuple relational calculus includes only *safe* tuple relational calculus expressions (i.e., those expressions that involve formulas whose domains are finite). Such expressions rule out the theoretical possibility of printing infinitely many or a very large number of tuples from a relation.

The domain relational calculus is built from the same operators as tuple relational calculus except that the basic entity of domain calculus is the domain variable. These variables are components of tuple variables. Safe domain relational calculus expressions are defined the same way as safe tuple relational calculus expressions.

A query language based on relational algebra is called prescriptive, because the algebraic operations are to be performed in a specific order. On the other hand, calculus-based query languages are descriptive, since they merely describe the defining characteristics of the desired result and the system determines what operations are to be performed. Most query languages are either algebra based or calculus based. SQL, however, is a hybrid between relational algebra and tuple relational calculus, since it includes both EXISTS from calculus and UNION, INTERSECT, and DIFF from algebra.

Query languages based on algebra or calculus are equivalent in their expressive power. The chapter contains proofs of three theorems showing that a query expression E expressed in relational algebra has an equivalent E', say, in tuple relational calculus, and an equivalent E'', say, in domain relational calculus. The proofs use the fact that of the eight algebraic operations, only five are primitive.

In the final section of the chapter we discussed two classification schemes of relational database systems, both introduced by Codd. One scheme classifies DBMSs with respect to four properties that were established by the Relational Task Group of the American National Standards Institute as a set of minimum criteria to be satisfied by a DBMS. Depending on whether a DBMS satisfies some or all of these criteria or whether it satisfies any additional criteria, we can define an entire spectrum of database systems. These are called tabular, minimally relational, relationally complete, and fully relational. Most of the existing database systems fall somewhere between being minimally relational and fully relational. The other classification scheme is based on the usage mode (i.e., interactive or embedded or both) of the data sublanguage supported by the DBMS. According to this scheme, a DBMS is uniform relational or nonuniform relational.

KEY WORDS

atom
bound variable
conjunction
database system, fully
  relational

database system,
  relationally complete
database system,
  semirelational
database system, tabular

REFERENCES AND FURTHER READING

The following references contain additional materials related to the topics covered in this chapter.

1. E. F. Codd, *Relational Completeness of Data Base Sublanguages,* Data Base Systems, Courant Computer Science Symposia Series, vol. 6, Prentice-Hall, Englewood Cliffs, NJ, 1972.

2. E. F. Codd, Relational Database: A Practical Foundation for Productivity, *Communications of the ACM,* vol. 25, no. 2, 1982, pp. 109–117.

3. C. J. Date, *An Introduction to Database Systems,* vol. I, 4th ed., Addison-Wesley, Reading, MA, 1986.

4. C. J. Date, *An Introduction to Database Systems,* vol. II, 3rd ed., Addison-Wesley, Reading, MA, 1983.

5. H. F. Korth and A. Silberschatz, *Database System Concepts,* McGraw-Hill, New York, 1986.

6. J. W. Schmidt and M. L. Brodie (eds.), *Relational Database Systems,* Springer-Verlag, New York, 1983.

7. J. D. Ullman, *Principles of Database Systems,* Computer Science Press, Rockville, MD, 1982.

8. C. C. Yang, *Relational Databases,* Prentice-Hall, Englewood Cliffs, NJ, 1986.

Codd's paper [1] contains a detailed discussion of tuple relational calculus and specifications of ALPHA, a calculus-based language proposed by Codd. However, ALPHA has never been implemented commercially. Codd's paper [2] and Date [4] provide one classification scheme of relational database systems. Schmidt and Brodie [6] discusses the other classification scheme in a foreword written by Codd. Tuple and domain relational calculus are treated extensively in Korth and Silberschatz [5], Ullman [7], and Yang [8]. Date's treatment of relational calculus [3] is less mathematical in treatment. The proofs of equivalence theorems on expressive power are taken from Ullman [7] and Yang [8]. Yang's proofs are more notation bound than are Ullman's.

The topics on mathematical prerequisites discussed in Section 4.2 can be found in any text on discrete mathematics for computer science. For example, the following is a good source:

B. KOLMAN and R. C. BUSBY, *Discrete Mathematical Structures for Computer Science,* Prentice-Hall, Englewood Cliff, NJ, 1984.

REVIEW QUESTIONS

1. Discuss why algebra-based languages are called prescriptive, whereas calculus-based languages are called descriptive.

2. Do you label SQL as descriptive or as prescriptive? Give reasons for your answer.

3. Why are the operations conjunction, disjunction, and negation regarded as the primitives of the five predicate logic operations?

4. Do you think that the universal and the existential quantifiers are mutually independent? Give reasons for your answer.

5. Define the terms *atom* and *formula* in tuple relational calculus.

6. What is a safe tuple relational calculus expression? Give an example?

7. How does a domain relational calculus expression differ from a tuple relational calculus expression?

8. Describe the DML capabilities beyond those that are covered by the algebra or the calculus.

9. Discuss the meaning of the statement: Query languages based on relational algebra, or tuple relational calculus, or domain relational calculus are equivalent in terms of expressive power.

10. Discuss the two classification schemes of relational database systems. To which category does SQL belong under each scheme? Explain your answer.

EXERCISES

1. Let A and B be two relations of degrees 4 and 2, respectively. Convert the relational algebra expressions E_1 and E_2 into **(a)** tuple relational calculus and **(b)** domain relational calculus.

$$E_1 = [(A \text{ MULT } B) \text{ WHERE } (2 = 4) \text{ OR } (1 = 6)] (1, 3, 5)$$
$$E_2 = [(B \text{ MULT } A) \text{ WHERE } (2 = 6) \text{ OR } (1 = 4)] (2, 4, 6)$$

2. Let R be a relation with attributes a, b, and c and S a relation with attributes d, e, and f. Give expressions in **(a)** tuple relational calculus and **(b)** domain relational calculus that are equivalent to the relational algebra expressions E_1, E_2, E_3, and E_4.

$$E_1 = [(R \text{ MULT } S) \text{ WHERE } c = d] (b, f)$$
$$E_2 = R \text{ DIFF } S$$
$$E_3 = R \text{ UNION } S$$
$$E_4 = R[a, b] \text{ INTERSECT } S[d, f]$$

3. Give the tuple and domain relational calculus versions of the queries given in Figure 2–11.

CHAPTER 5

QUERY LANGUAGES

5.1 QUERY LANGUAGE OVERVIEW

We have discussed query languages in Chapters 2 through 4. Three main features of a query language can be summarized as follows:

1. A query language is nonprocedural in nature so that the end user or the programmer specifies only *what* is to be retrieved and the DBMS determines *how* to retrieve that information. Although the degree of nonprocedurality varies according as the language is descriptive or prescriptive (see Section 4.4.1), a formal application program is not necessary to retrieve information.

2. A query language has an English-like syntax. Its reserved words, such as SELECT, FIND, DISPLAY, and MODIFY, are English verbs, and the format of a query in SQL or non-SQL languages resembles structured English closely.

3. Except for nested subqueries, the ordering of the qualifying clauses in a query is immaterial.

The query formulation in a nonrelational DBMS involves navigation through the schema structure. Consequently, the efficiency of the query formulation depends on the experience of the end user or programmer. In a relational database the user views the data as relations or tables and formulates queries in terms of the relational structure. Internally, the relational DBMS converts a query into an equivalent canonical form and then processes it. The user may write the same query in five alternative versions. But all of them will be converted to the same canonical form, at least theoretically. Thus the experience of the user formulating the query is somewhat irrelevant.

When the relational DBMS converts a query to its canonical form and selects an access strategy to process the query, the goal is to make the strategy optimal in terms of disk accesses and CPU utilization. Sometimes, the exact formulation of the query impacts on the optimality of the access strategy. As a result, the query optimization becomes an important issue in the performance of a relational DBMS. We now address this issue.

5.2 QUERY OPTIMIZATION

Suppose that a given query can be stated in multiple ways. Each way of writing the query suggests an implementation strategy. Although all of these implementations provide the same answer, their individual processing times may differ. A relational DBMS transforms the query, as entered by a user, into an equivalent query which can be computed more efficiently. This improvement of the strategy for processing a query is called *query optimization*. There is a close analogy between code optimization by a compiler and query optimization by a relational DBMS. It is quite possible that a query optimizer performs better than an experienced user, for the following two reasons:

1. The optimizer may have available to it the most current information on data values, which the human user does not have.
2. The optimizer may be able to evaluate a wider range of alternative strategies than would a user.

Query optimization is an important issue in any database system, because the difference in execution time between a good strategy and a bad one can be substantial. The overall goal for query optimization is to improve system performance. The optimizing strategy applies both to interactive queries and to queries embedded in a host language interface program.

The principle of economy plays a significant role in query optimization. It requires that optimization procedures should attempt either to maximize the output for a given number of resources or to minimize the resource usage for a given output. Query optimization tries to minimize the response time for a given query language and mix of query types in a given system environment. This general goal allows a number of different operational objective functions. The total cost to be minimized is the sum of the following four cost factors:

1. *Communication cost:* the cost of transmission of data from the site where they are stored to the sites where computations are performed and results are presented. These costs include the cost of the communication line, which is usually related to the time the line is open, and the cost for the delay in

processing caused by transmission. The latter, which is more important for query optimization, is often assumed to be a linear function of the number of data transmitted.

2. *Secondary storage access cost:* the cost of (or time for) loading data pages from secondary storage into main memory. This is influenced by the number of data to be retrieved (mainly by the size of intermediate results), the clustering of data on physical pages, the size of the available buffer space, and the speed of the devices used.

3. *Storage cost:* the cost of occupying secondary storage and memory buffers over time. Storage costs are relevant only if storage becomes a system bottleneck and if it can be varied from query to query.

4. *Computation cost:* the cost for (or time of) using the central processing unit (CPU).

The structure of query optimization algorithms is strongly influenced by the trade-off among these cost components. In a distributed database environment scattered over a large geographical area with relatively slow communication lines, communication delay dominates the cost, whereas the other factors are relevant only for local suboptimization. In a centralized database environment, the costs are dominated by the time for secondary storage accesses, although the CPU cost may be quite high for complex queries. In a locally distributed database environment, all factors have similar weights, leading to very complex cost functions and optimization procedures.

For centralized databases, communication costs are not considered because in such systems communication requirements are independent of the evaluation strategy. For the optimization of single queries, storage costs are usually assumed to be of secondary importance. They are considered only for the simultaneous optimization of multiple queries.

There remain the costs of secondary storage accesses, usually measured by the number of I/O operations, and the CPU usage, generally measured by the number of comparisons to be performed and called the run-time pathlength.

We now discuss each of these two topics separately.

1. *Number of I/O operations.* Fewer I/O operations usually lead to a better system performance. The number of I/O operations required to process a query depends primarily on the internal level (i.e., the physical structure of the database). The conceptual level (i.e., the logical structure of the database) also plays a role in that indexing and clustering of attributes are designed at this level. Both of these features affect the I/O performance. Most relational DBMSs support B-tree indices that can provide adequate performance for most applications. Some DBMSs provide hashing as well to handle those situations where B-tree indices are not adequate. Physical data clustering can also reduce the number of I/O operations by reducing disk accesses. A query optimizer always tries to utilize the clustering of data if one exists that matches the requirements of the query.

2. *Amount of CPU processing.* If the DBMS is a compiling system instead of an interpretive system, system performance can be improved by eliminating the following operations from its run-time pathlength:

a. Parsing the original user request

b. Detecting and reporting on system errors

c. Mapping logical-level names to physical-level addresses

d. Choosing an access strategy

e. Checking authorization

f. Generating machine code

The most significant factor from system performance standpoint is the selection of an access strategy (i.e., query optimization). The amount of CPU processing is considerably less for compiled systems than for interpretative systems.

5.3 METHODOLOGY OF QUERY OPTIMIZATION

The process of query optimization consists of the following three steps:

Step 1: Formulate an internal representation of the query. The query is expressed in terms of a nonprocedural language such as SQL. Any such language has its own reserved words and syntax. It is useful for the human end user but unsuited for an internal representation, which must be independent of specific features of a language. Hence before the query processing starts, the system must translate the query into a usable form. We can choose either the relational algebra or one of the two relational calculus versions of the query as its internal representation. We assume here that the relational algebra formalism is used as the basis of the internal representation. This means that the eight relational algebra operations—union, intersection, difference, Cartesian product, selection, projection, join, and division—are available for internal representation.

The first action the system must take on a query is to translate the query into its internal form. This translation process is similar to that done by the parser of a compiler. In the process of generating the internal form of the query, the parser checks the syntax of the user's query, verifies that the relation names appearing in the query are names of the relation in the database, and so on. If the query was expressed in terms of a view, the parser replaces all references to the view name with the relational algebra expression to compute a view.

Jarke and Koch [6, pp. 118–119] have discussed the use of query graphs and tableaus as alternative tools for internal representations, both of which are briefly described below, although they will not be used for our purposes.

Query Graphs. Two classes of query graphs can be distinguished: object graphs and operator graphs. Nodes in *object graphs* represent objects such as attributes and constants. Edges describe conditions that these objects are to satisfy. Object graphs contain the properties of the query result and are therefore closely related to the relational calculus. *Operator graphs* describe an operator-controlled data flow by representing operators as nodes that are connected by edges, indicating the direction of data movement. Operator graphs have been used for the representation of relational algebra expressions.

Query graphs have many attractive properties. The visual presentation of a query contributes to an easier understanding of its structural characteristics. In addition, graph theory offers a number of results useful for the automatic analysis of graphs: for example, discovery of cycles and tree property. Finally, an important advantage of query graphs is that they can easily be augmented with additional information, such as details of the physical data organization of a database.

Tableaus. *Tableaus* are tabular notations for a subset of relational calculus queries, characterized by the existence of only AND-connected terms and no universal quantifiers. Tableaus are specialized matrices, the columns of which correspond to the attributes of the underlying database schema. The first row of the matrix represents the summary and serves the same purpose as the target list of a relational calculus expression. The other rows describe the predicate. The symbols appearing in a tableau are distinguished variables (corresponding to free variables), nondistinguished variables (corresponding to existentially quantified variables), constants, blanks, and tags (indicating the range relation). Expressions containing disjunction (see union) and negation (set difference) can be represented by sets of tableaus.

Step 2: Convert the internal representation to an equivalent canonical form. After the query is converted to a relational algebra formulation as its internal representation, it is necessary to find an expression that is equivalent to the given algebraic expression but is more efficient to execute. Since relational algebra is prescriptive (see Section 4.4.1), the algebraic expression represents a particular sequence of operations. Since it is possible to express a given query in multiple ways using relational algebra, we need to find an expression that is equivalent to the given query and is more efficient for execution purpose. Such an expression is called the *canonical form* of the query in its algebraic version.

There are various transformation rules that are used to convert a given algebraic version into a canonical form. A set of such rules, not necessarily exhaustive, is given below.

(a) Rules involving Selection

1. Combine a sequence of selections into a single selection with a compound predicate, that is,

$$(\cdots ((R \text{ WHERE } p_1) \text{ WHERE } p_2) \cdots \text{ WHERE } p_n)$$

$$= (R \text{ WHERE } (p_1 \text{ AND } p_2 \text{ AND } \cdots \text{ AND } p_n))$$

2. Convert a compound predicate involving ANDs and ORs into *conjunctive normal form* where two or more subpredicates are connected by ANDs and each subpredicate consists of two simple predicates connected by OR, that is,

$$(R \text{ WHERE } p \text{ OR } (q \text{ AND } r)) = (R \text{ WHERE } (p \text{ OR } q) \text{ AND } (p \text{ OR } r))$$

3. Interchange selection with Cartesian product. Here three cases can arise:
   (i) $(R_1 \text{ MULT } R_2) \text{ WHERE } p = (R_1 \text{ WHERE } p) \text{ MULT } R_2$, if all the attributes mentioned in the predicate p belong to R_1
   (ii) $(R_1 \text{ MULT } R_2) \text{ WHERE } (p_1 \text{ AND } p_2) = (R_1 \text{ WHERE } p_1) \text{ MULT } (R_2 \text{ WHERE } p_2)$, if the attributes mentioned in predicate p_i belong only to the relation R_i, $i = 1, 2$
   (iii) $(R_1 \text{ MULT } R_2) \text{ WHERE } (p_1 \text{ AND } p_2) = ((R_1 \text{ WHERE } p_1) \text{ MULT } R_2) \text{ WHERE } p_2$, if the attributes mentioned in p_1 belong to R_1 alone but the attributes mentioned in p_2 belong to both R_1 and R_2

4. Interchange selection with union, that is,

$$(R_1 \text{ UNION } R_2) \text{ WHERE } p = (R_1 \text{ WHERE } p) \text{ UNION } (R_2 \text{ WHERE } p)$$

5. Interchange selection with set difference, that is,

$$(R_1 \text{ DIFF } R_2) \text{ WHERE } p = (R_1 \text{ WHERE } p) \text{ DIFF } (R_2 \text{ WHERE } p)$$

(b) Rules involving Projection

1. In a sequence of projections, ignore all except the last, that is,

$$(R[b_1, \ldots, b_m])[a_1, \ldots, a_n] = R[a_1, \ldots, a_n]$$

where attributes $a_1, \ldots, a_n$ are a subset of the attributes $b_1, \ldots, b_m$.

2. Interchange selection and projection operations, that is,

$$(R[a_1, \ldots, a_n]) \text{ WHERE } p = (R \text{ WHERE } p)[a_1, \ldots, a_n]$$

3. Interchange projection with Cartesian product, that is,

$$(R_1 \text{ MULT } R_2)[a_1, \ldots, a_n] = (R_1[b_1, \ldots, b_m]) \text{ MULT } (R_2[c_1, \ldots, c_k])$$

where $a_1, \ldots, a_n$ are a list of attributes of which $b_1, \ldots, b_m$ are attributes of R_1 and $c_1, \ldots, c_k$ are attributes of R_2.

4. Interchange projection with union, that is,

$$(R_1 \text{ UNION } R_2)[a_1, \ldots, a_n] = (R_1[a_1, \ldots, a_n]) \text{ UNION } (R_2[a_1, \ldots, a_n])$$

(c) Rule involving Join

Perform selection before join, that is,

$$(R_1 \text{ JOIN } R_2) \text{ WHERE } (p_1 \text{ AND } p_2)$$

$$= (R_1 \text{ WHERE } p_1) \text{ JOIN } (R_2 \text{ WHERE } p_2)$$

assuming that the predicate p_i involves the relation R_i, $i = 1, 2$.

The driving force behind all of these rules can be summarized as follows:

1. Perform selection operations as early as possible.
2. Perform projection operations as early as possible.
3. Retain only those attributes in the canonical form that are needed to process subsequent queries or that appear in the final result of the query.

Let us now examine the rationale of these transformation rules. The processing of a query becomes quicker if the number of disk accesses can be reduced, because the disk access speed is much slower than the memory speed. However, since the space in the memory is limited, the query processing can reduce the number of disk accesses only if all or most of the tuples in the relations referred to by the query can be fetched into memory. This requires that the numbers of tuples in the relations used by the query should be kept low. If a query involves join, selection, and projection, the selection and/or the projection should be done first and then the join should be performed. By doing the selection and/or projection at first, we reduce the number of target tuples in the component relations to be joined. By performing the join afterward, the total number of concatenated tuples is reduced. We now illustrate this concept with the following query (see Section 4.1):

List the department name and department head for each instructor whose rank is associate professor or professor.

This query can be processed in at least two different ways:

Case 1

1. Perform the join UNIV JOIN INSTR using DNO as the common attribute. Call this relation TEMP1.
2. Perform the selection

```
        TEMP1 WHERE (RANK = 'AssocProf' OR
                     RANK = 'Professor')
```

Call this relation TEMP2.
3. Perform the projection

```
        TEMP2 [DNAME, DHEAD]
```

Call this relation TEMP3. Then TEMP3 is the final result.

Case 2

1. Perform the selection

```
INSTR WHERE (RANK = 'AssocProf' OR
             RANK = 'Professor')
```

Call this relation TEMP4.

2. Perform the join TEMP4 JOIN UNIV using DNO as the common attribute. Call this relation TEMP5.

3. Perform the projection

```
TEMP5 [DNAME, DHEAD]
```

Call this relation TEMP6. Then TEMP6 is the final result.

Let us now assume the following:

UNIV has 50 rows.
INSTR has 1000 rows.
There are 100 professors and 200 associate professors.

We show below the total number of I/O operations needed for each of the two cases above:

Case 1

1. Read 50,000 (= 50 × 100) tuples; write 1000 tuples.
2. Write 300 (= 100 + 200) tuples.
3. Write 300 tuples.

Case 2

1. Read 1000 tuples; write 300 tuples.
2. read 1500 (= 300 × 50) tuples; write 300 tuples.
3. Write 300 tuples.

Thus in case 1 the total number of I/O operations is 51,600, while in case 2 that number is 3400. In other words, by performing the selection earlier, we have reduced the number of I/O operations by a factor of 15. Assuming that the number of tuple I/O is a measure of performance, case 2 is more than 15 times as efficient as case 1. This efficiency is achieved by performing the selection before the join operation.

Step 3: Select an optimal access path.   At the conclusion of step 2 the query is converted to an equivalent canonical expression by using one or more of the transformation rules. Next, the query optimizer examines a set of alternative implementation plans and selects the one that is the "cheapest," where the cost formula is based on the number of disk accesses involved and also the CPU utilization.

The basic strategy is to consider the existence of indices or other access paths, distribution of stored data values, physical clustering of records, and so on. The query expression involves a set of relational algebra operations such as selection, projection, and join. Each operation has an implementation procedure with an associated cost factor. The query optimizer selects one or more possible *access paths* consisting of the implementation procedures of all the operations involved in the query expression. In doing so, the optimizer uses information from the data dictionary regarding the current state of the database, such as existence of indices, clustering of relations, and estimates of sizes of the relations. The *optimal access path* is the one that minimizes the "cost" of processing the query. The procedure consists of the following steps:

1. Generate all reasonable logical access plans for evaluating the query. A logical access plan describes a sequence of operations or of intermediate results that start from the existing relations and lead to the final result of the query.
2. Augment the logical access plans by details of the physical representation of data (sort orders, existence of physical access paths, statistical information).
3. Choose the cheapest access plan by applying a model of access and processing costs.

The quality of the final solution plan is strongly influenced by the existing storage structures and access paths, which usually cannot be optimized for a single ad hoc query.

5.4 ALGORITHM FOR QUERY OPTIMIZATION

The canonical form of a query written in terms of relational algebraic operations can be represented as a tree. Its bottom nodes represent the relations used in the query, the nodes appearing progressively higher on the tree represent the various algebraic expressions used during the optimization process, and the topmost node represents the final result in the form of an algebraic expression. The query optimizer starts from the bottom and ends up at the top. The algorithm resulting from this tree traversal is the query optimization process. We can write the algorithm as follows:

1. Use rule (a)(1) of Section 5.3 to represent each sequence of selections as a single selection with a compound predicate.
2. For each selection, use rules (a)(1) through (a)(5) and (b)(2) of Section 5.3 to move the selection as far down the tree as possible.

3. For each projection, use rules (b)(1) through (b)(4) of Section 5.3 to move the projection as far down the tree as possible. Note that rule (b)(1) causes some projections to disappear and rule (b)(2) splits a projection into two projections, one of which can be migrated down the tree, if possible. Also, eliminate a projection if it projects an expression onto all its attributes.

4. Use rules (a)(1), (b)(1) and (b)(2) of Section 5.3 to combine sequences of selections and projections into a single selection, a single projection, or a selection followed by a projection.

5. Partition the interior nodes of the resulting tree into groups, as follows. Every interior node representing a binary operator (MULT, UNION, OR DIFF) is in a group along with any of its immediate ancestors that are labeled by a unary operator (i.e., selection or projection). Also include in the group any chain of descendants labeled by unary operators and terminating at a leaf, except in the case that the binary operator is a Cartesian product and not followed by a selection that combines with the product to form an equi-join.

6. Produce a program to evaluate each group in any order such that no group is evaluated prior to its descendant groups.

We now illustrate the foregoing algorithm with the query of Section 5.3:

Find the department name and department head for each instructor whose rank is Associate Professor or Professor.

The relational algebraic expression of this query is given by:

1. UNIV MULT INSTR (call this relation R_1)
2. R_1 WHERE (UNIV.DNO = INSTR.DNO AND (RANK = 'AssocProf' OR RANK = 'Professor')) (call this relation R_2)
3. R_2[DNAME, DHEAD]

Figure 5–1 shows the tree representation of the query above. We now apply rules 1 through 4 to convert the tree of Figure 5–1 to the tree of Figure 5–2. Rule 1 is already used in formulating step 1 of the query. Then rule 2 is used to push the selection

```
INSTR WHERE RANK = 'AssocProf'
         OR RANK = 'Professor'
```

below the Cartesian product MULT. Rules 3 and 4 then produce the rest of the tree. Note that the projection R_2[DNAME, DHEAD] cannot be pushed below the selection

```
R₁ WHERE UNIV.DNO = INSTR.DNO
```

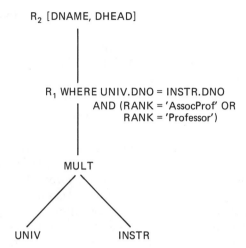

R₂ [DNAME, DHEAD]

R₁ WHERE UNIV.DNO = INSTR.DNO
    AND (RANK = 'AssocProf' OR
    RANK = 'Professor')

MULT

UNIV   INSTR

Figure 5–1 Tree representation of a query.

because then we lose the attribute DNO before performing the selection involving DNO.

Next, we split the tree of Figure 5–2 into two groups using rule 5 as follows:

1. Group 1 consists of the two nodes, INSTR WHERE . . . and UNIV MULT . . . , as indicated by the dashed line in Figure 5–3.
2. Group 2 consists of the remaining two upper nodes, R_1 WHERE . . . and R_2[DNAME, DHEAD], as indicated by the dashed line in Figure 5–3.

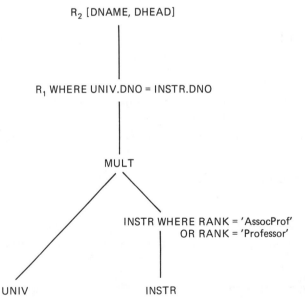

R₂ [DNAME, DHEAD]

R₁ WHERE UNIV.DNO = INSTR.DNO

MULT

INSTR WHERE RANK = 'AssocProf'
    OR RANK = 'Professor'

UNIV   INSTR

Figure 5–2 Query tree with optimization.

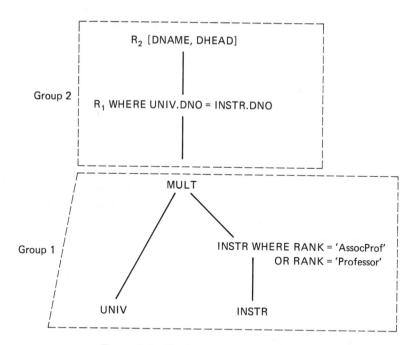

Figure 5–3 Final tree with grouped nodes.

Finally, we write a program to implement the operations in group 1 followed by those in group 2.

5.5 OPTIMIZATION IN SYSTEM R

The optimization in System R follows the generic methodology of Section 5.4, although some variations arise due to the specific syntax of SQL. The Research Storage Interface (RSI) of System R (see Section 2.3.1) performs the query optimization by choosing an optimal access path for each SELECT . . . FROM . . . WHERE statement in the query. Some of these statements may be nested inside others in case of a nested query. In that case the query optimizer executes the innermost block at first and then executes the remaining nested blocks in the order that is reverse of the order of their appearance in the query. Optimization occurs within each block.

For a given query block, there are two cases to consider, the first of which is a special case of the second:

1. For a block that involves just a selection and/or projection of a single relation, the optimizer uses statistical information from the system catalog, together with formulas for size estimates of intermediate results and for cost of low-level operations, to choose a strategy for constructing that selection and/or projection. The statistics maintained in the catalog are as follows:

a. Number of tuples in each relation
b. Number of pages occupied by each relation
c. Percentage of pages occupied by each relation with respect to all pages in the relevant portion of the database
d. Number of distinct data values for each index
e. Number of pages occupied by each index

These statistics are not updated every time the database is updated because of the overhead that such an approach would entail. Instead, they are updated in response to a special system utility called UPDATE STATISTICS which can be executed at any time. As a result, however, the optimizer may in fact be basing its decisions on information that is at least partially obsolete.

2. For a block that involves two or more relations to be joined together, with (probably) local selections and/or projections on individual relations, the optimizer

a. Treats each individual relation as in case 1
b. Decides on a sequence for performing the joins

However, operations a and b are not independent of each other.

For example, a given strategy for accessing an individual relation A might well be chosen precisely because it produces tuples of A in the order in which they are needed to perform a subsequent join of A with some other relation B.

Given a set of relations to be joined, the optimizer chooses a pair to be joined first, then a third to be joined to the result of joining the first two, and so on. In other words, it always treats an expression such as

$$A \text{ JOIN } B \text{ JOIN } C \text{ JOIN } D$$

(not intended to be genuine SQL syntax) in strictly nested fashion, that is, as

$$((A \text{ JOIN } B) \text{ JOIN } C) \text{ JOIN } D$$

System R optimizer chooses one of two methods for implementing any particular (binary) join, $A \text{ JOIN } B$, say. The two methods are the nested loop method and the sort/merge method. The choice between them is made on the basis of cost formulas. The two methods work as follows:

The *nested loop method* can be described by the following pseudocode algorithm:

```
scan relation A sequentially    (either via an index or
                                 in "physical" sequence);
```

```
for each tuple of A do;
  retrieve A-tuple;
  scan relation B looking for tuples matching that
  A-tuple                          (either via an index or
                                    in "physical" sequence);
  for each such B-tuple do;
    retrieve B-tuple;
    construct joined (A, B)-tuple;
  end;
end;
```

The *sort/merge method* basically consists of sorting the two relations into a sequence based on values of the joining attributes, and then applying the nested loop algorithm. However, certain improvements are now possible in that algorithm compared with the general case. First, physical sequence will now definitely be the most efficient basis for the two scans. Second, the two scans can be synchronized so that the complete join is constructed in a single pass over each of the two relations. For obvious reasons, this improved nested loop algorithm is usually referred to as a *"merge" process*.

5.6 ESTIMATION OF QUERY PROCESSING COST

The query processing cost plays an important role in the selection of an optimal access path. To estimate the cost the query optimizer uses various statistical information from the system catalog. The following three estimates are used most often:

1. Size of a Cartesian product
2. Number of tuples satisfying a given selection condition of the form

   attribute-name = value

3. Size of a natural join

We now give formulas for these estimates. Let R be a relation and $t(R)$ be a tuple in R. Let

n_R = number of tuples in R

$n_{t(R)}$ = number of bytes in $t(R)$

$v(a, R)$ = number of distinct values that appear in R for a given attribute a

We can now perform estimates 1 through 3 as follows:

1. Size of a Cartesian product R MULT $S = n_R \times n_S$.

2. We assume that each value of an attribute a appears with equal probability (i.e., the distribution of all possible attribute values is uniform). Then the number of tuples satisfying the selection condition R WHERE $a = $ 'A' can be estimated as

$$\frac{n_R}{v(a, R)}$$

Although the uniform distribution need not always hold, it provides a good approximation of reality. As a result, many query processors make this assumption when choosing an optimal access path.

3. In case of a natural join, we consider three cases. Let R and S be two relations that are joined together.

   a. If R and S have no common attributes, R JOIN S is the same as R MULT S. Hence the size of R JOIN $S = n_R \times n_S$, as in estimate 1.

   b. Let R and S have common attributes that form a key of R. Then we know that a tuple of S joins with exactly one tuple of R. Hence the size of R JOIN S cannot exceed the size of S, that is, size of R JOIN $S \leq n_S$.

   c. Let R and S have common attributes that do not form a key of either R or S. We assume that each value of a common attribute appears with equal probability, as in case (b). Suppose that a is a common attribute of R and S. Then the total number of tuples in S satisfying the selection condition S WHERE $a = $ 'A' is given by

$$\frac{n_S}{v(a, S)}$$

A tuple $t(R)$ in R is joined with each of the

$$\frac{n_S}{v(a, S)}$$

tuples in S and yields

$$\frac{n_S}{v(a, S)}$$

tuples in R JOIN S. Hence all of the tuples in R will produce a total number of

$$\frac{n_R \times n_S}{v(a, S)}$$

tuples in R JOIN S. Note that if we reverse the roles of R and S, the total number of tuples in S JOIN R, which is the same as R JOIN S, is

$$\frac{n_R \times n_S}{v(a, R)}$$

These two estimates are equal if

$$v(a, R) = v(a, S)$$

Otherwise, there will be some dangling tuples that do not participate in the join. In that case we take

$$\min\left(\frac{n_R \times n_S}{v(a, R)}, \frac{n_R \times n_S}{v(a, S)}\right)$$

as the estimate of the size of R JOIN S.

If we wish to maintain accurate statistics, then every time a relation is modified, it is necessary to update the statistics. This is a substantial amount of overhead (see Section 5.5). Therefore, most systems do not update the statistics on every modification. Instead, statistics are updated during periods of light load on the system. As a result, the statistics used for choosing a query processing strategy may not be accurate. However, if the interval between the update of the statistics is not too long, the statistics will be sufficiently accurate to provide a good estimation of the size of the results of expressions.

The cost of processing a query is measured in terms of I/O accesses (see Section 5.2). Using the estimates above, the query optimizer determines the number of I/O accesses for each access strategy, because each tuple is fetched from auxiliary storage to memory by means of an I/O access. Then the query optimizer develops estimates of the cost of implementing various alternative access paths. The cheapest access path is selected.

As an example, System R uses the cost formula

$$\text{cost} = \text{page fetches} + W \times (\text{RSI calls})$$

This cost is a weighted measure of I/O operations (pages fetched) and CPU used (instructions executed). W is an adjustable weighting factor between I/O and CPU. "RSI calls" is a predicted number of records returned from the RSS to be used in evaluating this query. Since most of System R's CPU time is spent in the RSS, the number of RSI calls is a good approximation for CPU utilization. Thus the choice of minimum cost path to process a query involves an attempt to minimize total resources required.

5.7 IMPACT OF INDEXING AND CLUSTERING ON QUERY OPTIMIZATION

Query optimization achieves fast data retrieval. The time for data retrieval can be reduced by

1. Indexing attributes in a relation
2. Using hashing algorithms

3. Clustering attributes common to multiple relations that are often joined together in a query

The cost-estimating procedures considered so far did not take into consideration the effects of indices, hash functions, and clustering. The presence of these tools significantly influences the selection of an optimal access strategy. We summarize our comments as follows:

1. Indices and hashing algorithms allow fast access to records containing a specific value of an indexed attribute.
2. Indices (although not most hash functions) allow the records of a file to be read in sorted order. It is efficient to read the records of a file in an order corresponding closely to physical order. If an index allows the records of a file to be read in an order that corresponds to the physical order of records, we call that index a *clustering index*. Clustering indices allow us to take advantage of the physical clustering of records into blocks.

5.8 FUTURE DIRECTIONS IN QUERY OPTIMIZATION

Query optimization research is still an active field. Promising directions include the development of simple, yet realistic cost estimates, the optimization of queries on databases with deductive or computational capabilities, and simultaneous optimization of multiple queries and update transactions. Other interesting areas are query optimization in database systems that utilize more advanced access paths, such as multiple-attribute indices or database machines, and query optimization in systems that work on the complex data structures required for artificial intelligence, office, statistical, decision support, or computer-aided design and manufacture applications.

5.9 SPECIFIC EXAMPLES OF QUERY LANGUAGES

In this section we give examples of various query languages that are based on relational algebra, tuple relational calculus, domain relational calculus, or a hybrid of algebra and calculus. In Section 5.9.1 we discuss QQL (Quick Query Language) based on relational algebra. QUEL (QUEry Language) based on tuple relational calculus is described in Section 5.9.2. In Section 5.9.3 we describe QBE (Query By Example) based on domain relational calculus. SQUARE (Specifying QUeries As Relational Expressions), whose basis is a hybrid of algebra and calculus, is described in Section 5.9.4. Finally, in Section 5.9.5 we introduce QBF (Query By Form), RBF (Report By Form), and GBF (Graph By Form), as examples of menu-driven form-based interfaces for query languages.

5.9.1 QQL (Quick Query Language)

QQL is the nonprocedural query language of LOGIX, a relational DBMS marketed by VenturCom, Inc. of Cambridge, Massachusetts. QQL is based on relational algebra. Figure 5–4 gives the LOGIX commands for relational algebra operations.
As an example, we give a QQL version of the query of Section 5.4:

> Find the department name and department head for each instructor whose rank is associate professor or professor.

The QQL version now follows:

```
join univ instr to newrel if
"rank = AssocProf or rank = Professor"
```

Note that LOGIX requires the names of relations in lowercase letters and the selection condition within quotation marks. Also, LOGIX does not have the equivalent of Cartesian product and division. The former can be implemented by "join" without a qualifying predicate, or by using the command "merge," which creates a relation with all attributes shared by the source relations and an additional attribute called TAG.

5.9.2 QUEL (QUEry Language)

QUEL is the query language of INGRES, a relational DBMS developed at the University of California in Berkeley and marketed by Relational Technology, Inc. QUEL is based on tuple relational calculus. For example, consider the following tuple relational calculus expression:

$$\{t^{(n)} \mid (\exists u^{(k)})(\exists v^{(m)})(R(u) \wedge S(v) \wedge (t(1) = u(1) \wedge \cdots \wedge (t(k)$$
$$= u(k)) \wedge (t(k + 1) = v(1)) \wedge \cdots \wedge (t(n) = v(m) \wedge \psi\}$$

where we assume that $n = k + m$, R and S have degrees k and m, respectively,

LOGIX Command	Relational Algebra Operations
union	union
common	intersection
diffa, diffb	difference
select	selection
project	projection
join	natural join

Figure 5–4 Relational algebra operations in QQL.

and ψ represents some additional condition without quantifiers. Then this expression can be written in QUEL as follows:

```
range of u is R
range of v is S
retrieve (u, v) where ψ'
```

Here ψ' is the QUEL expression for ψ. We now give the QUEL version of the query of Section 5.9.1:

```
range of u is UNIV
range of v is INSTR
retrieve (u.DNAME, u.DHEAD) where
     u.DNO = v.DNO and
     (v.RANK = "AssocProf" or v.RANK = "Professor")
```

5.9.3 QBE (Query by Example)

QBE (Query By Example) is a language developed by M. M. Zloof at the IBM Yorktown Heights Research Laboratory in 1975. It contains a number of features not present in relational algebra or calculus or in any of the implemented query languages we have discussed. It is based on domain relational calculus. Not the least of its special features is the fact that QBE is designed to be used sitting at a terminal, using a special screen editor to compose queries. A button on the terminal allows the user to call for one or more table skeletons, to be displayed on the screen. The user then names the relations and attributes represented by the skeleton, using the screen editor.

Queries are posed by using domain variables and constants, as in domain relational calculus, to form tuples that are in one of the relations whose skeletons appear on the screen. Certain of the variables, indicated by prefixing their name with P., are printed. All operators in QBE end in a dot, and the dot is not itself an operator. When a tuple or combination of tuples matching the conditions specified by the query are found, the components for those attributes preceded by P. are printed.

We now give the QBE version of the query of Section 5.9.1. Note that the user merely fills appropriate places in an empty table to formulate and print the query. Figure 5–5 gives the QBE version of this query. The skeletons of UNIV and INSTR are given in the figure. An entry of P. under DNAME and DHEAD indicates that these two attributes are to be printed. The selection criteria appear under RANK in INSTR. The fact that UNIV and INSTR are joined via DNO is indicated by entering a sample common value, -CS, under DNO in both relations. The domain relational calculus version of the query can be stated as follows:

UNIV	DNO	DNAME	DHEAD
	-CS	P.	P.

INSTR	INAME	IDEG	RANK	SSNO	SPCODE	DNO
			AssocProf Professor			-CS

Figure 5–5 Example of query using QBE.

$$\{t_1, t_2 \mid (\exists u_1)(\exists u_2)(\exists u_3)(\exists v_1)(\exists v_2)(\exists v_3)(\exists v_4)(\exists v_5)(\exists v_6)$$

$$(\text{UNIV}(u_1, u_2, u_3) \wedge \text{INSTR}(v_1, v_2, v_3, v_4, v_5, v_6))$$

$$\wedge (u_1 = v_6) \wedge (v_3 = \text{`AssocProf'} \vee v_3 = \text{`Professor'})\}$$

5.9.4 SQUARE (Specifying QUeries As Relational Expressions)

SQUARE was developed by IBM at the San Jose Research Laboratory during their work on System R. It later evolved into the query language SEQUEL, the predecessor of SQL. SQUARE is based on a hybrid of relational algebra and tuple ralational calculus. It supports the five relational algebra operations: union, difference, intersection, Cartesian product, and projection. The selection operation is done by using the tuple relational calculus notation. For example, R WHERE p is written as

$$\{r \mid R(r) \wedge p'\}$$

where p' is p written in tuple calculus notation. SQUARE also permits tuple variables.

The query of Section 5.9.1 can be written as follows in SQUARE:

DNAME, DHEAD **UNIV** DNO○DNO **INSTR** RANK ("AssocProf"
"Professor")

One of the problems with SQUARE is its reliance on subscripts. For using this language with a computer, we have to develop a syntax that places everything on a single line instead of the two-line notation shown above. But such syntax is not appealing. This eventually led to the replacement of SQUARE by SEQUEL, which has a syntax similar to that of SQL.

5.9.5 QBF (Query By Form), RBF (Report By Form), and GBF (Graph By Form)

QBF, RBF, and GBF are available in INGRES, a relational DBMS marketed by Relational Technology, Inc. They provide examples of menu-driven and form-driven interfaces to handle user queries, reports, and business graphics.

QBF is similar to QBE (see Section 5.9.3). QBF processes end-user queries through the use of forms. A *form* in INGRES is just a screen display version of a familiar hardcopy form. Such a form can be used both for input to the system from the user as well as output from the system to the user. QBF works in principle as follows:

1. INGRES automatically creates a default form for every table (base table or view) described in the system catalog. Each display field is labeled with the name of the corresponding database field and has a width that is determined from the data type of that database field. Figure 5–6 shows a default form for UNIV relation.

2. By calling up a copy of the default form on the screen and filling in some of the blank entries, the user can use that form to formulate simple queries concerning a table. Various control keys can be used during this process to step from field to field across the screen. After formulating a query, the user will choose the "Go" option from the menu, and INGRES will then retrieve the required records and display them one at a time in the same format (i.e., by means of the default form, but with all values filled in). The user can thus examine the records at leisure. This process is sometimes known as *database browsing*.

```
┌─────────────────────────────────────────────────────────────────┐
│                                                                   │
│   TABLE IS UNIV                                                    │
│                                                                   │
│                                                                   │
│   DNO:                 DNAME:                                      │
│                                                                   │
│                                                                   │
│   DHEAD:                                                           │
│                                                                   │
│                                                                   │
│                                                                   │
│                                                                   │
│   Help          Go            Query           End :               │
│                                                                   │
└─────────────────────────────────────────────────────────────────┘
```

Figure 5–6   Default form for UNIV.

GBF allows the user to issue simple queries against an INGRES database without requiring any knowledge of QUEL, the formal INGRES query language (see Section 5.9.2). QBF queries can involve base tables or views, joins of multiple tables, certain combinations of AND and OR, and the usual comparison operators (equals, less than, etc.). Also, if the default forms are not adequate for a specific application, INGRES allows the user to create new forms corresponding to joins of two or more tables. The *Visual Forms Editor* (VIFRED) can be used to create new forms from scratch.

RBF is a form-based system that allows the user to generate default reports interactively. It belongs to the report writer subsystem within INGRES. It is an interactive editor for those forms that make up a report specification. The user creates a new report specification by editing one of the default specifications using RBF.

GBF is the graphics component of INGRES. It is analogous to the report-writing component, except that the final "report" consists of a picture (i.e., a two-dimensional graph) rather than a simple table of rows and columns. For many kinds of data, a graph is a much more effective means of communication than a conventional report. GBF supports four types of graph: bar charts, pie charts, scatter graphs, and line plots. In all cases the data to be graphed consist of a table, derived in some way from the tables of the underlying database; GBF requires the user to define a query whose result is precisely the table in question. That table must have either two or three columns, referred to generically as the X, Y, and Z columns.

In general, the query can be specified via a QBF-like operation (if it is sufficiently simple), or via an explicit QUEL operation otherwise. The meanings of the three columns X, Y, and Z depend on the type of graph, as follows:

1. *Bar chart.* X represents the independent variable (the labels on the bars); Z (if present) represents labels of "subbars" within each bar. Y represents the dependent variable (the bar or "subbar" heights).

2. *Pie chart.* X represents the independent variable (the labels on the slice); Y represents the dependent variable (the slice areas). Z should not be present for this type of graph.

3. *Scatter graph.* X and Y represent (X, Y)-coordinates. For each value of Z, GBF will optionally attempt to find the straight line closely fitting the set of (X, Y) points ("linear regression").

4. *Line plot.* X and Y again represent (X, Y)-coordinates. For each value of Z, GBF will assume that the set of (X, Y) points represents a continuous function and will approximate that function by connecting adjacent points by means of a straight-line segment.

After specifying the query that defines the table to be graphed, the user can run that query and get GBF to create a resulting graph. Susequently, the user can modify that default graph specification, much as the user can modify a default report specification under RBF. Following are some of the changes the user can apply to the default graph specification:

1. *Bar charts*. The fill patterns for the bars can be changed.
2. *Scatter graphs*. The displayed character representing individual (X, Y)-points can be changed (on an individual Z-value basis). Linear regression can be requested.
3. *Line plots*. The character used to draw connecting lines can be changed (on an individual Z-value basis).
4. *All graphs except pie charts*. Axis origins can be changed. Axis scales can be set to logarithms (base 10). Axes can be labeled and/or can have specific values marked in a variety of fonts and font sizes. A grid can be superimposed on the graph.
5. *All graphs*. Placement details, title, and legend can be adjusted.

Like report specifications, graph specifications are kept in the INGRES system catalog.

We have provided a detailed description of QBF, RBF, and GBF as examples of menu-driven form-based interfaces. This is the current trend for vendors of relational database systems. These vendors try to address the needs of a growing volume of end users who are not experienced with the syntax and mechanism of query languages. Such users can enjoy the benefits of ad hoc queries, reports, and graphics without learning query languages if such form-based interfaces are available. SQL*FORMS, SQL*Reports, and SQL*Graphs, marketed by ORACLE Corporation, offer similar facilities within ORACLE.

5.10 APPLICATION GENERATORS

Application generators are rapid application development tools. They provide the application developer with a set of commands and menu-driven interfaces that can be used to implement an application without using a conventional programming language such as COBOL, FORTRAN, or Pascal. In this sense, an application generator can be regarded as an enhancement of QBF, RBF, and GBF discussed in Section 5.9.5.

The user of an application generator (i.e., the application designer) is thus presented with a very high-level application development language in which the primitive operations include not only the usual arithmetic and control flow facilities of conventional languages, but also facilities for database definition and access, terminal screen layout definition, screen input/output, screen data manipulation, and so on. Furthermore, the process of actually developing an application is typically done—at least in part—not by writing code in any conventional manner, but by conducting some kind of interactive dialogue with the system. Most generators are built around database management systems, since the definition and creation of a database are critical in the systems design process.

From the standpoint of the system life cycle, the generator attempts to reduce dramatically the time required in the programming and testing stages. This time saving in turn means that users will see the results from the development of a system much more quickly than if a procedural language is used.

5.11 OVERVIEW OF SQL

In this section we give an overview of SQL, because it has been accepted as the industry standard for nonprocedural database query languages. Many non-SQL relational DBMS vendors are now offering SQL interfaces to their products due to the importance of SQL. It has been estimated that in 1987 over 60 commercially available products supported some dialect of SQL.

In 1982 the American National Standards Institute (ANSI) chartered its Database Committee (X3H2) to develop a proposal for a standard relational language. The X3H2 proposal, which was finally ratified by ANSI in 1986, consisted essentially of the IBM dialect of SQL that formed a part of System R. It is quite likely that the X3H2 proposal will soon be accepted as an international standard by the International Standards Organization (ISO).

In 1989 a separate group called The SQL Access Group started an independent effort to develop a practical standard for database interoperability based on an open version of SQL. The Group is a confederation of such vendors as Digital Equipment Corporation, Oracle Corporation, Relational Technology Inc., Ashton-Tate, etc. The Group's efforts closely follow those of the ISO and the ANSI to establish a standard for SQL and for remote database access used in the distributed database systems.

Specific examples of some SQL commands used in ORACLE DBMS were given in earlier chapters. Here we present a set of basic SQL commands under three broad categories: data definition, data manipulation, and data control languages. The list is not exhaustive.

1. *Data definition commands*

```
a. CREATE TABLE table-name
              (attribute-name format,
               .....................
               attribute-name format);
```

An attribute may optionally be declared NOT NULL to exclude null values.

```
b. CREATE UNIQUE INDEX index-name ON
                   table-name (attribute-name);
```

The qualifier UNIQUE may be dropped to allow entry of the same value for the index repeatedly.

```
c. CREATE VIEW view-name AS selection-condition;
```

2. *Data manipulation commands*

```
a. INSERT INTO table-name VALUES (value-list);
b. UPDATE table-name SET
        attribute-name = value,
        ...................,
        attribute-name = value,
        WHERE selection-condition;
c. DELETE FROM table-name WHERE selection-condition;
d. ALTER TABLE table-name MODIFY
            (attribute-name format,
            ..................,
            attribute-name format);
e. ALTER TABLE table-name ADD
            (new-attribute-name format,
            ..................,
            new-attribute-name format);
f. DROP TABLE table-name;
g. DROP VIEW view-name;
h. RENAME table-name TO new-table-name;
i. DROP INDEX index-name;
j. SELECT * FROM table-name WHERE selection-condition;
k. SELECT attribute-name(s) FROM table-name
        WHERE selection-condition;
l. SELECT DISTINCT attribute-name(s) FROM
        table-name WHERE selection-condition
        GROUP BY attribute-name(s)
        HAVING expression
        ORDER BY attribute-name(s);
```

3. *Data control commands*
```
a. GRANT SELECT, UPDATE, INSERT ON table-name
                TO user-name;
b. REVOKE SELECT, UPDATE, INSERT ON table-name
                FROM user-name;
c. COMMIT
d. ROLLBACK
e. SET AUTOCOMMIT ON
f. SET AUTOCOMMIT OFF
g. SET AUTOCOMMIT IMMEDIATE
h. LOCK TABLE table-name, ...... , table-name
            IN SHARE MODE
```

5.12 SUMMARY

In this chapter we have discussed three major topics: query optimization, examples of specific query languages, and an overview of SQL. In a relational database the user formulates a query in a nonprocedural manner. The query optimizer of the DBMS transforms the query into an internal representation by using relational algebra or relational calculus. It then converts the internal representation into an equivalent canonical form. Various rules involving selection, projection, and join are used in this process. Finally, the query optimizer examines a set of alternative implementation plans and selects the one that involves the least number of disk accesses. Since the disk access speed is much slower than the memory speed, query processing becomes quicker if most of the relations that are manipulated can be brought into memory. Consequently, when a query is converted into a canonical form, the selections and projections are performed first, and then joins or Cartesian products are executed. This strategy reduces the sizes of the relations being worked on which can then be fetched into memory. The chapter contains a six-step algorithm for query optimization and illustrates it with an example. The query is represented as a tree that is traversed for processing the query. The goal of optimization is to minimize the tree traversal time. Also provided were several formulas to estimate the query processing cost, where the cost is measured in terms of disk accesses. A few comments are made on the optimization in System R and on the impact of indexing and clustering on query optimization.

The next segment gives some specific examples of a variety of query languages. QQL is based on pure relational algebra. QUEL and QBE are based on tuple relational calculus and domain relational calculus, respectively. SQUARE is based on a hybrid of relational algebra and tuple relational calculus. QBF, RBF, and GBF, all of which are available in INGRES, represent examples of menu-driven and prompt-driven interfaces to handle user queries, reports, and business graphics. They can be regarded as precursors of more versatile application development tools, usually called application generators.

The chapter closes with an overview of the basic SQL commands.

KEY WORDS

access path	communication cost
access path, optimal	computation cost
access strategy	conjunctive normal form
application generators	CPU processing
B-tree	database browsing
canonical form	GBF
clustering index	hashing

I/O operations	query optimizer
internal representation	query processing cost
join	RBF
merge process	relational algebra
	operations
nested loop method	runtime pathlength
nonprocedural	secondary storage
object graph	access cost
operator graph	selection
optimal access path	sort/merge method
projection	SQL
QBE	SQUARE
QBF	storage cost
QQL	System R
QUEL	tableau
query graph	tree representation
query language	VIFRED
query optimization	X3H2

REFERENCES AND FURTHER READING

The following references contain additional materials related to the topics covered in this chapter.

1. M. W. BLASGEN et al., System R: Architectural Overview, *IBM Systems Journal,* vol. 20, no. 1, 1981, pp. 41–62.

2. C. J. DATE, *Introduction to Database Systems,* vol. I, 4th ed., Addison-Wesley, Reading, MA, 1986.

3. C. J. DATE, *Relational Database Selected Writings,* Addison-Wesley, Reading, MA, 1986.

4. C. J. DATE, *The SQL Standard,* Addison-Wesley, Reading, MA, 1987.

5. R. FINKELSTEIN, Lingua Franca for Database, *PC Technical Journal,* December 1987, pp. 53–68.

6. M. JARKE and J. KOCH, Query Optimization in Database System, *ACM Computing Surveys,* vol. 16, no. 2, June 1984, pp. 111–152.

7. H. F. KORTH and A. SILBERSCHATZ, *Database System Concepts,* McGraw-Hill, New York, 1986.

8. J. D. ULLMAN, *Principles of Database Systems,* Computer Science Press, Rockville, MD, 1982.

9. C. C. YANG, *Relational Databases,* Prentice-Hall, Englewood Cliffs, NJ, 1986.

Date [3] and Korth and Silberschatz [7] have discussed the rationale of query optimization in terms of reduced I/O operations and shortening the run-time pathlength. The paper by Jarke and Koch [6] provides a comprehensive treatment of the query optimization process. The materials discussed in Sections 5.2 and 5.3 depend on this paper. Date [2] has given a treatment that follows [6]. The internal representation of a query and the formulation of a canonical form are discussed in Date [2], Korth and Silberschatz [7], and Ullman [8]. The algorithm to optimize a query appears in Ullman [8]. Ullman also discusses optimization algorithms used in System R and QUEL. Specific optimizing techniques used in System R are available in Blasgen et al. [1]. The estimation of query processing cost has been treated in detail by Korth and Silberschatz [7] and Ullman [8].

A variety of query languages have been described in detail by Ullman [8] and Yang [9]. More specifically, Ullman has discussed ISBL, SQUARE, SEQUEL, QUEL, and QBE. Yang has discussed ISBL, QUEL, QBE, and PROLOG. The specifics of SQL can be found in any SQL manual. Date [4] contains a detailed treatment of SQL, as proposed by the American National Standards Institute, and also some criticisms of SQL. Finkelstein [5] provides a quick overview of SQL, including a section on the history of SQL.

REVIEW QUESTIONS

1. Discuss three main features of a query language. Illustrate each feature with examples using SQL.
2. Why is query optimization necessary in a relational database as opposed to a non-relational database?
3. Discuss the two principal factors determining the system performance.
4. What is run-time pathlength?
5. Describe briefly the three-step methodology of query optimization.
6. What is a canonical form of a query? Formulate the rules involving selection, projection, and join that are used to derive the canonical form.
7. Why are selection and projection pushed as far as possible down the tree representing a query for optimization?
8. Discuss the nested loop method and the sort/merge method used by System R to optimize the implementation of a binary join. Give examples to illustrate your answer.
9. How do you measure the "cost" of processing a query?
10. Explain the formulas that can estimate the size of a natural join.
11. Define the term *clustering index*. How is it related to query optimization?
12. Explain the usage of application generators.

EXERCISES

1. (a) Consider the following three queries involving LHUDB:

   (1) List the student name, student major, student advisor, rank of advisor, and advisor's department name.

(2) List the course name, course instructor's name, and instructor's department name.

(3) List the course name, section number, names of students enrolled in the course, and the course instructor's name.

For each query, answer the following questions:
  (i) Give a relational algebra expression of the query.
  (ii) Draw a tree representation of the expression in part (i).
  (iii) Use the algorithm of Section 5.4 to optimize the query.
  (iv) Draw a revised tree showing the optimized version of the query.
  (v) Draw a tree showing the grouping of nodes to implement the version in part (iv).

(b) Each query listed in part (a) involves one or more joins. Assume the following sizes of the relations in LHUDB:

Relation Name	Number of Tuples
UNIV	30
INSTR	450
STUDNT	6000
CRSE	700

Estimate the size of each join used in the queries. [You have to make some reasonable assumptions regarding the variable $v(a, R)$ for applying the formulas of Section 5.6.]

2. Let R_1, R_2, and R_3 be three relations with respective attributes p, q, r; r, s, t; and t, u. Let the sizes of R_1, R_2, and R_3 be 10,000, 15,000, and 8000 tuples, respectively. Estimate the size of

$$R_1 \text{ JOIN } R_2 \text{ JOIN } R_3$$

and give a tree representation of this expression in the following two cases.
(a) Attributes p, r, t are primary keys of R_1, R_2, and R_3, respectively.
(b) No primary keys exist; instead, assume that

$$v(r, R_1) = 9000$$

$$v(r, R_2) = 11,000$$

$$v(t, R_2) = 500$$

$$v(t, R_3) = 1000$$

CHAPTER 6

NORMALIZATION
AND RELATIONAL DATA MODELS

6.1 NORMALIZATION PROCESS AND FIRST NORMAL FORM

The process of normalization is related to the theory of logical database design. We address this topic in detail in Chapter 9. So in this chapter we merely discuss normalization theory and point out later that normalization is a tool to be used for an efficient database design.

We have seen in Chapter 1 that a relational database always involves some data redundancy. This is needed to link multiple relations while performing a join operation. However, the data redundancy must be kept at the minimum level. Normalization process provides a systematic way of ensuring the minimum possible redundancy of data among the relations in a logical database design. It is based on the principle that ideally a given fact about an entity should appear only in one place, but can be repeated if *absolutely* necessary.

Normalization theory is built around the concept of *normal forms*. A relation is said to be in a particular normal form if it satisfies a certain specified set of conditions. Various normal forms have been defined. In this chapter we discuss only the following types:

1. First normal form or 1NF
2. Second normal form or 2NF
3. Third normal form or 3NF
4. Boyce–Codd normal form or BCNF
5. Fourth normal form or 4NF

6. Fifth normal form or 5NF, which is also called project join normal form or PJNF

A normal form of type (n) is also of types ($n - i$), where $i = 0, 1, \ldots, 5$ and a type is assumed to be a positive integer.

Codd originally defined 1NF, 2NF, and 3NF in 1972. The motivation behind Codd's definitions was that 1NF and 2NF are not desirable for a good database design and that relations should be in 3NF. Codd's original definition of 3NF suffered from certain inadequacies. A revised (stronger) definition, due to Boyce and Codd, appeared in 1974. This definition was stronger in the sense that any relation that was in 3NF by the new definition was certainly in 3NF by the old, but a relation could be in 3NF by the old definition and not by the new. The new 3NF is sometimes called Boyce–Codd normal form (BCNF) to distinguish it from the old form. Subsequently, in 1977, Fagin defined a new "fourth" normal form (4NF), and more recently, in 1979, he introduced another normal form, which he called projection-join normal form (PJ-NF or 5NF).

A relation is in the *first normal form* (1NF) if it satisfies the following conditions:

1. No attribute has repeated or array values.
2. No duplicate tuples exist.
3. The order of appearance of the attributes is immaterial.

Every relation in a relational database is at least in 1NF (i.e., it is normalized). For example, UNIV, STUDNT, CRSE, CRSELST, and SPCODE are all in 1NF.

An *unnormalized* relation allows repeated or array values for its attributes. Thus INSTR is unnormalized, because the attribute IDEG accepts array values such as 'BA, MA, PhD' and 'MA, MS, PhD'. Some relational DBMSs allow the existence of unnormalized relations.

6.2 FUNCTIONAL DEPENDENCIES

Functional dependencies represent a set of constraints that apply to the entities in a relational database. When we combine attributes to constitute a relation and declare candidate key(s) for the relation, we ensure that the functional dependencies hold. A large body of formal theory has been developed for the functional dependencies. In general, if we are given a set of functional dependencies, they may imply that other functional dependencies hold also. In this section we consider the following two dependencies: (1) functional dependency (FD) and (2) full functional dependency (FFD).

Given a relation R, an attribute y is *functionally dependent* on another attribute x if and only if each x-value in R has associated with it exactly one y-

value, irrespective of any additions, deletions, or changes at any given time. We also say that *x functionally determines* y. In symbols we write $R.x \rightarrow R.y$. Here x and y can be composite attributes. The notion of FD is an extension of the concept of a single-valued mathematical function. In fact, let X and Y be the sets of all possible x- and y-values in R. Then the FD

$$R.x \rightarrow R.y$$

is represented by the function

$$f: X \rightarrow Y$$

such that each $x \in X$ has a unique image $f(x) = y \in Y$.

If x is a composite attribute in R, then y is *fully functionally dependent* (FFD) on x if $R.x \rightarrow R.y$, and $R.z \rightarrow R.y$ does not hold for any proper subset z of x in R. Clearly, FFD implies FD, but not conversely.

As an example we note that the attributes DNAME and DHEAD are functionally dependent on the attribute DNO in the relation UNIV. Again, in the relation INSTR, the attribute DNO is functionally dependent on SSNO and RANK, but not fully functionally dependent on them, because DNO depends on SSNO alone.

The FDs in a given relation are represented by means of a *functional dependency diagram* or FD diagram, for short. An FD such as $R.x \rightarrow R.y$ can be represented as follows in an FD diagram:

$$\boxed{x} \quad \rightarrow \quad \boxed{y}$$

Figure 6–1 shows some FDs in the relations UNIV, INSTR, and STUDNT.

For an efficient and consistent logical database design it is necessary to determine the full set of FDs among the attributes. In 1974, W. W. Armstrong introduced a set of axioms, subsequently called *Armstrong's axioms*, to generate the complete set of FDs from a given starter set.

Let S be a set of FDs and let $\overline{S}$ be the set of all FDs logically deducible from S. Then $\overline{S}$ is called the *closure* of S and can be derived by applying the following rules on the attributes of S:

1. *Reflexivity.* If X is a set of attributes and $Y \subset X$, then $X \rightarrow Y$ holds.
2. *Augmentation.* If $X \rightarrow Y$ holds and W is a set of attributes, then $W \wedge X \rightarrow W \wedge Y$ holds, where $\wedge$ is the conjunction operation.
3. *Transitivity.* If $X \rightarrow Y$ and $Y \rightarrow Z$ hold, then $X \rightarrow Z$ holds.
4. *Union.* If $X \rightarrow Y$ and $X \rightarrow Z$ hold, then $X \rightarrow Y \wedge Z$ hold.
5. *Decomposition.* If $X \rightarrow Y \wedge Z$ holds, then $X \rightarrow Y$ and $X \rightarrow Z$ hold.
6. *Pseudotransitivity.* If $X \rightarrow Y$ and $W \wedge Y \rightarrow Z$ hold, then $X \wedge W \rightarrow Z$ holds.

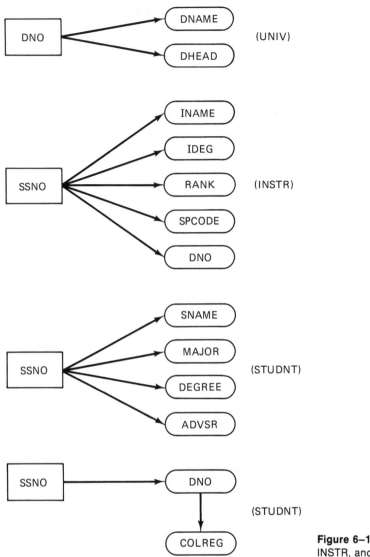

Figure 6–1 Sample FDs for UNIV, INSTR, and STUDNT.

Rules 1 through 3 are called Armstrong's axioms. They are called *sound* because they do not generate any incorrect FDs. They are also *complete* because they allow us to determine the entire closure S. However, if S is fairly large, it is a tiresome process to compute S by using rules 1 through 6. Korth and Silberschatz [4, pp. 187, 223] have given two algorithms in pseudo Pascal to compute $\overline{S}$ from a given S.

6.3 SECOND AND THIRD NORMAL FORMS

A relation is said to be in *second normal form* (2NF) if it is in first normal form and one of the following conditions applies:

1. Key consists of a single attribute.
2. No nonkey attribute exists.
3. Every nonkey attribute fully functionally depends on the entire key, which is composite.

For example, UNIV is in second normal form, assuming that DNO is the key. But CRSE is not so. If we take CNO and SECNO as the composite key, the nonkey attribute CNAME depends only on CNO, not on SECNO. In other words, CNAME does not fully functionally depend on the entire key (CNO, SECNO).

Let R be a relation with the key attribute x, which may be composite, and two nonkey attributes y and z such that the FD $R.y \rightarrow R.z$ holds that does not involve x. Then we say that a *transitive dependency* (TD) exists among the attributes of R. In case of TD, we note that the two separate FDs hold, that is,

$$R.x \rightarrow R.y \qquad \text{and} \qquad R.y \rightarrow R.z$$

which together yield a third FD

$$R.x \rightarrow R.z$$

Hence the name *transitive dependency*.

A relation is said to be in *third normal form* (3NF) if it is in second normal form and if there is no transitive dependency among its attributes.

Theoretically, 3NF is regarded as a highly desirable feature. Relations in 2NF may lead to some update anomalies, to be discussed later, that do not occur for relations in 3NF. The FDs involved in 2NF are dependencies of a nonkey attribute on the key, whereas the TDs in 3NF involve dependencies among nonkey attributes that do not involve the key. We now take an example to illustrate 3NFs. The relation STUDNT in LHUDB has the attribute SSNO as key. Hence it is in 2NF. However, a TD exists among DNO and COLREG, since DNO functionally determines COLREG without involving the key SSNO. For example, DNO = 'CS' belongs to COLREG = 'Arts/Sc.' independent of any specific student. Hence STUDNT is not in 3NF. It should be noted here though that a TD does not occur if there is an FD among nonkey attributes that involves the key. For instance, the nonkey attribute SNAME functionally determines the other nonkey attributes MAJOR, DEGREE, ADVSR, and DNO. But these FDs are not TDs, since all of them involve the key SSNO.

The importance of 3NF arises out of the fact that a non-3NF relation may involve some update anomalies. As an example, refer to the Customer Master File of Figure 1–1. We can design it as a relation with attributes.

Customer Number
Customer Name
Customer Address
Credit Code
Credit Description

This satisfies conditions 1 through 3 of Section 6.1 and hence is in first normal form. Using the Customer Number as a key, we can see that this is also in second normal form. But since the Credit Code determines the Credit Description and since this dependency does not involve the key attribute, Customer Number, there is a transitive dependency among the attributes. Hence the relation is not in the third normal form.

To illustrate the difficulty encountered with relations that are not in third normal forms, suppose that the Customer relation has the following values:

Customer Number	Customer Name	Customer Address	Credit Code	Credit Description
1	Smith	Boston	A2	Very good
2	Jones	Allentown	B	Good
3	Brown	New York	X	Not determined
4	Adams	Boston	B	Good
5	Blake	Cambridge	A2	Very good

If the tuple for Customer Number = '3' is deleted, the information about credit code X is also gone. This situation can be remedied by splitting Customer relation into two separate relations, Cust and Credit, each of which is in 3NF, as shown below:

Cust Relation	Credit Relation
Customer Number	Credit Code
Customer Name	Credit Description
Customer Address	
Credit Code	

When we delete the tuple for Customer Number = '3', the data on customer number 3 is gone from Cust relation (which is the file on current customers), but the Credit (which is a master list of all possible credit codes and descriptions) will still contain data on credit code X.

In general, a relation not in 3NF can be decomposed into two or more relations each of which is in 3NF; similarly, a relation not in 2NF can be decomposed into two or more relations, each in 2NF, and so on. The main issue to be addressed here is whether we lose any information or introduce any new information as a result of this decomposition process. This topic is known as *nonloss decomposition* of relations. We discuss it in the next section.

6.4 NONLOSS DECOMPOSITION OF RELATIONS

Let R be a relation and let $R_1, \ldots, R_n$ be a set of projections of R on its attributes such that $R_1, \ldots, R_n$ can be joined together via some common attribute(s) to reproduce R. If $t \in R$ is any tuple, t gives rise to one tuple t_i in each R_i, $i = 1, \ldots, n$. These n tuples t_i can be combined to reproduce t when we form the join R_1 JOIN $R_2 \cdots$ JOIN R_n. In other words, we always have

$$R \subset R_1 \text{ JOIN } R_2 \cdots \text{ JOIN } R_n$$

that is, every tuple in R appears in the join on the right. The relations $R_1, \ldots, R_n$ are called a *decomposition* of the relation R. In general, the right side contains more tuples than R (i.e., $R \neq R_1$ JOIN $R_2 \cdots$ JOIN R_n).

A decomposition $(R_1, \ldots, R_n)$ of a relation R is called a *nonloss decomposition* of R if

$$R = R_1 \text{ JOIN } R_2 \cdots \text{ JOIN } R_n$$

always holds. For example, let us take R = Customer, R_1 = Cust, and R_2 = Credit (see Section 6.3). Then we always have

$$R = R_1 \text{ JOIN } R_2$$

Hence R_1 and R_2 form a nonloss decomposition of R. We now describe a general criterion to ensure that a decomposition is nonloss.

Let R be any relation and let S be a set of FDs in R. Let R_1 and R_2 form a decomposition of R. This decomposition is nonloss if at least one of the following FDs belongs to S:

1. Attribute(s) in R_1 functionally depend on the common attribute(s) of R_1 and R_2.
2. Attribute(s) in R_2 functionally depend on the common attribute(s) of R_1 and R_2.

For the example given above, where R = Customer, R_1 = Cust, and R_2 = Credit, we note that the common attribute of R_1 and R_2 is Credit Code and the remaining attribute in R_2 (i.e., Credit Description) functionally depends on Credit Code. This explains why R_1 and R_2 form a nonloss decomposition of R.

In 1971, I. J. Heath proved the following special case of the general result above: If a relation R with attributes x, y, and z satisfies the FD $R.x \rightarrow R.y$, the two projections $R_1[x, y]$ and $R_2[x, z]$ always constitute a nonloss decomposition of R.

The motivations behind a nonloss decomposition of a relation is that no information should be lost during the decomposition process. Hence any information that can be derived from the original structure can also be derived from the new structure. The converse is not true. The new structure can contain information that could not be represented in the original. In this sense the new structure may be regarded as a slightly more faithful representation of the real world.

6.5 BOYCE–CODD NORMAL FORM

Let R be a relation with attributes $a_1, \ldots, a_n$. An attribute a_i, $i = 1, 2, \ldots, n$, is a *determinant* of R if at least another attribute in R is fully functionally dependent on a_i. We define R to be in *Boyce–Codd normal form* (BCNF) if every determinant is a candidate key. The definition of BCNF is conceptually simpler, because it makes no explicit reference to 1NF, 2NF, or 3NF. BCNF is strictly stronger than 3NF and a relation in 3NF but not in BCNF can be nonloss decomposed into two or more relations in BCNF.

As an example, UNIV is in BCNF. It has two determinants, DNO and DNAME, both of which are candidate keys. On the other hand, CRSLST (see Figure 2–1) is in 3NF, but not in BCNF. Taking the composite attribute (CNO, SECNO, SID, OFRNG) as the candidate key, we see that no transitive dependency exists in CRSLST and hence CRSLST is in 3NF. But the attribute CNO is a determinant since SECNO fully functionally depends on CNO, although CNO is not a candidate key. Hence CRSLST is not in BCNF.

6.6 FOURTH NORMAL FORM

Let R be a relation with attributes $a_1, \ldots, a_n$. We say that there is a *multivalued dependency* (MVD) of an attribute a_j on another attribute a_i, if given any value of a_i there is a set of zero or more associated values of a_j such that the latter set is not connected in any way to the values of the attributes in the subset $R - a_i - a_j$. In symbols, we write $a_i \rightarrow \rightarrow a_j$, and say that a_i *multidetermines* a_j in the relation R.

MVDs are a generalization of FDs in the sense that every FD is an MVD, but the converse is not true (i.e., there exist MVDs that are not FDs). A relation R is said to be in *fourth normal form* (4NF) if whenever there exists an MVD in R of the form $A \rightarrow \rightarrow B$, all attributes of R are also functionally dependent on A. In other words, R is in 4NF if R is in BCNF, and every MVD is also an FD in R. A relation not in 4NF can always be nonloss decomposed into two or more relations in 4NF. The relation UNIV is in 4NF because it is in BCNF and no MVD exists in UNIV.

6.7 FIFTH NORMAL FORM

The concept of a fifth normal form depends on join dependency. It is possible to construct relations that cannot be nonloss decomposed into two projections, but can be so decomposed into three or more projections. This means that if R is such a relation, its decomposition into two projections R_1 and R_2, say, produces spurious tuples in R_1 JOIN R_2 (i.e., tuples that do not exist in R). In other words, R is not equivalent to R_1 JOIN R_2. However, R can be broken into three or more projections $R_1, \ldots, R_n$ such that

$$R = R_1 \text{ JOIN } R_2 \cdots \text{ JOIN } R_n, \quad n > 2$$

The spurious tuples disappear when the final set of n (> 2) joins are performed.

A relation R satisfies the *join dependency* (JD), written as

$$*(R_1, R_2, \ldots, R_n)$$

if R is equal to the join of its projections on $R_1, R_2, \ldots, R_n$, where $R_1, R_2, \ldots, R_n$ are subsets of the set of attributes of R. We say that R is in *fifth normal form* (5NF) if every JD in R is implied by the candidate keys of R. As an example, UNIV is in 5NF, since UNIV can be written as the join of two binary relations

```
UNIV₁ = (DNO, DNAME)
UNIV₂ = (DNO, DHEAD)
```

Also this JD [i.e., $*(\text{UNIV}_1, \text{UNIV}_2)$] is implied by the candidate keys DNO and DNAME.

Some authors call 5NF a *project join normal* from (PJNF).

6.8 CONCLUDING REMARKS ON NORMALIZATION

The theory of functional dependency, which includes FD, MVD, and JD, is an area of active research. It leads to the concept of normalization that involves the six normal forms. However, normalization beyond the 3NF is rarely done in practice. Date [1, p. 390] comments that 5NF relations are "pathological cases and likely to be rare in practice." Although BCNF and 4NF may be less rare than 5NF, they are still highly theoretical in nature. Regarding 3NF, it should be pointed out here that there is nothing sacred about a relation being in 3NF. Usually, a relation in first and second normal form exhibits certain anomalies with respect to insertion, deletion, or update of tuples, whereas a relation in third normal form does not have such problems. Consequently, a relation in third normal form is preferred.

Let us consider a relation NAMADDR which is used for generating mailing labels. The structure of NAMADDR is as follows:

```
NAMADDR ( NAME     CHAR (30),
          STREET   CHAR (50),
          CITY     CHAR (20),
          STATE    CHAR (2),
          ZIP      NUM  (5) )
```

Declaring NAME as the primary key, we note that NAMADDR is in 2NF. But there is a transitive dependency among CITY, STATE, and ZIP, since the FD

```
ZIP → (CITY, STATE)
```

does not involve the primary key NAME. Hence NAMADDR is not in 3NF. If we insist that relations must be in 3NF, we have to decompose NAMADDR into two relations, NAMSTR and ZIPCODE, say, as follows:

```
NAMSTR  ( NAME     CHAR (30),
          STREET   CHAR (50),
          ZIP      NUM  (5) )

ZIPCODE ( CITY     CHAR (20),
          STATE    CHAR (2),
          ZIP      NUM  (5) )
```

Then NAMADDR is derived as NAMSTR JOIN ZIPCODE via the common attribute ZIP. However, realistically, it is better to sacrifice 3NF and use the single relation NAMADDR to generate the mailing labels.

The theory of normalization forms an integral part of logical database design, discussed in Chapter 9. Normalization pertains to a single relation at a time. Interrelational dependencies are handled by the referential and relational integrity requirements (see Chapter 2). A sound logical database design should include both normalization and integrity issues.

When we systematically reduce a relation in 1NF into multiple relations in 2NF, and then into 3NF, and so on, we always insist on the nonloss decomposition process; that is, no information should be lost nor should spurious tuples appear as a result of the decomposition. Date [1, pp. 390–391] has formulated the successive decomposition process as a set of rules as follows:

1. Take projections of the original 1NF relation to eliminate any non-FDs. This will produce a collection of 2NF relations.

2. Take projections of these 2NF relations to eliminate any transitive dependencies. This will produce a collection of 3NF relations.

3. Take projections of these 3NF relations to eliminate any remaining functional dependencies in which the determinant is not a candidate key. This will produce a collection of BCNF relations. (*Note:* Steps 1 through 3 can be condensed into the single guideline "Take projections of the original relation to eliminate FDs in which the determinant is not a candidate key.")

4. Take projections of these BCNF relations to eliminate any multivalued dependencies that are not also functional dependencies. This will produce a collection of 4NF relations. (*Note:* In practice it is usual to eliminate these MVDs before applying the other steps above.)

5. Take projections of these 4NF relations to eliminate any join dependencies that are not implied by the candidate keys (although perhaps we should add "if you can find them"). This step will produce a collection of relations in 5NF.

The higher levels of normalization are important for database designers because they make the structure of the database easier to understand. As a result, the end users also benefit from them. However, the impact of normalization on system performance is less significant. The system will function perfectly well if relations are only in 2NF, say. The update anomalies may occur at times, but they will not break down the system. For instance, the loss of information on Credit Code = X, as described in Section 6.3, will probably not happen in reality, because there will be many other tuples with Credit Code = X, and the chance of all of them being deleted at the same time is almost nil.

Database designs that are based on 3NF tend to involve a lot of small relations (i.e., relations with a small number of attributes per relation). In most of the current systems, each relation typically maps to a single stored file. Consequently, a large number of small relations can have undesirable performance implications. In a sense, 3NF requirement optimizes update at the cost of retrieval. It eliminates a variety of update anomalies, but it can lead to the need for a large number of joins to be performed for data retrieval. The example of the relation NAMADDR given at the beginning of this section illustrates this point.

6.9 RELATIONAL DATA MODELS

Normalization theory emphasizes the doctrine that each relation should represent a single atomic fact. The various dependencies provide a tool to ensure the atomicity of a relation. To address the issue of one fact for each relation, various authors have proposed alternative relational data models. In the three following subsections we discuss three such models. A *relational data model* consists of three components:

1. Relational database
2. Relational operations (algebra or calculus)
3. Relational rules (entity, referential, and relational integrity)

A relation is typically an n-ary relation (i.e., it consists of n attributes and hence is said to be of *degree n*).

In 1976, Hall and Falkenburg proposed the irreducible relational model, and in 1978, Kent proposed the binary relational model as two alternative relational data models to replace the more widely used n-ary relational models. Their main criticism against the latter was that it was too much implementation oriented. From 1974 through 1981, a variety of authors proposed a third alternative called the functional model. The most notable among them are Abrial (1974), Senko (1975), Bracchi (1976), Sharman (1977), Munz (1980), and Shipman (1981). In Sections 6.9.1, 6.9.2, and 6.9.3 we discuss the binary, irreducible, and functional data models, respectively.

6.9.1 Binary Relational Model

Each binary relation represents a single atomic fact: a correspondence between a key and a nonkey attribute, where the key consists of only one attribute. Consequently, every binary relation is in 3NF. However, the fact that every relation in a database is binary does not necessarily mean that the database is good. In fact, binary relations require more redundancy of attributes in relations than n-ary relations require. Access operations tend to be more complex in the binary approach than in the n-ary approach, because the former involves more joins for data retrieval.

As an example, the ternary relation UNIV can be decomposed into two binary relations, $UNIV_1$ and $UNIV_2$, say, as follows:

```
UNIV₁(DNO,DNAME)
UNIV₂(DNO,DHEAD),
```

where DNO is the key in each relation.

If an n-ary relation has a composite key, its decomposition into binary relations becomes a bit tricky. Either the composite attributes must be renamed as a single attribute key or the composite attributes must be broken down into different attributes for different binary relations. For instance, CRSE has a composite key (CNO, SECNO). Note that CNAME and DNO are determined by CNO alone, but INAME is determined by the pair (CNO, SECNO). Hence CRSE can be decomposed into the following three binary relations:

1. $CRSE_1$ (CNO, CNAME)
2. $CRSE_2$ (CNO, DNO)
3. $CRSE_3$ (CSECNO, INAME).

In relation 3 CSECNO consists of both CNO and SECNO and hence has the format CHAR (7). Typical values of CSECNO can be CS22501, CS57904, and so on, where the first five characters represent the CNO and the last two digits represent SECNO (see Figure 2–2).

6.9.2 Irreducible Relational Model

An *n*-ary relation is broken down into two or more subrelations such that none of them is reducible anymore, although none may be a binary relation. Each subrelation is then irreducible in that it represents a single atomic fact and consists of

1. A primary key, possibly composite
2. At most one other attribute, which may be composite

Theorem.   Every binary relation is irreducible, but not conversely.

Proof. Let *R* be a binary relation. Then *R* consists of two attributes, one key and the other nonkey. Hence *R* is an irreducible relation by the definition above.

Conversely, consider the relation UNIV. It has a primary key DNO and has another nonkey composite attribute (DNAME, DHEAD). Hence it is irreducible. But UNIV is not binary because it has more than two attributes.

6.9.3 Functional Data Model

The *functional data model* is the most popular of the irreducible approaches. It involves *entities*, which are represented by unary relations, and *functions*, which are represented by binary relations. The notion of a function is borrowed from mathematics.

As examples, let us consider the relations UNIV and INSTR. UNIV consists of 3-tuples, each of which represents a unique department within the university. Similarly, INSTR consists of 6-tuples, each of which represents a unique instructor. Hence UNIV and INSTR can be regarded as unary relations identifying departments and instructors, respectively. Each attribute of UNIV and INSTR is then represented as a function from the relation as domain to the set of all possible values of the attribute as range. Thus the attributes of UNIV are given by the following functions:

```
  DNO : UNIV → CHAR2
DNAME : UNIV → CHAR25
DHEAD : UNIV → CHAR20
```

This means that DNO, as a function, maps a tuple of UNIV into an element of CHAR2 which consists of all two-character strings. Thus, given a tuple t of UNIV, there exists exactly one value of DNO, say CS, in the range CHAR2 corresponding to t under the function DNO. Each function is indeed a binary relation. The function DNO, for instance, consists of all pairs (t, d), where t is a tuple in UNIV and d is a value of DNO.

The attributes of INSTR can be written as follows:

```
     INAME : INSTR → CHAR20
      IDEG : INSTR → CHAR10
    SPCODE : INSTR → NUM2
      Rank : INSTR → CHAR10
      SSNO : INSTR → NUM9
INSTR-UNIV : INSTR → UNIV
```

The last function, INSTR-UNIV, is interpreted as follows:

> INSTR-UNIV is a function from the unary relation INSTR identifying a unique instructor tuple to the unary relation UNIV identifying a unique department tuple.

To define DNO as an attribute of INSTR, we need to use the composite function

```
DNO ○ INSTR-UNIV : INSTR → CHAR2
```

The composite function is used in the functional data model in order to represent attributes that link two or more n-ary relations. As indicated above, the composite function DNO ○ INSTR-UNIV maps a tuple t of INSTR into an element of CHAR2 that represents the value of DNO appearing in the tuple t.

6.9.4 Use of the Functional Model in the Query Language

Using a functional model it is possible to define a query language that has intuitive appeal. It uses the notion of inverse of a function and composition of two functions, which are now defined. Given two functions $f: X \rightarrow Y$ and $g: Y \rightarrow Z$, the *composite function* $f \circ g: X \rightarrow Z$ is defined as follows:

$$(f \circ g)(x) = g(f(x)), \qquad \forall x \in X$$

The definition is meaningful, because for every $x \in X$, $f(x) \in Y$ always, and hence $g(f(x)) \in Z$.

Next, given a function $f: X \rightarrow Y$, the *inverse function* $f^{-1}: Y \rightarrow X$ is defined as follows:

$$f^{-1}(y) = x \quad \text{if and only if} \quad y = f(x), \qquad \forall y \in Y$$

This definition is meaningful if f is a bijective mapping (i.e., f is one-to-one and onto).

We now show the representation of the following query using functional data model:

Find the department name of each instructor whose rank is associate professor.

Figure 6–2 shows a functional representation of the UNIV and INSTR relations. Each circle represents either a unary relation or the range of a function corresponding to an attribute. Each arrow represents a function.

In the functional data model the preceding query can be written as follows:

```
DNAME o INSTR-UNIV o (RANK)⁻¹ ('AssocProf')
```

The query is processed as follows (see Figure 6–3):

1. The function $(RANK)^{-1}:CHAR10 \rightarrow INSTR$ returns three tuples of INSTR with INAMEs

    Deb Kumar Roy

    Cathy Doucette

    Jack Adams

    since each of these tuples has RANK = 'AssocProf'.

2. The function INSTR-UNIV:INSTR $\rightarrow$ UNIV returns three tuples of UNIV by matching the DNO values of the three tuples in step 1 with those of the tuples in UNIV. Thereby the three tuples of UNIV with DNO = 'MA', 'HS', and 'CS' are retrieved.

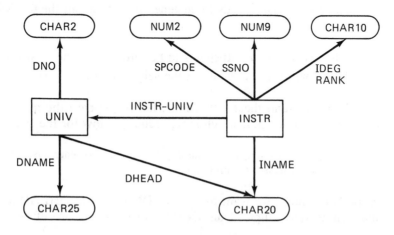

Figure 6–2 Functional representation of UNIV and INSTR.

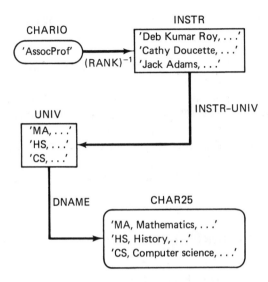

CHARIO

'AssocProf'

$(RANK)^{-1}$

INSTR

'Deb Kumar Roy, . . .'
'Cathy Doucette, . . .'
'Jack Adams, . . .'

INSTR–UNIV

UNIV

'MA, . . .'
'HS, . . .'
'CS, . . .'

DNAME   CHAR25

'MA, Mathematics, . . .'
'HS, History, . . .'
'CS, Computer science, . . .'

Figure 6–3 Functional representation of a query.

3. Finally, the function DNAME:UNIV → CHAR25 returns the DNAME values of the three tuples above in step 2, that is, the values

Mathematics, History, Computer Science

A function in the mathematical sense is understood to be single valued. This means that if $f: X \rightarrow Y$ is a function, then for every $x \in X$ its image $f(x) \in Y$ is unique. We note that this restriction does not apply to the inverse function $(RANK)^{-1}$ in the example above. Given a single element 'AssocProf' in the domain CHAR10 of $(RANK)^{-1}$, there are three images: the three tuples in the unary relation INSTR. In this sense, $(RANK)^{-1}$ is defined as multiple valued.

The query above needs to be generalized to admit the following two extensions:

1. Allow two or more attributes to be retrieved at the final stage.

2. Allow two or more values in the selection criteria.

To understand these extensions, let us compare the query of this section with that of Section 5.4, which is reproduced below for the sake of reference:

Find the department name and department head of each instructor whose rank is associate professor or professor.

In the latter query we want to retrieve DNAME and DHEAD at the final stage and want to select tuples from INSTR satisfying any one of two conditions

```
RANK = 'AssocProf'   or   RANK = 'Professor'
```

A modified version of the earlier query can be written as follows to accommodate the two extensions above:

```
{DNAME, DHEAD} o INSTR-UNIV o
          (RANK)⁻¹ ({'Assoc Prof', 'Professor'})}
```

This notation is a shorthand for the following expanded form:

```
DHEAD o (DNAME)⁻¹ (DNAME o INSTR-UNIV o ((RANK)⁻¹
               ('Professor') ∪ (RANK)⁻¹ ('AssocProf')))
```

The expression above is implemented as follows:

1. $(RANK)^{-1}$ ('Professor') $\cup$ $(RANK)^{-1}$ ('AssocProf') returns seven tuples of INSTR with INAMEs

> Lee Kunkel
>
> Albert Roby
>
> Raj Chandra Mittra
>
> Brady Jackson
>
> Deb Kumar Roy
>
> Cathy Doucette
>
> Jack Adams

2. INSTR-UNIV then returns the five tuples from UNIV with DNO values EN, CS, MA, HS, EE. Since 'RL' does not appear in UNIV as a valid DNO, it is not returned by INSTR-UNIV.

3. DNAME returns the corresponding DNAME values

> English
>
> Computer Science
>
> Mathematics
>
> History
>
> Electrical Engineering

These five values are stored in a temporary location for future display.

4. $(DNAME)^{-1}$ returns the five tuples in UNIV corresponding to the five DNAME values above.

5. DHEAD maps each of these five tuples into CHAR25 and returns the DHEAD values

> Lee Kunkel

Albert Roby

Deb Kumar Roy

Cathy Doucette

Raj Chandra Mittra

6. The query processor finally returns the five pairs of matching (DNAME, DHEAD) values from steps 3 and 5.

6.10 SUMMARY

In this chapter we have presented the normalization concepts and three data models as alternatives for n-ary relational data models. Normalization is related to the topic of logical database design. Its goal is to improve the efficiency of the design. This is achieved by the requirement that a relation should be in a particular normal form. As a minimum, every n-ary relation is in first normal form since no array values are allowed there. An unnormalized relation, on the other hand, allows array values for its attributes.

The concepts of second- and higher-order normal forms involve functional dependencies of various types. A relation is in second normal form if it is in first normal form and every nonkey attribute is fully functionally dependent on the key attribute(s). If there is a functional dependency among nonkey attributes that does not involve the key, there exists a transitive dependency among the attributes of the relation. If a relation is in 2NF and no transitive dependency exists among its attributes, the relation is in 3NF, which is regarded as a desirable feature of a relation. Examples are given in the chapter to show that certain update anomalies may exist if a relation is not in 3NF.

A relation in 2NF but not in 3NF can always be decomposed into two or more relations, each of which is in 3NF, via projections. When we perform this decomposition, we ensure that no existing information is lost. This means that by joining the projections we should be able to get back the original relation. This is known as the nonloss decomposition of information.

There are three more normal forms of order higher than the third: Boyce–Codd, fourth, and fifth. Their definitions involve multivalued dependency and functional dependency. However, these forms are primarily of theoretical interest. In practical applications we rarely encounter relations that are higher than 3NF. Sometimes we do not insist on even 3NF in consideration of retrieval efficiency. Normalization introduces a trade-off decision between update efficiency and retrieval efficiency.

In the last section three other data models that have been proposed as alternatives to the n-ary relations have been discussed. These are binary data model, irreducible data model, and functional data model. Binary and irreducible data models are refinements of the n-ary relational data model in that they both insist on the principle that a relation should represent a single atomic fact. The functional data model uses unary and binary relations, the latter being used for defining functions that represent attributes of each relation. The functional data model provides a basis of defining query languages in terms of composition of functions and inverse functions. Several examples are provided to illustrate this point.

KEY WORDS

Armstrong's axioms
augmentation
binary data model
Boyce-Codd normal
  form
complete axiom
composite function
decomposition
determinant
entity
fifth normal form
first normal form
fourth normal form
full functional
  dependency
fully functionally
  dependent
function
functional data model
functional dependency
functional dependency
  diagram

functionally dependent
functionally determines
Heath's theorem
inverse function
irreducible data model
join dependency
multidetermine
multivalued dependency
normal form
nonloss decomposition
normalization
project join normal form
pseudotransitivity
query language
reflexivity
second normal form
sound axiom
third normal form
transitive dependency
transitivity
union
unnormalized relation

REFERENCES AND FURTHER READING

The following references contain additional materials related to the topics covered in this chapter.

1. C. J. DATE, *Introduction to Database Systems,* vol. I, 4th ed., Addison-Wesley, Reading, MA, 1986.
2. C. J. DATE, *Introduction to Database Systems,* vol. II, 3rd ed., Addison-Wesley, Reading, MA, 1983.

3. C. J. DATE, *Relational Database Selected Writings,* Addison-Wesley, Reading, MA, 1986.

4. H. F. KORTH and A. SILBERSCHATZ, *Database System Concepts,* McGraw-Hill, New York, 1986.

5. J. D. ULLMAN, *Principles of Database Systems,* Computer Science Press, Rockville, MD, 1982.

Date [1, Chapter 17], Korth and Silberschatz [4, Chapter 6], and Ullman [5, Chapter 7] have discussed the theory of normalization with a variety of examples. The last two references are especially heavy on the mathematical theory of functional dependencies and nonloss decomposition of information. Date [2, pp. 199–210] provides some insight on alternative data models, including the two schools of modeling, which may be called record-like and graph-like. The *n*-ary relational models belong to the record-like school, and the irreducible data models belong to the graph-like school. Date [3, Chapter 6] contains some valuable discussions about third normal forms and their implications. He contends that the third normal form is not a panacea. I personally subscribe to this contention on the basis of my industry experience.

REVIEW QUESTIONS

1. Why is normalization needed? Give an example of an unnormalized relation. Convert it into a relation in 1NF.

2. Define the terms *functional dependency, full functional dependency,* and *transitive dependency.* Explain their differences with examples.

3. Do you agree with the following statement? The definition of 2NF involves the functional dependency on key attributes, while that of 3NF involves the functional dependency on nonkey attributes. Justify your answer with adequate examples.

4. What are Armstrong's axioms? Explain their usage in determining functional dependencies.

5. Why are Armstrong's axioms called sound and complete?

6. Explain the concept of nonloss decomposition of relations.

7. How can a relation in 2NF be nonloss decomposed into two or more relations in 3NF? Give examples.

8. Define multivalued dependency and fourth normal forms.

9. What is join dependency? How is it related to the fifth normal form?

10. Do you think that 3NF should be a requirement for efficient database design? What are the trade-offs between update and retrieval processes in a 3NF environment?

11. What is the difference between a binary and an irreducible data model?

12. Describe how relations and attributes are represented in a functional data model.

EXERCISES

1. Examine the relations CRSE, CRSLST, STUDNT, and SPECL from LHUDB to see if each one is in 3NF. Decompose those relations that are not in 3NF into two or more relations, each in 3NF. Is every decomposition that you do a nonloss decomposition?

2. Determine *all* FDS and FFDs in CRSE and CRSLST. Draw an FD diagram for each dependency. Verify Armstrong's axioms for each FD that you have listed.

3. Select two decompositions from Exercise 1 that are nonloss. Verify that the criterion of nonloss decomposition (see Section 6.4) is verified in each case.

4. Give the functional data model representations of the following queries.
   (a) Student name, major adviser name, advisor rank, and department name of the students Roger Brown Smith, Steve Levin, and Beverly Black.
   (b) Course name, instructor name, and department name of the courses CS225, CS547, EN604, and MA611.
   (c) Course name, section number, student name, and instructor name of the courses CS579 and MA611.

5. Prove that a binary relation is in 3NF and BCNF.

6. Let R be a relation with attributes a, b, and c. Let $R_1 = R[a, b]$ and $R_2 = R[a, c]$ be two projections of R. Prove the following theorems.
   (a) $R = R_1$ JOIN R_2 if the FD $a \rightarrow b$ holds in R.
   (b) The FDs $a \rightarrow b$ and $b \rightarrow c$ together imply the FD $a \rightarrow c$.
   (c) The FDs $a \rightarrow b$ and $b \rightarrow c$ together imply the FD $a \rightarrow b \wedge c$.
   (d) The FDs $b \rightarrow a$ and $c \rightarrow a$ together imply the FD $b \wedge c \rightarrow a$.

CHAPTER 7

NONRELATIONAL DATA MODELS

7.1 THREE NONRELATIONAL DATA MODELS

In this chapter we describe the basics of three nonrelational data models: (1) hierarchical, (2) network, and (3) inverted file. In the first six chapters we have laid down the foundation of relational data model. To understand and appreciate the relative advantages and disadvantages of a relational database system versus a nonrelational database system, it is essential to have an understanding of the latter. The three data models above have the following common features:

1. All of them are older than the relational data model.
2. No mathematical theory underlies any of these models.
3. They operate at a lower level of abstraction than relational data models. The processing of a query takes place in a record-at-a-time environment, while in a relational system the data retrieval occurs in a group mode (i.e., a group of records is retrieved in response to a query).
4. The hierarchical and network models represent an abstraction of the pointer chain file organization that is implemented via an owner–member scheme in the database.
5. The inverted file model represents an abstraction of the indexed sequential file organization as applied to the database.
6. None of the three models offers a truly nonprocedural query language. The user in every case is an application programmer who uses a procedural query language or a host language interface to generate reports. No system-initiated query optimization occurs. An optimization, if any, is performed by the user.

7. An end user of any of these models cannot perform an ad hoc query without navigating through the schema structure of the database. As a result, if the end user is not a programmer, he or she has to be supported by means of canned reports produced by means of on-line application programs.

Because of the popularity of the relational data models, many nonrelational data models now offer a relational front end whereby an end user gets a relational view of a nonrelational database. IDMS/R, marketed by Cullinet, is a case in point. However, such "relational" databases are less efficient than is a genuinely relational database. In Sections 7.2 through 7.4 we discuss the hierarchical data model, in Sections 7.5 through 7.7 describe the network data model, and in Sections 7.8 and 7.9 introduce the inverted file data model.

7.2 HIERARCHICAL SCHEMA

A hierarchical schema appears like a *tree* that starts with a *root node* and branches out into multiple lower-level *subtrees*. Each level is connected with the higher-level nodes by means of owner–member (also called parent–child) relationships, whereby an owner can have zero or more members. To reach a member node at level *n*, one has to start at the root node and traverse the tree via owner–member linkages until the node at level *n* is reached..

The basic entity of a hierarchical schema is *record type*, which can be regarded as an unnormalized relation. Individual values of a record type are called *record occurrences*. Each node in the tree represents a record type. The information that is represented in a relational schema by means of foreign keys is represented in a hierarchical schema by means of owner–member linkages. All nonroot nodes in the tree are called *dependent* record types. Figure 7–1 gives the

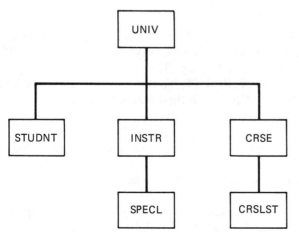

Figure 7–1   Hierarchical schema of LHUDB.

hierarchical schema of the LHUDB database. This is really the hierarchical version of Figure 1–4. The database consists of six record types with the following respective contents:

```
UNIV     DNO      CHAR(2)
         DNAME    CHAR(25)
         DHEAD    CHAR(20)


STUDNT   SNAME    CHAR(20)
         SSNO     INT(9)
         MAJOR    CHAR(15)
         DEGREE   CHAR(10)
         ADVSR    CHAR(20)
         COLREG   CHAR(15)


INSTR    INAME    CHAR(20)
         IDEG     CHAR(10)
         SPCODE   INT(2)
         RANK     CHAR(10)
         SSNO     INT(9)


CRSE     CNO      CHAR(5)
         CNAME    CHAR(20)
         INAME    CHAR(20)
         SECNO    INT(2)


CRSLST   SID      INT(9)
         GRADE    CHAR(2)
         OFRNG    CHAR(8)


SPECL    SPCODE   INT(2)
         SPNAME   CHAR(20)
```

In Figure 7–1, UNIV is the root node and all other record types are dependent nodes. UNIV is the owner of the record types STUDNT, INSTR, and CRSE, which are the member record types. Similarly, INSTR is the owner of SPECL and CRSE is the owner of CRSLST. To reach the record type CRSLST, for example, one has to start at UNIV and then follow the path

$$UNIV \rightarrow CRSE \rightarrow CRSLST$$

down the tree. Figure 7–2 gives an example of some record occurrences of the schema.

The three levels of a hierarchical schema can be described as follows:

1. *External level:* predesigned reports generated by application programmers in procedural language; ad hoc query capabillity not available

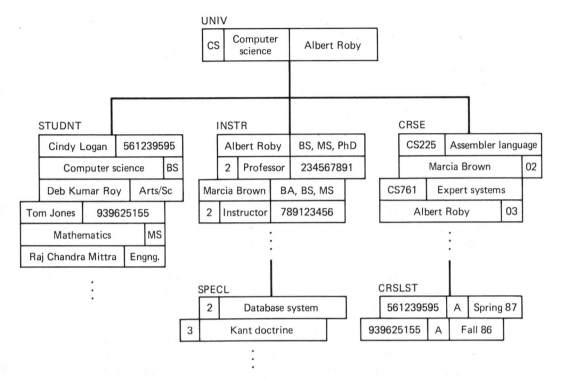

Figure 7–2   Sample record occurrences of LHUDB.

2. *Conceptual level:* complete description of the record types and owner–member linkages

3. *Internal level:* physical storage of data in disk files supporting the conceptual level

As noted in Section 7.1, a hierarchical data model does not have a nonprocedural query language. The user has to navigate through the schema diagram in order to design a program in response to an ad hoc query. Programming capability in a procedural language is needed.

Information Management System (IMS) is one of the oldest hierarchical DBMS packages still in use. In the next section we use IMS to illustrate the concepts introduced above.

7.3 HIERARCHICAL SCHEMA USING IMS

IMS was designed and implemented by IBM on System 360 and was released in 1968. Initially, it was intended for batch applications alone. But now end users can be supported by means of appropriate on-line applications programs.

The physical database record (PDBR) is the basic building block in IMS. A PDBR consists of a hierarchical arrangement of segments. A *segment* consists of a set of related fields. The top segment in the PDBR is the root segment. A PDBR consists of the *root segment* and a hierarchical arrangement of subordinate segments called *child segments*. The PDBR can be either a PDBR type or a PDBR occurrence. For example, Figure 7–1 is the PDBR type of LHUDB and Figure 7–2 consists of a few PDBR occurrences of the same database.

The PDBR type is described by a *database description* (DBD) in IMS. A DBD is the IMS equivalent of the CREATE TABLE statement of SQL. The DBD appears as a set of macro statements that define the segments and fields within a PDBR. These macro statements are coded by a programmer, then assembled into object form, and finally stored in a library by the IMS control program. Figure 7–3 shows a partial DBD for the PDBR of Figure 7–1. It contains statements for the segments UNIV and INSTR only. The statements in Figure 7–3 have been numbered only for reference; normally, they are not numbered.

Statement 1 assigns the name LHUDB to the database shown in Figure 7–3. Statement 2 then defines the root segment. This segment type is assigned the name UNIV and is defined as 47 bytes in length. All names in IMS are limited to a maximum length of eight characters.

Statements 3 through 5 define the three field types that are included in UNIV. Each FIELD definition statement defines the name, length, and starting position within the segment. Statement 3 contains the clause NAME = (DNO, SEQ). This clause defines DNO to be the sequence field for UNIV root segment type. As a result, physical database record occurrences within LHUDB data base are sequenced in ascending department number sequence.

Statement 6 defines the INSTR segment type. The clause PARENT = UNIV in this segment defines INSTR as a child segment of UNIV. The segment is 51 bytes in length.

```
 1.   DBD     NAME = LHUDB
 2.   SEGM    NAME = UNIV,        BYTES = 47,   PARENT = 0
 3.   FIELD   NAME = (DNO, SEQ),  BYTES = 3 ,   START  = 1
 4.   FIELD   NAME = DNAME,       BYTES = 25,   START  = 4
 5.   FIELD   NAME = DHEAD,       BYTES = 20,   START  = 29
 6.   SEGM    NAME = INSTR        BYTES = 51    PARENT = UNIV
 7.   FIELD   NAME = INAME,       BYTES = 20    START  = 1
 8.   FIELD   NAME = IDEG,        BYTES = 10    START  = 21
 9.   FIELD   NAME = SPCODE,      BYTES = 2,    START  = 31
10.   FIELD   NAME = RANK,        BYTES = 10,   START  = 33
11.   FIELD   NAME = (SSNO, SEQ), BYTES = 9,    START  = 43
.................................................................
.................................................................
```

Figure 7–3 Partial hierarchical DBD for LHUDB.

Statement 11 defines the SSNO field type within the INSTR segment type. The clause NAME = (SSNO, SEQ) means that for each occurrence of a parent UNIV segment type, occurrences of the child INSTR segment type are stored in ascending sequence according to the SSNO field. For example, in Figure 7–2, the segment for 'Albert Roby' occurs before the segment for 'Marcia Brown'. All occurrences of child segments of a particular parent occurrence are referred to as *twins*.

We note that the notion of ordering is critical to the hierarchical data structure. This is the reason for associating DNO in UNIV and SSNO in INSTR with the clause SEQ (see statements 3 and 11 in Figure 7–3). Also, the hierarchical schema supports referential integrity to some extent. For example, no child segment is allowed to exist without its parent segment. If a parent segment is deleted, IMS will automatically delete the entire subtree rooted at that segment. Similarly, a child segment cannot be inserted unless its parent already exists.

7.4 DATA MANIPULATION IN A HIERARCHICAL DATABASE

A hierarchical data manipulation language (DML) consists of a set of operators that process data represented in the form of trees. Such operators perform the following functions:

1. Locate a specific tree in the database.
2. Move from one tree starting at a node to another such tree starting at a different node.
3. Move from one node to another within a tree by moving up and down the various hierarchical paths.
4. Move from one node to another by following pointers implementing the owner–member linkages.
5. Insert a new record occurrence at a specific node in the tree.
6. Delete or modify an existing record occurrence at a specific node in the tree.

Steps 1 through 4 relate to data retrievals while steps 5 and 6 correspond to data updates. We now illustrate steps 1 through 4 with the following query:

List the department name and the department head for each instructor whose rank is Associate Professor or Professor.

The following pseudocode describes how the report above can be generated:

1. Locate the first record occurrence of the record type UNIV.
2. Locate all twin record occurrences of the record type INSTR that have the record occurrence in step 1 as the parent segment.

3. Locate the field occurrence RANK within each INSTR record occurrence in step 2.

4. If RANK = 'AssocProf' or RANK = 'Professor', retrieve values of DNAME and DHEAD from the record occurrence of step 1; otherwise, go to the next twin record occurrence INSTR.

5. When all twin record occurrences of INSTR are finished, go to the next record occurrence of the present segment UNIV.

6. Repeat steps 2 through 5 until all record occurrences of the record type UNIV are finished.

7. Return all DNAME and DHEAD values retrieved during the process above.

7.5 DATA MANIPULATION USING IMS

The IMS data manipulation language is called Data Language I or DL/I. DL/I consists of a set of commands that are used with a host language (COBOL, PL/I, or 370 Assembler Language). The application program invokes these commands by means of subroutine calls. Figure 7–4 gives a list of the basic commands of DL/I. We now illustrate some of these commands with examples from LHUDB.

    1. *Direct retrieval*

> *Query:* Retrieve the first record occurrence within the record type STUDNT who is a mathematics major.
>
> *DL/I command:* `GU UNIV, STUDNT WHERE MAJOR = 'Mathematics';`
>
> *Comment:* GU is really a misnomer; its operations is to "get first." It retrieves the first record occurrence satisfying a given pred-

Command	Function
GET UNIQUE (GU)	Direct retrieval of a segment
GET NEXT (GN)	Sequential retrieval of a segment
GET NEXT WITHIN PARENT (GNP)	Sequential retrieval within the current parent segment
GET HOLD (GHU, GHN, GHNP)	Same as GU, GN, and GNP, respectively, but with subsegment delete or replacement capability
INSERT (ISRT)	Insert a new segment
DELETE (DLET)	Delete an existing segment
REPLACE (REPL)	Update an existing segment

Figure 7–4 Basic DL/I commands.

icate. The predicate is called a *segment search argument* (SSA). Thus

$$\text{MAJOR} = \text{'Mathematics'}$$

is an SSA here.

2. *Path call*

> *Query:* Retrieve the first student who is a mathematics major and his or her department record occurrence.
>
> *DL/I command:* `GU STUDNT * D, WHERE MAJOR = 'Mathematics';`
>
> *Comment:* GU normally retrieves the segment at the end of its search path (i.e., STUDNT segment in this case). By using the command code D here the query retrieves the parent segment UNIV as well. Command codes always follow the segment name to which they apply and are separated from it by an asterisk.

3. *Sequential retrieval within parent*

> *Query:* Retrieve all student record occurrences for the mathematics department.
>
> *DL/I command:*
> ```
> GU UNIV WHERE DNO = 'MA';
>     do until no more STUDNTs under current
>     UNIV;
>     GNP STUDNT;
>     end;
> ```
>
> *Comment:* GU points to the record occurrence in UNIV for which DNO = 'MA' (i.e., for the mathematics department). GNP starts with this record as the current database position and the parent segment and retrieves all STUDNT record occurrences under the loop execution.

4. *Segment insertion*

> *Query:* Insert a new course for the mathematics department.
>
> *DL/I command:* `ISRT UNIV WHERE DNO = 'MA', CRSE;`
>
> *Comment:* ISRT command identifies the parent segment as the record occurrence of the mathematics department. CRSE then builds the new child segment CRSE.

7.6 LOGICAL HIERARCHICAL DATABASE

A logical hierarchical database corresponds to the external level of the database, as described in Section 7.2. To generate a predesigned report from one or more physical databases it is necessary to define a *logical hierarchical database*. The latter can be regarded as the hierarchical version of a view in a relational database. A logical hierarchical database allows the user to see the data in a hierarchic arrangement in the underlying physical database(s).

A logical hierarchical database is defined by means of a logical DBD, which can be defined over multiple physical DBDs. A *logical database* (LDB) in IMS consists of all occurrences of a *logical database record* (LDBR) type. Each LDBR type is a subset of one or more corresponding PDBR types. Like a view in a relational database, an LDB has no existence of its own. An LDB is formed from a PDB as follows:

1. Root segment of LDB is same as root segment of PDB.
2. Fields of an LDBR segment can be a subset of the corresponding PDBR segment and can be rearranged within that LDBR segment.
3. A new segment can be added at any point as the child of an existing segment provided only that it does not affect any existing parent–child relationship.
4. Any segment except the root segment of a PDBR may be omitted from an LDBR. If a segment type in the PDBR is omitted, all its dependent segments are also omitted.

Figure 7–5 shows an example of an LDB called STUDENT-LIST that contains the list of all students enrolled in a given course offered by a given depart-

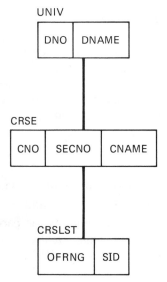

Figure 7–5 Example of an LDB.

ment. Each LDBR type is defined by a series of statements called a *program communication block* (PCB). Figure 7–6 shows the PCB for the LDBR STU-DENT-LIST of Figure 7–5. Statement 1 defines the program communication block. The clause TYPE = DB is required for each PCB that defines a database (as opposed to an on-line transaction). The clause DBNAME = LHUDB specifies that the DBD for the underlying database is LHUDB (as defined in Figure 7–3).

The clause KEYLEN = 18 defines the maximum length of the concatenated key for the hierarchical path in this LDBR. In the LDBR shown in Figure 7–5, the hierarchical path consists of the UNIV, CRSE, and CRSLST segment types. The fields on which these segments are sequenced, and the field lengths, are the following: DNO, 3 bytes; CNO, 5 bytes; SECNO, 2 bytes; OFRNG, 8 bytes. Thus KEYLEN = 3 + 5 + 2 + 8 or 18 bytes. The KEYLEN clause is used by IMS to reserve space for concatenated keys in retrieving segments.

Statements 2 through 4 define the segments from the PDBR that are to be included in this LDBR. The term SENSEG means "sensitive segment." Segments from the PDBR that are included in an LDBR are said to be "sensitive" (the term can also be applied to fields that are to be included). In this PCB, the sensitive segments are UNIV, CRSE, and CRSLST.

The term PROCOPT in Figure 7–6 stands for "processing options." The PROCOPT clause specifies the operations that a user of this LDBR can perform against each segment. In Figure 7–6 the clause PROCOPT = G specifies that a user can only "get" (G) or retrieve each segment occurrence. Other options that can be specified are I ("insert"), R ("replace"), and D ("delete"). Also, any combination of these options may be specified.

Each user may have one or more program communication blocks. The set of all PCBs for a given user is called a *program specification block* (PSB). The PSB for each user is assembled and stored in a system library by the IMS control program. The control program extracts the PSB from the library when a user program is executed.

In a logical hierarchical database the referential integrity is introduced by the following rule: For every segment that is a logical parent or a logical child, or a physical parent that has a physical child that is also a logical child, the physical DBD for that segment must specify an insert rule, a delete rule, and an update rule. These rules govern the effect of ISRT, DLET, and REPL operations on the segment concerned.

```
1.   PCB      TYPE = DB,    DNAME = LHUDB, KEYLEN = 18
2.   SENSEG   NAME = UNIV,    PROCOPT = G
3.   SENSEG   NAME = CRSE,     PROCOPT = G
4.   SENSEG   NAME = CRSLST, PROCOPT = G
```

Figure 7–6   PCB for LDBR STUDENT-LIST.

7.7 DBTG/CODASYL REPORT

The network data model was introduced as an improvement of the hierarchical data model. During the late 1960s the COnference of DAta System Languages (CODASYL) committee was formed as a voluntary group of individuals representing hardware and software vendors, academic institutions, and major developers and users of data processing systems. The initial assignment of CODASYL was to discuss changes of COBOL and to write position papers in that area. The committee soon formed a subgroup called the Data Base Task Group (DBTG) that concentrated on specifications for a network database system, initially conceived as an improvement of a hierarchical database. DBTG published its first report in preliminary form in 1969 and in a finished form in 1971. This report contained detailed specifications of data definition and data manipulation languages of a network database system. Subsequent updates of this report were published in 1978 and 1981. Most of the currently existing network DBMSs follow these specifications.

In 1984, ANSI Database Committee X3H2 produced a document called Draft Proposed Network Database Language NDL. This document defined a proposed standard network database language NDL that was based on the specifications of the original CODASYL/DBTG report of 1971.

A network database is an extension of a hierarchical database in that a set (see Section 7.9) in the former can have one or more owners and zero or more members, while the equivalent of a set in the latter can have only one owner and zero members. In fact, the concept of a set does not exist in the hierarchical database.

The function of a set is implemented via links or pointers. Also, in a hierarchical database one can reach a record occurrence at any level by starting at the root and following the hierarchical sequence leading to the desired record. In a network data model it is possible to define pointers from the root node to any desired record type, so that one can directly reach that record type without going through a hierarchical sequence.

7.8 NETWORK SCHEMA

The DBTG report specified three types of languages that a network database must have:

1. *Schema data definition language.* The schema DDL describes the network structure of the database at the conceptual level. As a minimum, it must contain the following information:

    a. Definition of each record type (i.e., name and length)

    b. Definition of each field in a record type (i.e., name, data type, and length)

    c. Definition of a set type (i.e., name, owner, member, and type)

2. *Subschema data definition language.* The subschema DDL defines subsets of the network schema and may be regarded as the network equivalent of a view in a relational database. As a minimum it must provide the following information:

    a. Specification of schema record types that are used
    b. Specifications of data items in the record types that are used
    c. Specifications of set types linking the record types that are used

One cannot define in the subschema any new set type or any new record type that spans two or more schema records, which do not already exist in the schema.

3. *Data manipulation language.* As with the DML in a relational database, the network DML handles both data retrieval and data updates. However, only procedural commands are available and the user must navigate through the schema using the DML commands.

The DBTG proposals also called for extensive capabilities to define security controls in the schema DDL. Many initial implementations of the DBTG model chose not to include these capabilities, since it was felt that given computing power in the early 1970s, database processing performance would be seriously deterred by such overhead. Today, inclusion of security controls is a standard feature of DBTG implementations. Also standard today are nonprocedural (non-record-at-a-time) query languages for DBTG implementations that permit retrieval (but often not update) to be accomplished in fewer statements and less programming time than in conventional procedural languages such as COBOL or FORTRAN.

7.9 DBTG SET TYPE

A *set type* in DBTG sense is the link between two distinct record types, one of which is the owner of the set and the other is the member of the set. A set type in a network data model can be of 1:1 or 1:N type. Each occurrence of a given set consists of one or more occurrences of its owner and zero or more occurrences of its member. DBTG does *not* support M:N types. However, subsequently, some vendors offered network DBMSs supporting sets of both N:1 and M:N types. MDBSIII is an example of such a DBMS.

Given a particular set type S with owner record type P and member record type C, the following must hold:

    1. Each occurrence of P is the owner in *exactly* one occurrence of S.
    2. Each occurrence of C is a member in *at most* one occurrence of S.

Set type is implemented by a chain of pointers that originates at the owner occurrence, runs through all the member occurrences, and finally returns to the owner occurrence. Any other implementation method is functionally equivalent to the pointer chain method.

7.10 CURRENCY INDICATORS IN NETWORK SCHEMA

Currency indicators in network schema are a generalization of current position in a file. For each program running under its control, the network DBMS maintains a table of currency indicators. A *currency indicator* is an object whose value is either null or is the address of a stored record in the database. It is really a database pointer. A null currency indicator identifies no record. The currency indicators for a given program, called a *run-unit* in network schema, identify the record occurrence most recently accessed by that program. In other words, a currency indicator represents the most recent value of the record or set accessed by the program.

In case of a record type R, the most recently accessed R occurrence is referred to as the current R occurrence. For a set type S, the most recently accessed record occurrence that participates in an occurrence of S may be either an owner occurrence or a member occurrence. It is always referred to as the current record of set type S which uniquely identifies the set occurrence that contains the current record of set type S. It is called the current S occurrence.

The most recently accessed record occurrence, no matter what its type and no matter what sets it participates in, is referred to as the current record of the run unit (usually abbreviated as *current of run unit*). Current of run unit is the most important currency of all for the purpose of data manipulation in a network schema. It can refer to the FIRST or LAST within a given set type or to the NEXT or PRIOR with respect to a given record occurrence within a given set occurrence.

Currency indicators are updated each time a record occurrence is accessed. Currency indicator updating may be suppressed under application program control to maintain a desired reference point. The programmer must be well aware of the effect that each DML statement has on currency indicator status.

7.11 EXAMPLES USING VAX-11 DBMS

VAX-11 DBMS is a network-type DBMS marketed by Digital Equipment Corporation. It separates data definition from application programming by making the data definition part of a program a separate unit referenced by the program at compile time.

When compiled by the VAX-11 DBMS DDL compiler, data definitions are stored in a central repository called the *common data dictionary* (CDD). The

CDD contains the logical definition of the database (the schema), the specification of how the database is physically stored on mass storage devices (the storage schema), and the individual user views of that database (subschemas). The person who is designing, implementing, and administering database is responsible for writing the schema, storage schema, and subschemas.

A system utility called DBO/CREATE creates the database from the schema. The database consists of *database storage files* and the *database root files*. The storage files are for data storage and the root file contains the *data definition control blocks* (DDCBs) used by *Database Control System* or DBCS, the run-time controller of VAX-11 DBMS. The DBCS fills a variety of roles in VAX-11 DBMS. Its major functions are to monitor database usage, act as an intermediary between VAX-11 DBMS and VAX/VMS, and manipulate database records on behalf of user programs. The DBO/CREATE utility also establishes pointers between the root file and the CDD; these pointers assure that the root file is associated with the schema.

When an application program is compiled, the VAX-11 COBOL compiler, the VAX-11 FORTRAN DML preprocessor, or a VAX-11 DBMS system utility named DBO/WORK—AREA extracts the necessary subschema data definitions from the CDD. The *User Work Area* (UWA) is a location where the DBCS delivers all data called for by a program. It is also where the DBCS picks up all data from a program.

7.11.1 Schema DDL for LHUDB

Figure 7–7 gives the network schema diagram for LHUDB. It is similar to Figure 7–1 except that specific pointers have been set up explicitly to represent the set types

```
SYS-STUD
SYS-CRSE
SYS-UNIV
UNIV-STUD
UNIV-INST
UNIV-CRSE
INST-SPEC
CRSE-CRSL
```

Each set type is named with the following convention:

1. If the owner is SYSTEM, the first three characters of the name is SYS and the last four characters are taken from the member.
2. Otherwise, the owner name provides the first four characters and the member name provides the last four characters.

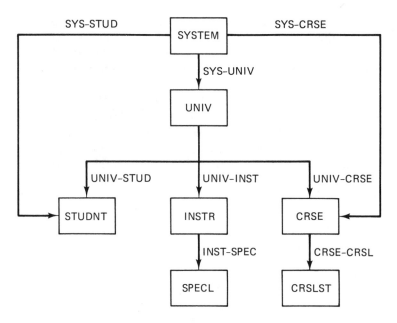

Figure 7-7 Network schema for LHUDB.

In a VAX-11 DBMS database, all SYSTEM-owned set types are called *singular*. Unlike a hierarchical schema, it is possible to define a singular set type whose member is several levels away from the SYSTEM (see the comment at the end of Section 7.7). This makes specific report generation somewhat simpler.

The definitions of the record types in Figure 7-7 are the same as those of Figure 7-1. Figure 7-8 shows a partial schema DDL for Figure 7-7.

Line 1 gives the schema a name. Line 2 defines a record type UNIV. Lines 3 through 5 define the data elements or fields within the record type UNIV. Lines 6 through 12 similarly define the record type STUDNT. Lines 13 through 19 define the singular set type SYS-UNIV with owner SYSTEM and member UNIV. This set type has exactly one occurrence with a hypothetical SYSTEM record occurrence as owner and all UNIV record occurrences as members in ascending order of the sorting key DNO (see lines 18 and 19). Line 16 states that a member record occurrence is automatically inserted into the set when it is stored in the database. Line 17 states that a member record occurrence cannot be removed from the set occurrence without removing the record itself. Lines 20 through 24 have similar meanings of the set type UNIV-STUD. Line 25 states that a new member record occurrence is stored immediately after the current member record occurrence in the set.

```
 1.   SCHEMA NAME IS LHUDB
 2.   RECORD NAME IS UNIV
 3.   ITEM DNO TYPE CHAR 8
 4.   ITEM DNAME TYPE CHAR 25
 5.   ITEM DHEAD TYPE CHAR 20

 6.   RECORD NAME IS STUDNT
 7.   ITEM SNAME TYPE CHAR 20
 8.   ITEM SSNO TYPE UNSIGNED NUMERIC 9
 9.   ITEM MAJOR TYPE CHAR 15
10.   ITEM DEGREE TYPE CHAR 10
11.   ITEM ADVSR TYPE CHAR 20
12.   ITEM COLREG TYPE CHAR 15

13.   SET NAME IS SYS-UNIV
14.   OWNER IS SYSTEM
15.   MEMBER IS UNIV
16.   INSERTION IS AUTOMATIC
17.   RETENTION IS FIXED
18.   ORDER IS SORTED BY
19.   ASCENDING DNO

20.   SET NAME IS UNIV-STUD
21.   OWNER IS UNIV
22.   MEMBER IS STUD
23.   INSERTION IS AUTOMATIC
24.   RETENTION IS FIXED
25.   ORDER IS NEXT
. . . . . . . . . . . . . . . . . . .
```

Figure 7–8   Partial schema DDL for LHUDB.

7.11.2 Subschema DDL for STUDENT-LIST

We next give the VAX-11 DBMS version of the subschema STUDENT-LIST shown in Figure 7–5. A subschema is often called a *user view*. Any particular user view is a substructure of the underlying schema structure, derived from that underlying structure in accordance with the following rules:

1. Any field type can be omitted.
2. Any record type can be omitted.
3. Any set type can be omitted.
4. If a given record type is omitted, all set types in which that record type participates (as either owner or member) must be omitted also.

Figure 7–9 gives the VAX-11 DBMS code for the user view STUDENT-LIST.

Lines 1 and 2 of Figure 7–9 identify the subschema and its parent schema. Lines 3 through 12 describe the three record types and lines 13 through 16 describe the four set types of the subschema.

7.11.3 Sample DML for LHUDB

In this section we give DML codes for the four reports described in Section 7.5.

1. Retrieve the first record occurrence within the record type STUDNT who is a mathematics major.

```
FETCH FIRST STUDNT WITHIN SYS-STUD
        WHERE MAJOR EQ 'MATHEMATICS'
```

2. Retrieve the first student who is a mathematics major and his or her department record occurrence.

```
FETCH FIRST STUDNT WITHIN SYS-STUD
        WHERE MAJOR EQ 'MATHEMATICS'
FETCH OWNER WITHIN UNIV-STUD
```

3. Retrieve all student record occurrences for the mathematics department.

```
1.   SUBSCHEMA NAME IS STUDENT-LIST
2.   FOR LHUDB SCHEMA
3.   RECORD NAME IS UNIV
4.   ITEM DNO TYPE IS CHAR 20
5.   ITEM DNAME TYPE IS CHAR 25

6.   RECORD NAME IS CRSE
7.   ITEM CNO TYPE IS CHAR 5
8.   ITEM SECNO TYPE IS UNSIGNED NUMERIC 2
9.   ITEM CNAME TYPE IS CHAR 20

10.  RECORD NAME IS CRSLST
11.  ITEM OFRNG TYPE IS CHAR 8
12.  ITEM SID TYPE IS UNSIGNED NUMERIC 9

13.  SET NAME IS SYS-UNIV
14.  SET NAME IS SYS-CRSE
15.  SET NAME IS UNIV-CRSE
16.  SET NAME IS CRSE-CRSL
```

Figure 7–9 Possible subschema for STUDENT-LIST.

```
FETCH FIRST UNIV WITHIN SYS-UNIV WHERE DNO EQ 'MA'
              do while more records
FETCH NEXT STUDNT WITHIN UNIV-STUDNT
```

4. Insert a new course for the mathematics department.

```
FIND FIRST UNIV WITHIN SYS-UNIV WHERE DNO EQ 'MA'
STORE CRSE WITHIN UNIV-CRSE
```

7.11.4 Basic DML Commands in VAX-11 DBMS

Data retrieval is accomplished by the following five commands:

1. FIND: locates a record in the database and makes it the current record
2. GET: moves data item values from the current record to the user's area
3. FETCH: locates a record in the database and retrieves its data item values (equivalent to FIND followed by GET)
4. KEEP: "remembers" a record so that the user can access it or modify it later and be sure it has not been changed by another user
5. FREE: releases references to records in currency indicators or keeplists

Update functions are implemented by the following six commands:

1. STORE: adds a new record to the database.
2. MODIFY: changes the contents of selected data items in the current record; can also change the order of members in a set
3. ERASE: deletes the current record—and often related records as well—from the database
4. CONNECT: inserts the current record into one or more sets
5. DISCONNECT: removes the current record from one or more sets
6. RECONNECT: moves the current record from one occurrence of a set type to another

7.12 INVERTED FILE DATA MODEL

An *inverted file data model* is similar to a relational data model at a lower level of abstraction. This means that the user has to do a housekeeping job in such a database and that direct join of two or more files (available in a relational database) is not possible. The user or programmer must know how the joining is done and what kind of correspondence exists among records in the two files to be joined (e.g., one record of the first file being joined to many records of the second file, etc.).

In an inverted file data model no hierarchical schema structure exists and hence there are no owner–member relationships. The database consists of a set of separate files with some common fields to link them together. Each file may have one or more fields as primary and secondary keys. An *inverted list* is a list of all records in a file having a given value of primary or secondary key. Searching the database becomes quicker via the inverted lists. Files can be interconnected using the inversion method.

Several DBMSs are currently available that use inverted file data model. Examples are: ADABAS, Model 204, System 1022, and so on. In case of System 1022, for example, the user must specifically OPEN files (which are called *datasets*) for data retrieval or update. The projection operation is not available and the user must write a small macro using the DUMP command in order to implement projection. Similarly, SELECT or JOIN does not exist in System 1022 and the user must write a small command file (called .DMC file in System 1022) using the MAP command to perform a join of two or more tables.

As a general comment about inverted file data models we can say that a user has to specify an access path for his or her query and that access to files is possible either through physical sequence path or through inverted lists. Terms such as FIRST, LAST, and NEXT are used in queries as in a network database. At the time of insertion of a record into a file a record-id is assigned to the record and this record-id can be used for retrieving information from the file. Data manipulation is done more at a physical storage level than at a logical level.

7.13 EXAMPLES USING SYSTEM 1022

In this section we provide some examples of data retrieval and update commands using System 1022 in order to illustrate inverted file DBMSs. System 1022 was marketed by Software House of Cambridge, Massachusetts, and runs on DEC-10 machines. It was later modified for the VAX machines and renamed System 1032. Software House provided detailed conversion methods for converting applications from System 1022 to System 1032.

Let us take the following query (used in Chapter 5):

List the department names and department heads for all instructors whose rank is associate professor or professor.

We assume that the System 1022 database contains the six datasets of LHUDB. The following code then generates the desired report:

```
OPEN INSTR UNIV
FIND RANK 'AssocProf' OR 'Professor'
MAP TO UNIV VIA DNO
CLOSE INSTR UNIV
```

The example above shows that the user interaction is at a lower level in System 1022 than in a typical relational database.

System 1022 does not support projection. To extract the student names, their major fields, and their degrees, say, the following code is needed:

```
OPEN STUDNT
SEARCH SNAME MAJOR DEGREE
DUMP SET STDLST
CLOSE STUDNT
```

The dataset STDLST must be created before issuing the foregoing commands.

Update in System 1022 is done by means of ADD, CHANGE, and DELETE commands. They operate in a manner similar to updating a relational database. However, a dataset must be OPENed before updating and CLOSEd after updating. Such housekeeping chores are the responsibility of the user. The KEY command builds a new primary key table for one or more attributes, and the UNKEY command removes a primary key table from an attribute. These are similar to the CREATE UNIQUE INDEX and DROP INDEX commands of SQL, respectively. Bulk updates of datasets are done by the TRANSACT command. The updates are made to the current dataset called the MASTER dataset. The transaction records, called TRANSACTIONS, are supplied in another dataset or in an ASCII file. The user must write a command file to update datasets using the TRANSACT command.

7.14 CONCLUDING REMARKS

The hierarchical and network data models differ significantly from the relational data model in both DDL and DML features, as seen earlier. Except for very simple queries, both models require small programs or macros to respond to a user's query. See example 3 in Section 7.5 and Section 7.11.3 for specific examples.

The inverted file data model is similar to a relational data model with respect to DDL commands, because owner–member relationships or set types do not exist there. Also, attributes are repeated among files, as in a relational database, to join multiple files. But the DML commands operate at a lower level than in a relational database, as shown in Section 7.13.

7.15 SUMMARY

This chapter has provided a brief survey of three nonrelational data models: hierarchical, network, and inverted file. These models are older than the relational model and are presented here to show the relative advantages of the relational data model. In both hierarchical and network data models, data are stored in a hierarchical tree form and are viewed in an owner–member or a parent–child relationship. Access to a particular record is available via this hierarchy. Set types in a network data model provide linkages among record types.

To illustrate the schema structure of a hierarchical or a network data model, the database LHUDB is represented using both data models. IMS is used as an example of a hierarchical DBMS and samples of DDL and DML commands in IMS are given. Sample queries from LHUDB also appear as examples using IMS. The network data model is illustrated with the VAX-11 DBMS, a network DBMS from Digital Equipment Corporation. Sample queries from LHUDB are given.

Both hierarchical and network data models offer subschemas as user views or external levels. However, a truly nonprogrammer end user cannot use the hierarchical or network data models, since navigation through the schema or the subschema is necessary for formulating a query.

The chapter closes with a discussion of the inverted file data model, which is similar to a relational data model at a lower level of abstraction. The DDL commands of an inverted file DBMS are quite similar to those of a relational DBMS. But the DML commands for data retrieval and update are quite different from those of a relational DBMS. Examples from System 1022, an inverted file DBMS, show that even simple queries have to be processed via a command file.

KEY WORDS

child segment
CODASYL
Common Data
  Dictionary (CDD)
conceptual level
Conference of Data
  System Languages
  (CODASYL)
currency indicator
current of run unit
Data Base Task Group
  (DBTG)
data definition control
  block (DDCB)
Data Language I (DL/I)
data model, hierarchical
data model, inverted file
data model, network
data model, relational

Database Control
  System (DBCS)
database description
  (DBD)
database root file
database storage file
dataset
dependent node
external level
hierarchical schema
Information
  Management System
  (IMS)
internal level
inverted file data model
inverted list
logical database (LDB)
logical database record
  (LDBR)

logical hierarchical database	root segment
	run unit
Network Database Language (NDL)	schema data definition language
network schema	segment
owner/member linkage	segment search argument (SSA)
parent-child linkage	
physical database record (PDBR)	sensitive segment
	set occurrence
program communication block (PCB)	set type
	singular set type
program specification block (PSB)	subschema data definition language
query language	subtree
query optimization	System 1022
record occurrence	tree
record type	twins
record type, dependent	user view
relational front-end	User Work Area (UWA)
root node	X3H2

REFERENCES AND FURTHER READING

The following references contain additional materials related to the topics covered in this chapter.

1. S. ATRE, *Data Base: Structured Techniques for Design, Performance, and Management,* Wiley, New York, 1980.

2. C. J. DATE, *An Introduction to Database Systems,* vol. I, 4th ed., Addison-Wesley, Reading, MA, 1986.

3. Digital Equipment Corporation, *VAX-11 DBMS Database Administration Manual,* Order No. AA-J966A-TE.

4. IBM Corporation, *Information Management System/Virtual Storage General Information Manual,* IBM Form No. GH20-1260.

5. FRED R. MCFADDEN and JEFFREY A. HOFFER, *Data Base Management,* Benjamin-Cummings, Menlo Park, CA, 1985.

6. Software House, Cambridge, MA, *System 1022 Database Management System User's Reference Manual,*

Two of the three nonrelational data models, hierarchical and network, are treated adequately in any standard database text. For example, Atre [1], Date [2], and McFadden and Hoffer [5] have discussed these two data models. By contrast, the inverted file data model is not a standard topic. Date [2] has discussed it in a separate chapter and Atre [1] has provided some scanty discussions (pp. 257–266, 280–287) with ADABAS as an example. References 3, 4, and 6 are manuals of VAX-11 DBMS, IMS, and System 1022, respectively. Detailed treatment of DDL and DML of these DBMSs can be found in these manuals.

REVIEW QUESTIONS

1. What are the three nonrelational data models? Enumerate some of their common features.
2. What is a relational front end of a nonrelational database system? Give an example.
3. Describe the structure of a hierarchical schema. Give an example other than the LHUDB.
4. Distinguish between the following pairs.
   (a) Record type and record occurrence.
   (b) Set type and set occurrence.
5. Why is a hierarchical schema said to have a tree structure?
6. Describe the basic data manipulation process in a hierarchical database.
7. What is a logical hierarchical database? How does it compare with the subschema in a network database and with the view in a relational database?
8. Define the terms *program communication block* and *program specification block*.
9. Discuss the three types of languages that a network database should have.
10. Describe the role of currency indicators in a network data model.
11. What is an inverted file data model? How does it differ from a relational data model?
12. Explain the role of macros or command files in performing data retrievals or updates in a nonrelational data model.

EXERCISES

Figure 7–10 represents a network schema of a personnel database.

1. Define an appropriate DBD for the database using a hierarchical schema. Assume appropriate data elements in each record type.
2. Define a PCB for the logical hierarchical database containing information of employees and their dependents.
3. Formulate IMS and VAX-11 DBMS commands for the following queries.
   (a) List of all programmer employees with their dependents and skills.
   (b) List of all job classifications by department.
   (c) List of all employees without dependents.
4. Reformulate the queries in Exercise 3 using VAX-11 DBMS and assuming that no singular set types exist in the schema.

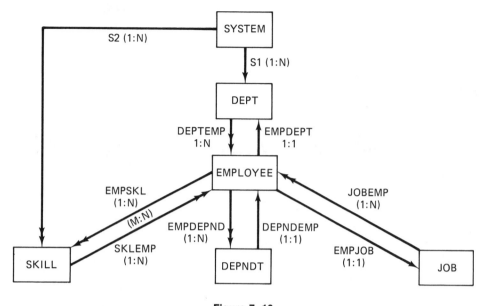

Figure 7–10

5. Define the schema of Exercise 4 using an inverted file data model.
6. Formulate the queries in Exercise 3 using System 1022.

CHAPTER 8

ENTITY–RELATIONSHIP DATA MODEL

8.1 RATIONALE FOR THE ENTITY–RELATIONSHIP DATA MODEL

We have discussed the relational data model in Chapter 2 and three nonrelational data models in Chapter 7. Regarding the inverted file data model as a low level of relational data model and also noting that the hierarchical data model is a special case of the network data model, we can say that there are two significant types of data models used in databases, network and relational. Each model has its own advantages and disadvantages.

The main advantage of the relational data model is its flat file structure. However, data redundancy among the relations leads to some inefficiency with respect to storage and multiple updates. The network data model is better in both of these features, but its schema structure is quite cumbersome to understand and manipulate.

The entity–relationship data model introduced by P. P. Chen in 1976 seeks to combine the best features of the network and the relational models. It accepts the flat file structure of the relational data model and combines that with the set type feature of network models. It adopts the view that the real world consists of entities and relationships. Chen proposed this model to offer a unified view of data. As such it includes the relational and the network data models as special cases. It offers a high degree of data independence and uses set theory and relational calculus in designing its query language.

The notions of entity and relationship were used by Bachman in designing the Bachman diagram of conceptual level of a database (see Section 1.7). Bachman described his ideas in a paper, "Data Structure Diagrams," published in 1969 in

Data Base, Journal of the ACM SIGBDP, vol. 1, no. 2. Thus Chen's proposal of 1976 came as a refinement of Bachman's concept. The entity–relationship concept is used in Chapter 9 as a synthetic approach to design a relational database.

8.2 ENTITY AND RELATIONSHIP RELATIONS

An entity–relationship data model consists of two types of relations, an entity relation and a relationship relation. An *entity* is a thing that can be distinctly identified. Thus a specific person, company, or event is an entity. A *relationship* is an association between two entities. Thus "father–son" is a relationship between two "person" entities.

An *entity relation* is a group of entities of the same type. UNIV is an entity relation consisting of all the department entities of the Long Hill University. There is a predicate associated with each entity relation to determine if a given entity belongs to the relation. In fact, an entity relation is the same as an *n*-ary relation in a relational model. Each entity is represented by a tuple of the relation.

A *relationship relation* is a group of relationships of the same type. Formally, it is a mathematical relation on *n* entity relations, where $n \geq 2$. If $E_1, \ldots, E_n$ are *n* entity relations, a relationship relation R is a subset of the Cartesian product

$$E_1 \times \cdots \times E_n = \{(e_1, \ldots, e_n) \mid e_i \in E_i, i = 1, \ldots, n\}$$

where $(e_1, \ldots, e_n)$ is a relationship. As an example, consider the two entity relations UNIV and INSTR. Since each instructor belongs to one department, we can define a relationship relation UNIV-INSTR to denote the association between these two entity relations. Since only two entity relations are involved, UNIV-INSTR is an example of a binary relationship relation.

The *role* of an entity in a relationship relation is represented by the entity relations that are linked together by the relationship relation. Thus UNIV and INSTR are the roles of UNIV-INSTR.

The term *attribute* has the same meaning as in a relational model. The term *value set* is used in the sense of domain in a relational model.

An *entity primary key* (PK) of an entity relation is a group of attributes of the entity relation such that the group uniquely identifies a tuple. For example, DNO and SSNO are, respectively, the PKs in UNIV and INSTR.

In a relational model, two or more relations are linked via repeated attributes among them so that the relations can be joined as needed. In an entity–relationship model, the entity relations mostly do not contain repeated attributes. As such they resemble the record types of a network model. A relationship relation contains, as a minimum, the PKs of all the entity relations that are linked by it. As such it corresponds to a set type in a network model. Accordingly, the entity and relationship relations of LHUDB can be represented as follows:

Entity Relations

```
(1) UNIV
        DNO      CHAR(2)    PK
        DNAME    CHAR(25)
        DHEAD    CHAR(20)

(2) INSTR
        INAME    CHAR(20)
        IDEG     CHAR(10)
        SPCODE   INT(2)
        RANK     CHAR(10)
        ISSNO    INT(9)     PK

(3) STUDNT
        SNAME    CHAR(20)
        SSNO     INT(9)     PK
        MAJOR    CHAR(15)
        DEGREE   CHAR(10)
        ADVSR    CHAR(20)

(4) CRSE
        CNO      CHAR(5)    PK
        CNAME    CHAR(20)
        SECNO    INT(2)     PK

(5) CRSLST
        SID      INT(9)     PK
        GRADE    CHAR(2)
        OFRNG    CHAR(8)    PK
        CNO      CHAR(5)    PK

(6) SPECL
        SPCODE   INT(2)     PK
        SPNAME   CHAR(20)
```

Relationship Relations

```
(1) UNIV-INSTR
        DNO      CHAR(2)    PK
        ISSNO    INT(9)     PK

(2) UNIV-STUDNT
        DNO      CHAR(2)    PK
        SSNO     INT(9)     PK
        COLREG   CHAR(15)

(3) UNIV-CRSE
        DNO      CHAR(2)    PK
        CNO      CHAR(5)    PK
```

```
(4) INSTR-STUDENT
            ISSNO    INT(9)    PK
            SSNO     INT(9)    PK

(5) INSTR-CRSE
            ISSNO    INT(9)    PK
            CNO      CHAR(5)   PK
            SECNO    INT(2)    PK

(6) INSTR-SPECL
            ISSNO    INT(9)    PK
            SPCODE   INT(2)    PK

(7) CRSE-CRSLST
            CNO      CHAR(5)   PK
            SECNO    INT(2)    PK
            OFRNG    CHAR(8)   PK
            SID      INT(9)    PK
```

8.3 ENTITY–RELATIONSHIP DIAGRAMS

There are three symbols used in an entity–relationship model. A rectangular box represents an entity relation and a diamond-shaped box represents a relationship relation. A large rectangle containing a small rectangle within itself represents a *weak entity relation*. The latter is an entity relation that depends on another entity relation for its existence and includes the PK of the latter among its own primary key (PK). For example, CRSLST is a weak entity relation that depends on CRSE for its PK so that the composite attribute set (SID, OFRNG, CNO) becomes the PK of CRSLST, where CNO is a part of the PK of CRSE. Figure 8–1 shows these three symbols.

A relationship relation can be of four types: 1:1 (one–one), 1:M (one–many), N:1 (many–one), and M:N (many–many). Each line connecting an entity relation to a relationship relation has a symbol such as 1, M, or N marked against it to indicate the type of the relationship relation. For example, in Figure 8–2, INSTR-STUDNT is a relationship relation of type M:N, UNIV-CRSE is of type 1:N, and so on. Also, CRSLST is a weak entity relation, while, CRSE, DEPT, and so on, are regular entity relations.

A relationship relation is called *weak* if at least one of the entity relations associated with it is a weak entity relation. Thus CRSE-CRSLST is a weak relationship relation. No special symbol is used to designate a weak relationship relation. We close this section with the following comments:

1. A relationship relation may involve more than two entity relations.
2. There may be two or more relationship relations involving only two entity relations.

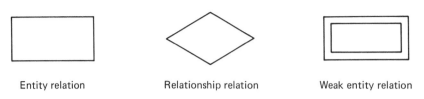

Entity relation   Relationship relation   Weak entity relation

Figure 8–1   Entity and relationship relation symbols.

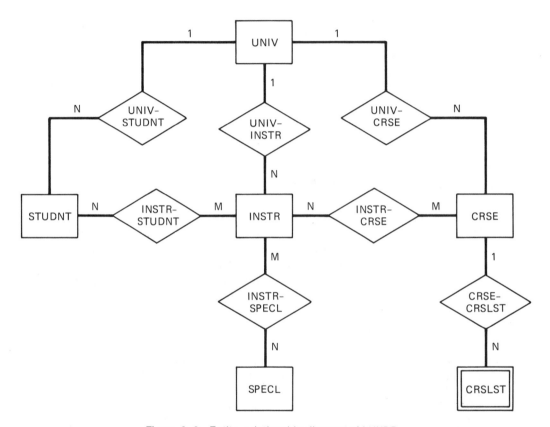

Figure 8–2   Entity–relationship diagram of LHUDB.

8.4 DATA DEFINITION LANGUAGE IN THE ENTITY–RELATIONSHIP MODEL

In his paper [1, pp. 21–22] Chen proposed a syntax for a DDL for the entity–relationship schema. There are five types of DECLARE statements in this DDL. The first DECLARE contains the definitions of all attributes and their respective value sets for the entire database. Then there are two DECLARE statements for regular and weak entity relations, and two additional DECLARE statements for regular and weak relationship relations. The syntax of these statements is given below:

```
(1) DECLARE VALUE-SETS REPRESENTATION ALLOWABLE-VALUES
            (list of all attributes, value sets,
            representations,
            and allowable values)
(2) DECLARE REGULAR ENTITY RELATION entity-name
            ATTRIBUTE/VALUE-SETS:
                 (list of attribute/value set)
            PRIMARY KEY:
                 (name of PK)
(3) DECLARE WEAK ENTITY RELATION entity-name
            ATTRIBUTE/VALUE-SETS:
                 (list of attribute/value set)
            PRIMARY KEY:
                 (name of PK)
            regular entity PK THROUGH weak-relationship
(4) DECLARE REGULAR RELATIONSHIP RELATION relationship-
       name
            ROLE/ENTITY-RELATION.PK/MAX-NO-OF-ENTITIES
                 (list of entity/attribute)
            ATTRIBUTE/VALUE-SET:
                 (list of attribute/value set; may be empty
                 list)
(5) DECLARE WEAK RELATIONSHIP RELATION relationship-name
            ROLE/ENTITY-RELATION.PK/MAX-NO-OF-ENTITIES
                 (list of entity/attribute)
            EXISTENCE OF weak-entity DEPENDS ON EXISTENCE
                 OF regular-entity
```

We now illustrate the foregoing syntax with examples from LHUDB.

```
(1) DECLARE VALUE-SETS REPRESENTATION ALLOWABLE-VALUES

                DNO         CHARACTER(2)      ALL
                DNAME       CHARACTER(25)     ALL
                DHEAD       CHARACTER(20)     ALL
                INAME       CHARACTER(20)     ALL
                IDEG        CHARACTER(10)     ALL
                SPCODE      INTEGER(2)        (1, 60)
                RANK        CHARACTER(10)     ALL
                .....................................
                .....................................
```

```
(2) DECLARE REGULAR ENTITY RELATION UNIV
                ATTRIBUTE/VALUE-SET:
                     DNO/DNO
                     DNAME/DNAME
                     DHEAD/(FIRST-NAME, MI, LAST-NAME)
                PRIMARY KEY:
                     DNO
(3) DECLARE REGULAR RELATIONSHIP RELATION UNIV-INSTR
                ROLE/ENTITY-RELATION.PK/MAX-NO-OF-ENTITIES
                     UNIV/UNIV.PK/1
                     INSTR/INSTR.PK/N   (1:N mapping)
                ATTRIBUTE/VALUE-SET:
(4) DECLARE WEAK ENTITY RELATION CRSLST
                ATTRIBUTE/VALUE-SET:
                     SID/SID
                     GRADE/GRADE
                     OFRNG/OFRNG
                     CNO/CNO
                PRIMARY KEY:
                     SID
                     OFRNG
                     CNO THROUGH CRSE-CRSLST
(5) DECLARE WEAK RELATIONSHIP RELATION CRSE-CRSLST
                ROLE/ENTITY-RELATION.PK/MAX-NO-OF-ENTITIES
                     CNO/CRSE.PK/1
                     SECNO/CRSE.PK/1
                     OFRNG/CRSLST.PK/N
                     SID/CRSLST.PK/N  (1:N mapping)
                EXISTENCE OF CRSLST DEPENDS ON EXISTENCE OF CRS
```

The remaining entity and relationship relations can be DECLAREd similarly.

As of now no commercially available DBMS exists that implements the entity–relationship model of Chen. Hence the DDL statements above must be interpreted as theoretical. Also, any relational DBMS can implement an entity–relationship database, although less efficiently than for a truly relational database. Hence the data integrity issues (see Section 2.7) for an entity–relationship database can be handled the same way as in a relational database. Chen [1, pp. 22–23] has given examples of such data integrity issues.

8.5 DATA MANIPULATION LANGUAGE IN THE ENTITY–RELATIONSHIP MODEL

Chen did not propose any DML for his entity–relationship model. Instead, he gave samples of queries using both relational calculus formalism and SQL version [1, pp. 23–25]. This is meaningful since an entity–relationship database can be implemented using a relational DBMS. As an example, we provide below the two formulations of the following query:

Print a list of all students enrolled in CS579, section 01, for spring 1988.

1. *SQL version*

```
SELECT SNAME, SSNO, FROM STUDNT WHERE SSNO IN
   (SELECT SID FROM CRSE-CRSLST WHERE
      CNO = 'CS579' AND SECNO = '01' AND
      OFRNG = 'SPRING88');
```

2. *Relational calculus version*

$$\{t^{(2)} \mid (\exists u^{(5)}) \ (\exists v^{(4)}) \ (STUDNT(u) \wedge CRSE\text{-}CRSLST(v)$$
$$\wedge u(2) = v(4) \wedge (v(1) = 'CS579' \wedge v(2) = '01' \wedge$$
$$v(3) = 'SPRING88'))\}$$

As for update operations (i.e., insert, modify, or delete), Chen provided only the logic for these operations instead of sample codes. The logic takes care of referential integrity issues, as shown below [1, pp. 24–25]:

1. *Insertion*
    a. *Operation:* Create an entity tuple with a given entity-PK.
       Integrity: Check whether PK already exists or is acceptable.
    b. *Operation:* Create a relationship tuple with given entity PKs.
       Integrity: Check whether the entity PKs exist.
    c. *Operation:* Insert values in an entity tuple or a relationship tuple.
       Integrity: Check whether the values are acceptable.

2. *Modification*
    a. *Operation:* Update a value in an entity tuple.
       Integrity: If the value is not part of an entity PK, no checking is needed; if the value is part of an entity PK:
         • Change the entity PKs in all related relationship relations.
         • Change PKs of other entities that use this value as part of their PKs.
    b. *Operation:* Update a value in a relationship tuple.
       Integrity: None, since a relationship attribute is either an entity PK or is a new attribute not dependent on an entity PK.

3. *Deletion*
    a. *Operation:* Delete an entity tuple.
       Integrity: Delete any entity tuple whose existence depends on this entity tuple; delete relationship tuples associated with this entity.

    b. *Operation:*   Delete a relationship tuple.
          Integrity: None

8.6 DERIVATION OF A RELATIONAL MODEL FROM THE ENTITY–RELATIONSHIP MODEL

A relational model can be easily derived from an entity–relationship model as follows:

1. Each entity relation becomes a relation in the relational model.
2. The attributes of each relationship relation are included, as needed, in the appropriate relations derived in step 1. The criterion for inclusion is to allow a minimum level of data duplication so that the relations in the relational model can be joined, if necessary, by using the repeated attributes.
3. The key attribute(s) of the relations are derived from the PKs of the corresponding entity and relationship relations.
4. Finally, the relations in the relational model are modified so as to be in 3NF as far as practicable.

8.7 DERIVATION OF A NETWORK MODEL FROM THE ENTITY–RELATIONSHIP MODEL

We need to consider two cases in order to convert an entity–relationship model to a network model.

Case 1. None of the relationship relations in the entity–relationship model is of M:N type. In this case, each entity relation becomes a record type and each relationship relation becomes a set type in the network model. The roles of the relationship relation become the owner and the member of the corresponding set type.

Case 2. At least one relationship relation is of the type M:N. If the network model is strictly of CODASYL type, no M:N set type is allowed. Hence an M:N relationship relation is replaced by two 1:N set types in opposite directions. For example, let an entity–relationship model contain a relationship relation R of type M:N and with roles A and B. In the network model we replace R by two set types R_1 and R_2, each of type 1:N. Here R_1 has owner A and member B, while R_2 has owner B and member A (see Figure 8–3). If the network model is of extended CODASYL type so that it admits M:N set types, an M:N relationship relation can be converted directly to an M:N set type.

In both cases discussed above, additional modifications and rearrangement of attributes may be needed in order to derive the final form of the network

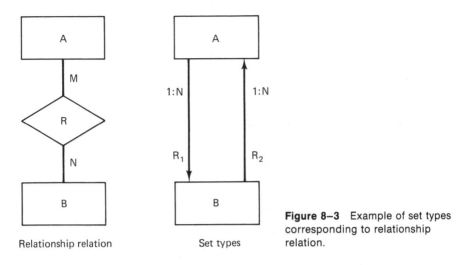

Relationship relation   Set types

Figure 8–3 Example of set types corresponding to relationship relation.

schema. In his paper [1, pp. 30–32] Chen proposed the criteria of a *data structure diagram* as a vehicle to convert relationship relations into set types. The treatment described above (cases 1 and 2) is based on the concept of a data structure diagram. The latter merely converts the associations of a relationship relation into appropriate set types.

8.8 COMPARISON OF RELATIONAL, NETWORK, AND ENTITY–RELATIONSHIP MODELS

From a conceptual level the entity–relationship model includes both relational and network models as special cases (see Sections 8.6 and 8.7). Since a hierarchical model can be regarded as a special case of network model and an inverted file model as a low-level version of relational model, we may say that the entity–relationship model can produce as special cases all the other relational and nonrelational models *at a conceptual level*. Figure 8–4 shows a tree diagram in support of this claim.

The same item is referred to by different names in different models. For example, an entity in the entity–relationship model becomes a record type in a network model. Figure 8–5 gives a table of equivalent terms among the three models: entity–relationship, relational, and network.

We close this section with a checklist of items to be included in the conceptual level in each of the three data models: network, relational, and entity–relationship.

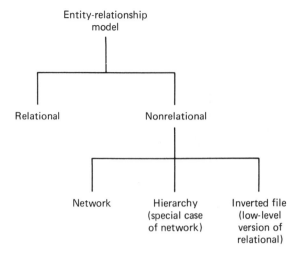

Figure 8–4 Tree diagram of data model.

(a) Network model

1. Diagram of the network schema
2. Listing of each record type, which must include the name of each field, the description of each field, and the format of each field
3. Listing of each set type, which must include the owner of the set, the member of the set, and the type of the set (e.g., 1:1, 1:N, M:N, N:1)

(b) Relational model

1. Listing of each relation, which must include all the attribute names, all attribute descriptions, and all attribute formats

	Data Model		
Item	Network	Relational	Entity–Relationship
Data element or field	Data element, data item, field	Attribute, column	Attribute, column
Record	Record occurrence	Row, tuple	Row, tuple
Link between two records	Set type, association (specify owner, member, and type: 1:1, 1:N, N:1, M:N)	N/A (implemented via repeated attributes among relations)	Relationship set, relationship relation (specify type: 1:1, 1:N, N:1, M:N)
File	Record type	Relation, table, dataset	Entity relation

Figure 8–5 Equivalent terms.

2. Key attribute(s) for each relation, if any

3. Determination of whether the relation is in third normal form

(c) Entity–relationship model

1. Diagram of the entity–relationship schema

2. Listing of each entity relation, which must include all the attributes, value sets, representations, and allowable values

3. Listing of each relationship relation, which must include all its attributes, its type (i.e., 1:1, 1:N, M:N), descriptions of attributes, their representations, and roles

4. Key attribute(s) of each entity and each relationship relation

8.9 UNIFIED APPROACH FOR DATA MODELING

Subsequent to Chen's proposal for entity–relationship data model several similar attempts were made by other authors. The common goal was to prescribe a vehicle for uniform data modeling whereby all of the existing data models could be brought under a single framework. Two major attempts in this regard were made by Codd and Date.

Codd [2] introduced the extended relational model RM/T with the assumption that the real world can be modeled in terms of *entities*. Date has described the basic features of RM/T as follows [5, pp. 241–242]: Entities are represented by *E-relations* and *P-relations*, both of which are specialized forms of the general *n*-ary relation; E-relations are used to record the fact that certain entities exist, and P-relations are used to record certain properties of those entities. A variety of relationship can exist among entities; for example, two or more entities may be linked together in an *association*, or a given entity type T1 may be a *subtype* of some other type T2; that is, every entity of type T1 is necessarily also an entity of type T2. RM/T includes a formal *catalog structure* by which such relationship can be made known to the system; the system is therefore capable of enforcing a variety of *integrity constraints* that are implied by the existence of such relationships (e.g., it can enforce the constraint that the entities participating in an association must exist before the association itself is allowed to exist). Finally, a number of high-level *operators* are provided to facilitate the manipulation of the various RM/T objects (E-relations, P-relations, catalog entries, etc.).

Codd introduced four types of entities: characteristic, associative, kernel, and designative. They handled a variety of situations involving entities, such as linkage among entities, designation of an entity related to another entity, and so on. As such Codd's RM/T model was more elaborate than Chen's entity–relationship model, but it did not offer any substantially different approach. Codd included both DDL and DML commands for the RM/T model.

Date [4] proposed a new language called UDL that supported all three data models—relational, network, and hierarchical—in a uniform and consistent manner. UDL appeared as a tightly coupled extension of a 3GL such as COBOL or PL/I. The motivation behind UDL was to offer a unified view of the three models similar to the tree structure shown in Figure 8–4.

UDL recognized two basic types of record sets, *basesets* and *fansets*. A baseset is similar to a record type in a network model and a fanset is similar to a set type in a network model. Thus the features of the UDL were quite similar to those of the entity–relationship model if we identify a baseset with an entity relation and a fanset with a relationship relation.

UDL was designed with an "onion-layer" structure in order to reflect the unified view. The DDL part of UDL contained a core set of commands to define a relational schema. This core set was a subset of another set of commands needed to define a hierarchical schema, and the latter set was a subset of the still bigger (and the final) set of commands needed to define a network schema. The same architecture was applicable to DML part of UDL. Thus the core set of relational DML commands within UDL was purely nonprocedural, the most important statement being FIND (similar to SELECT in SQL). As this core set expanded to include hierarchical and network structures, more and more procedural commands were introduced. For example, a loop was handled by a statement like

```
DO records WHERE selection-condition WHILE loop-condition;
```

The decision making was handled by a statement like

```
IF EXISTS decision-condition
   THEN;
ELSE action;
```

Date recognized [5, p. 204] that "there is virtually no chance of any kind of UDL product ever appearing." Thus UDL now remains a theoretical product that provides a consistent treatment of the network and the relational approaches.

8.10 APPLICATION OF THE ENTITY–RELATIONSHIP MODEL TO SYSTEM ANALYSIS

The entity–relationship model proposed by Chen was never commercially implemented as a DBMS. However, the concepts of entity and relationship are now used as tools for the structured analysis phase of system development. To develop an application system for a business organization, it is necessary to model the operation of the organization. This involves the identification of individual business data types and the multiple relationships that exist among them to represent business rules of the company. For example, a company can have business data types such as vendor, product, and customer and may have policies or rules such as "a vendor may supply one or more products" that involve relationships between the two data types, vendor and product.

For the purpose of system analysis, we define an *entity* to be anything of significance in the company about which information must be gathered and stored. Each entity has a separate and distinct existence of its own. A *relationship* describes what one entity has to do with another. It shows the association between two or more entities. As such, a relationship often represents specific operational or organizational rules of the company. It embodies business functions by formulating what the enterprise actually does or is required to do. Entity and relationship are represented by the same symbols, as mentioned in Section 8.3.

Once entities and relationships are defined for the organization, entity–relationship diagrams are prepared. The purpose of these diagrams is to highlight the major objects that the application system must deal with as well as to emphasize the relationships among these objects. For a complex application system, the information modeled by the entity–relationship diagrams is as important as the processing that is modeled by the data flow diagrams. In fact, the data flow diagrams and the entity–relationship diagrams describe two different aspects of the same system. There is a one-to-one correspondence between these two sets of diagrams that the system analyst can check to ensure that he or she has a consistent model. For example, each data store in a data flow diagram should correspond to an entity in the entity–relationship diagram.

Chen is currently chairman of a software consulting firm, Chen and Associates, in Baton Rouge, Louisiana. In September 1986 he introduced a PC-based software called ER-Designer that implements the entity–relationship modeling for system analysis. It allows users to enter data into a PC for automatic creation and manipulation of entity–relationship diagrams and incorporates information to be used for design of application systems. ER-Designer contains an internal data dictionary that maintains the relationships among data types and attributes and performs consistency checking. In addition, this software can be used with SchemaGen, another package from Chen and Associates, to generate the database schema for a specific DBMS such as ORACLE and INGRES. The user can use the entity–relationship diagrams produced by ER-Designer to create the database file structures.

8.11 SUMMARY

In this chapter we have discussed the entity–relationship model first introduced by Chen in 1976. This data model combines the flat file structure of a relational database with the set type concept of a network database. Two basic concepts used in the model are entity relation and relationship relation. An entity is a thing that can be distinctly identified. A relationship is an association between two entities. The terms *attribute* and *primary key* (PK, in Chen's notation) have the same meaning as in the relational model.

An entity–relationship database consists of entity relations and relationship relations. Attributes are usually not repeated among the entity relations. Relationship relations provide linkages among entity relations and as such contain the PKs of these entity relations as attributes. A relationship relation can be of four types: 1:1, 1:N, N:1, and M:N. The structure of an entity–relationship database is represented graphically by entity–relationship diagrams, which are modifications of Bachman diagrams.

Next we discussed the data definition language (DDL) introduced by Chen. The syntax of the DDL distinguishes between regular and weak entity relations as well as between regular and weak relationship relations. Chen did not introduce any specific syntax for the data manipulation language (DML). Instead, he used SQL-like query language and also used relational calculus formalisms. The chapter contains several examples of the DDL and DML using the entity–relationship version of the LHUDB database.

Both relational and network models can be derived as special cases of the entity–relationship model. Precise step-by-step methodology of the derivation process is provided. Since a hierarchical data model is a special case of the network data model and an inverted file data model can be regarded as a low-level version of the relational model, we may say that the entity–relationship data model includes all relational and nonrelational data models as special cases.

Subsequent to Chen's proposal, several attempts were made to introduce database languages to unify all the data models. Codd's extended relational model RM/T and Date's unified database language (UDL) are two examples of these attempts. Both are discussed in this chapter.

In the closing section of the chapter we describe the application of entity–relationship model to system analysis and design. During the analysis phase, specific data objects of the company are captured as entities, and operational constraints or policies are embodied as relationships. During the design stage these entities and relationships help the system analyst to create the structure of the database. ER-Designer, a PC-based software marketed by Chen and Associates, can implement the entity–relationship modeling for system analysis and design.

KEY WORDS

association

attribute

Bachman diagram

baseset

catalog structure

Chen, P. P.

conceptual level

data definition language
  (DDL)

data flow diagram

data manipulation
  language (DML)

data model, entity–
  relationship
data model, network
data model, relational
data modeling
data structure diagram
E-relation
entity
entity primary key
entity relation
entity relation, regular
entity relation, weak
entity–relationship
  diagram
ER-Designer
extended relational
  model RM/T
fanset
integrity constraint
operator

P-relation
PK (see entity primary
  key)
relational calculus
relationship
relationship relation
relationship relation,
  regular
relationship relation,
  type of
relationship relation,
  weak
role
SchemaGen
SQL
structured analysis
subtype
unified data language
  (UDL)
value set

REFERENCES AND FURTHER READING

The following references contain additional materials related to the topics covered in this chapter.

1. PETER P.-S. CHEN, The Entity–Relationship Model: Toward a Unified View of Data, *ACM Transactions on Database Systems,* vol. 1, no. 1, March 1976, pp. 9–36.
2. E. F. CODD, Extending the Database Relational Model to Capture More Meaning, *ACM Transactions on Data Systems,* vol. 4, December 1979.
3. C. J. DATE, *An Introduction to Database Systems,* vol. II, 3rd ed., Addison-Wesley, Reading, MA, 1983.
4. C. J. DATE, An Introduction to the Unified Database Language (UDL), *Proc. 6th International Conference on Very Large Databases,* October 1980.
5. C. J. DATE, *Relational Database Selected Writings,* Addison-Wesley, Reading, MA, 1986.
6. H. F. KORTH and A. SILBERSCHATZ, *Database System Concepts,* McGraw-Hill, New York, 1986.
7. E. YOURDON, *Managing the Structured Techniques,* Yourdon Press, Englewood Cliffs, NJ, 1986.

Chen's paper [1] contains the most detailed treatment of entity–relationship data models. The specific DDL syntax of the entity–relationship data sublanguage appears there. Since the paper was published before the recent advances of relational databases, some of the comments made by Chen may appear too simplistic. Date [5, Chapter 11] contains a detailed treatment of the unified database language or UDL. Date [3, Chapter 6] discusses the extended relational model RM/T. Korth and Silberschatz [6, Chapter 2] provides a basic discussion of the entity–relationship models but no references are made to the DDL and DML proposed by Chen [1]. Yourdon [7] is a good source of information on structured analysis and the use of entity–relationship modeling in system design.

REVIEW QUESTIONS

1. In what sense can you say that the entity–relationship model combines the best features of both relational and network models? How can you derive each of these two models from the entity–relationship model?
2. Define an entity relation and a relationship relation. Give examples of your own.
3. Define the terms *role*, *attribute*, *value set*, and *entity primary key* (PK) in an entity–relationship database.
4. How do you define the PKs in a relationship relation? Is there a possibility that a relationship relation may not be in third normal form? Give examples to explain your answer.
5. Describe the types of a relationship relation. How many possible types are there?
6. How do you define the PKs of weak entity and weak relationship relations?
7. Explain why a relational DBMS can be used to implement an entity–relationship database?
8. How can you convert an M:N set type in a network database to one or more relationship relations in an entity–relationship database?
9. Describe briefly the two attempts, RM/T and UDL, of unifying the relational and the nonrelational data models.
10. Discuss the use of entity–relationship diagrams as a tool for system analysis.
11. In what sense can you say that a relationship relation represents an operational constraint of an organization?

EXERCISES

Refer to the personnel database diagram given in Chapter 7 Exercises (Figure 7–10). Design an entity–relationship database using this diagram as follows:

1. Prepare all the entity and relationship relations.
2. Design an entity–relationship diagram for this database.
3. Prepare DDL statements for each entity and each relationship relation using Chen's DDL syntax (see Section 8.4).

4. Formulate DML statements for the following queries by using (a) SQL and
   (b) relational calculus formalism.
   (i) List of all programmer employees with their dependents and skills.
   (ii) List of all job classifications by department.
   (iii) List of all employees without dependents.

CHAPTER 9

DESIGN, IMPLEMENTATION, AND MAINTENANCE OF RELATIONAL DATABASES

9.1. SCOPE OF THE CHAPTER

The design and implementation of a database are quite complex. Once a database is implemented, it is necessary to maintain it. The maintenance of a database is more complicated than that of a file processing system. Accordingly, we address all of these issues in this chapter.

Given a business problem involving database design, one has to analyze it and establish that a database is warranted. This happens during the detailed system design phase of system development. We assume that the developers decide to build a relational database and hence need a relational DBMS to implement it.

The analysis and design of a relational database are described here without reference to any particular DBMS. But the implementation and maintenance issues cannot be described without reference to a specific DBMS. We have used ORACLE for this purpose, because we have already used ORACLE in many of the earlier chapters.

The job of a database administrator (DBA) is to ensure a smooth operation of the database. The DBA has to interface with a wide variety of people, such as users, management, technical staff, and vendors. In this chapter we explore these different roles of a DBA.

The DBA is also responsible to ensure data independence, data security and privacy, system backup and recovery, and database restructure. Since the data in a database are used by multiple users, these issues become highly important. We discuss them and explain how a sophisticated DBMS can handle these concerns. The database restructure, however, is a massive problem for a large database.

We close this chapter with a discussion of the data dictionary, which has often been described as a "database about the database." A data dictionary contains information about all the relations and their component attributes and keys belonging to the database. It provides information about both the conceptual and internal levels. In the chapter we explain all these issues and emphasize that the data dictionary plays a critical role in maintaining data integrity.

9.2 ROLE OF THE DATABASE IN THE SYSTEM LIFE CYCLE

There are five principal phases of system development:

1. Problem definition and feasibility study
2. System analysis
3. Preliminary system design
4. Detailed system design
5. System implementation, maintenance, and evaluation

These five phases are grouped into three logical categories: system analysis, consisting of phases 1 and 2; system design, consisting of phases 3 and 4; and system implementation, consisting of phase 5. Clearly, the distinction between phases 1 and 2 is one of degree, not of kind. In other words, phase 1 starts at a superficial level that is pursued and described in more detail in phase 2. A similar comment applies to phases 3 and 4. The only distinction between phases 4 and 5 is that in phase 4 the physical system is designed on paper, whereas in phase 5 that "paper" system is converted into electronics.

The entire system development process is interactive in nature. As each phase concludes, the system team prepares a report containing findings and recommendations as the end product of that phase. The customer reviews the report and provides suggestions and/or corrections. Once the report is approved by customer, work starts on the next phase. Thus a continuous dialogue must be ongoing between the customer and the system team during the entire system development process.

As the system development proceeds through the successive phases of system analysis, preliminary design, detailed design, and implementation, the system life cycle nears its end phase. Then the maintenance of the operational system continues.

During the detailed system design phase the record and file structures of the system are prepared. The decision about the need for a database is made at this time. We now assume that a relational database is needed and that ORACLE will be used for implementing it.

9.3 ANALYSIS AND DESIGN OF A RELATIONAL DATABASE

There are two situations in which a relational database is designed:

1. No prior database exists so that the collection and analysis of data start from a scratch.
2. A relational database currently exists that has to be restructured for improved performance or new user requirements.

The *synthetic approach* is used to address situation 1 and the *analytic approach* to address situation 2. We now describe each method separately. We assume that as a result of the first three phases of the system life cycle we have collected all the necessary data, know the reports that are to be generated from the system, and have established the frequency of retrieval and update of the data. Kroenke [6, Chapter 11] and Mittra [7, Sections 5.6 and 9.6) may be consulted for insight into data collection and user requirements issues.

9.4 SYNTHETIC APPROACH

The synthetic approach is based on the extended relational data model RM/T proposed by Codd (see Section 8.9). The concept of *entity* is basic for this approach. An entity is any distinguishable object about which we want to store information in the database. The methodology consists of two steps:

1. Identify all the entities, attributes, and primary and foreign keys.
2. Record the design information in a pseudo DDL resembling SQL.

9.4.1 Identification of Entities, Attributes, and Keys

There are three types of entities: (1) kernel, (2) association, and (3) characteristic. A *kernel* is an independent entity that has an existence of its own. During implementation it gets its own base table. The design process starts by identifying the kernel entities at first. A kernel is the same as the regular entity relation of Chen (see Section 8.3). An *association* is a one–many, many–one, or many–many relationship among two or more kernel entities. The association is called *n*-ary if it links *n* ($\geq$ 2) kernels. Each association is mapped onto its own base table during implementation. An association is the same as a relationship relation of Chen (see Section 8.3). Finally, a *characteristic* is an entity whose sole function is to describe or characterize some other kernel or association. It thus depends on another entity. As such it resembles a weak entity relation or a weak relationship relation of Chen (see Section 8.3). The relationship between a characteristic and the kernel or association that it characterizes is of the many–one type.

Examples of kernels, association, and characteristics can be taken from the LHUDB. As outlined in Sections 8.2 and 8.3, all the regular entity relations, such as UNIV, INSTR, and STUDNT, are kernels; all the regular relationship relations, such as UNIV-INSTR, INSTR-STUDNT, and UNIV-CRSE, are associations; and CRSLST and CRSE-CRSLST are characteristics.

The three types of entities form the basic building blocks of a database. We next need to determine their attributes. An *attribute* in an entity (kernel, association, or characteristic) describes some property of that entity that needs to be recorded in the database. Sometimes the same property may belong to multiple entities, in which case it translates into an attribute appearing in an association or among multiple kernels. The most difficult situation arises when we come up with a property to be recorded in the database, but we do not know which entity or entities should have that property. The objective is to map the property in question into an attribute in at least one entity of any type.

Finally, we have to identify the primary and foreign keys. Using the concept of functional dependency and normalization, we identify single or multiple attributes in a kernel as *primary key* if that group of attributes uniquely determines a tuple of the kernel. The primary key of an association or a characteristic is selected from that of the kernels that are linked up by the association or that are characterized by the characteristic. The *foreign key* of an entity of any type is selected in such a way that two or more entities can be joined by using them. We observe that the value of a foreign key must match the value of some primary key. Hence the same design principle that is used for a primary key also applies to a foreign key.

We can summarize the synthetic approach by the following checklist:

1. Determine all the kernels at first.

2. Identify the attributes of each kernel.

3. Designate one or more of the attributes of a kernel as its primary key.

4. Determine all the associations using the linkage requirements among the kernels.

5. Identify the attributes of each association.

6. Designate one or more of these attributes as the primary key and the foreign key.

7. Determine all the characteristics using the kernels and associations.

8. Identify the attributes of each characteristic.

9. Designate one or more of these attributes as the primary key and the foreign key.

10. Repeat steps 1 through 9 until the design satisfies the normalization principles. Ideally, each entity should be in third normal form.

9.4.2 Pseudo DDL for Recording Design Information

The database design information is recorded for future implementation in two ways:

1. A set of entity–relationship diagrams
2. A set of pseudo DDL statements closely resembling the SQL DDL statements and profusely commented in plain English

We have already seen the entity–relationship diagrams in Section 8.3. In the rest of this section we describe the pseudo DDL syntax with examples taken from LHUDB.

The general syntax of the pseudo DDL includes the entity name, entity type, attribute list, primary key, foreign key, and foreign key linkage with other entities. The syntax is given below.

```
CREATE TABLE entity-name    /* any English comment
        TYPE entity-type
        ATTRIBUTES  (attribute-list)
        PRIMARY KEY (attribute-list)
        FOREIGN KEY (attribute-name IDENTIFIES entity-
                    name).
```

We now illustrate the foregoing syntax with these examples, one of each entity type.

1. *Kernel*

```
CREATE TABLE UNIV     /* UNIV maps to a base table
TYPE KERNEL
ATTRIBUTES
 (DNO     CHAR(2),   /* name and format of
  DNAME   CHAR(25),  /* each attribute
  DHEAD   CHAR(20))
PRIMARY KEY (DNO)     /* no foreign key exists
```

2. *Associations*

```
CREATE TABLE UNIV-INSTR  /* maps to a base table
        TYPE ASSOCIATION  /* links two kernels
        ATTRIBUTES        /* UNIV and INSTR
         (DNO      CHAR(2)
          ISSNO    INT(9)
        PRIMARY KEY (DNO, ISSNO)
        FOREIGN KEY (DNO IDENTIFIES UNIV)
                        /* DNO matches primary
                        /* key of UNIV
```

```
         FOREIGN KEY (ISSNO IDENTIFIES INSTR)
                              /* ISSNO matches primary
                              /* key of INSTR
```

3. *Characteristics*

```
CREATE TABLE CRSLST          /* maps to a base table
         TYPE CHARACTERISTIC /* depends for its
                             /* existence
         ATTRIBUTES          /* on the kernel CRSE
           (SID    INT(9),
            GRADE  CHAR(2),
            OFRNG  CHAR(8),
            CNO    CHAR(5))
         PRIMARY KEY (SID, OFRNG, CNO)
                              /* CNO is the primary
                              /* key of kernel CRSE
         FOREIGN KEY (SID IDENTIFIES STUDNT)
                              /* SID matches primary key
                              /* SSNO of STUDNT
         FOREIGN KEY (CNO IDENTIFIES CRSE)
                              /* CNO matches primary
                              /* key of CRSE
```

9.5 ANALYTIC APPROACH

The analytic approach applies when a database already exists and needs modification for some reason, such as performance improvement or storing more information. This is called database restructuring and is usually a quite involved job. The modification takes place in two steps: (1) modify the structure of the existing database, and (2) modify the applications that use the old database structure. We now address each issue separately.

9.5.1 Modification of the Database Structure

The goal is to apply normalization theory and put each relation in third normal form (3NF). This means that large relations (i.e., relations with more than 12 attributes, say) are broken into smaller relations. To satisfy the functional dependency constraints, we need to have relations with fewer attributes. When a large relation is broken into multiple smaller size relations, we have to redefine and reallocate the primary and foreign keys. We assume that a database design specification document exists that provides all the information on relations, attributes, primary keys (often called indexed attributes), clustering, and so on. In addition, if information on integrity is also available, so much the better. Alternatively, we can use the internal data dictionary maintained by the relational DBMS that implemented the database.

We now summarize the steps used for the structure modification process:

1. Make a complete list of all relations, views, and indices in the database.
2. Prepare a common data dictionary (CDD) using ORACLE that will contain the following information, as a minimum, for each attribute:
   a. Attribute name
   b. Name of each application using the attribute
   c. Alias of the attribute for each application
   d. Name of each relation using the attribute
   e. Format (i.e., length and type)
   f. Description
   g. Source (i.e., how input)
   h. Destination [i.e., report(s) using the attribute]
3. The structure and contents of CDD will have to be finalized after some experiments with collected data.
4. Transfer the information from CDD into a matrix format to identify duplication of data among applications.
5. Prepare a master list of required attributes without any duplications.
6. Distribute these attributes among newly constructed relations that should be in third normal form as far as practicable.
7. Decide on the choice of indices, both single and concatenated.
8. Explore the possibility of clustering attributes among the tables.
9. Prepare complete documentations for the entire project. This will be an ongoing task from the beginning of the project.

9.5.2 Modification of the Application Code

An application developed using a database refers to the relations, attributes, and keys of the database. So when the database structure is modified, the portions of the application code referring to the database structure must be modified also. Data retrieval and update routines, query formulations, host language interface commands, and so on, must be examined and changed, as needed. If code is used to enforce referential and relational integrity, that code must be changed, too.

9.6 ENTITY SUBTYPES AND SUPERTYPES

An entity type Y is a *subtype* of entity type X if every instance of Y is always an instance of X. In this case we also say that entity type X is a *supertype* of entity type Y. As an example, let us consider the entity STUDNT of LHUDB. We split the entity into two separate entities:

```
STUDNT (SNAME, SSNO, DEGREE, ADVSR, DNO, COLREG)
STUDNT-MAJ (SSNO, MAJOR)
```

Then STUDNT is a supertype of STUDNT-MAJ, since every student with a major field is a student in the first place. Also, STUDNT-MAJ is a subtype of STUDNT.

If Y is a subtype of X, every attribute of X also belongs to Y. This leads to a *type hierarchy* in the following sense: A supertype produces a generalization hierarchy of its subtype, and a subtype yields a specialization hierarchy of its supertype.

The concept of subtype and supertype plays an important role in avoiding null values in relations. We recall that the entity integrity rule mandates that no primary key can have null values. In general, avoiding null values is a good idea, because they often lead to unpredicted results during retrieval of data.

Referring to Figure 2–2, we find that the relation STUDNT admits null values for the attribute MAJOR when a student (e.g., Steve Levin) does not have a major field of study. This situation can be avoided by declaring STUDNT without the attribute MAJOR as a supertype and STUDNT-MAJ as a subtype, as described earlier in this section. The contents of these two relations are given in Figures 9–1 and 9–2. The attribute SSNO is the primary key in both relations. Such a representation is logically cleaner than that involving just a single relation.

STUDNT   (shown in two parts)

SNAME	SSNO	DEGREE	ADVSR
Roger Brown Smith	556123959	BS	Jack Adams
Cindy Logan	561239595	BS	Deb Kumar Roy
Benjamin Johnson	612395999	NONE	
Steve Levin	126939555	BA	Lee Kunkel
Tom Jones	939625155	MS	Raj Chandra Mitra
Beverley Black	512559369	PhD	Lee Kunkel

STUDNT   (SNAME repeated for continuity)

SNAME	DNO	COLREG
Roger Brown Smith	BI	Arts & Sci.
Cindy Logan	MA	Arts & Sci.
Benjamin Johnson	BA	Business
Steve Levin	EN	Arts & Sci.
Tom Jones	EE	Engineering
Beverley Black	EN	Arts & Sci.

Figure 9–1   STUDNT without MAJOR.

SSNO	MAJOR
556123959	Biology
561239595	Computer Science
612395999	NDEG
939625155	Mathematics
512559369	English

Figure 9–2 STUDNT-MAJ relation.

Theoretically, the type hierarchy can be taken down to any number of levels. An entity supertype X may be broken into subtypes $Y_1, Y_2, \ldots, Y_n$ according to one categorization, into subtypes $Z_1, Z_2, \ldots, Z_m$ according to another, and each of $Y_1, Y_2, \ldots, Y_n, Z_1, \ldots, Z_m$ may in turn be further subdivided into additional subtypes, and so on. Avoidance of null values should be taken as a design criterion in both synthetic and analytic approaches. Type hierarchy provides a mechanism to enforce this criterion.

9.7 INDEXING AND DENORMALIZATION

Indexing is the process of implementing the primary keys. It optimizes data retrieval at the cost of update; that is, it speeds up retrieval but slows down the update process (see Section 2.1.4). Normalization may be regarded as optimizing for update at the cost of retrieval. A fully normalized database tends to require less processing on update but more on retrieval, since normalization up to 3NF produces relations with fewer attributes. To avoid this problem, sometimes denormalization is desirable. This leads us to the following design guideline (Date [3, p. 462]): If two items of information are very frequently retrieved together and are only very infrequently updated, and if normalization up to 3NF separates these two items, the design should be denormalized slightly to bring these items back together again.

9.8 IMPLEMENTATION OF A RELATIONAL DATABASE

We assume that the database, whether newly designed or restructured, will be implemented using ORACLE. The following steps need be taken to convert the pseudo DDL of Section 9.4.2 into SQL of ORACLE:

1. Use CREATE TABLE command to set up each relation corresponding to any entity type (i.e., kernel, association, or characteristic).
2. Use CREATE UNIQUE INDEX command to set up the primary key of each relation.

3. Include each foreign key as a set of repeated attributes among the relations.

4. Use NOT NULL clause in CREATE TABLE commands to enforce the entity integrity rule for each primary key.

5. Use appropriate code to enforce the referential and relational integrity constraints.

6. If tables are clustered, use CREATE CLUSTER command to set up the clustering of tables and their attributes.

7. Use SQL Loader utility to load data into each table from ASCII source data files.

9.9 DATABASE MAINTENANCE

Once the database is designed and implemented, the database maintenance function starts. This function can be broken down into the following four broad categories: (1) daily operation, (2) backup and recovery, (3) performance, and (4) security. In the next four sections we discuss these four issues. Actual examples from ORACLE version 5.1.24 are given.

9.9.1 Daily Operation of the Database

The daily operation of the database system requires that all applications dependent on the database run smoothly and error-free and that the database update operations are successful. Two specific issues are addressed here: (1) upgrading the DBMS to a new version, and (2) changing the environment from stand-alone to clustered. These topics are discussed in the next two subsections.

(a) Upgrading DBMS to new version.   Suppose that the DBMS is upgraded from its current version X to a new version Y. Use the following steps:

1. Backup the complete database (i.e., all data and index files).
2. Shut down the DBMS [i.e., make it unavailable to users (ORACLE command: IOR SHUT)].
3. Backup all system and temporary files (ORACLE calls them .DBS and BI files).
4. Install the new version Y using the installation procedure. Set up a new dictionary to hold files for version Y. If version X is also retained, there will be two directories, one for version X and the other for version Y.
5. Install all other DBMS products dependent on version Y.
6. Initialize the database (ORACLE command: IOR INIT).
7. Rebuild the terminal definition files (ORACLE command: CRTINS).

8. Build new system views and tables specific to version Y (ORACLE command: NEWCAT.ORA).

9. Reload all data and index tables under the new version Y using its own directory. (ORACLE calls this process a full database import, which is menu driven.)

10. Start the DBMS in version Y (ORACLE command: IOR W).

If we want to retain both versions X and Y, we must create two separate directories, as noted in step 4, and then repeat the steps for version X separately. Finally, it is necessary to create the DBA.COM files for each version of DBMS so that the DBA.COM file of each version can point to that version after a user logs in.

(b) Clustering process for DBMS.   The computer on which the DBMS is installed may operate as a single stand-alone machine or as a *node* in a clustered configuration consisting of multiple machines, each machine being a node in the cluster. The nodes share disk and tape devices and a common file system. The *cluster* is configured so as to present an identical user environment on every node. The nodes communicate with one another via a data communication network such as DECNET for VAX machines. However, each node in a cluster boots and fails separately. The main advantages of a cluster environment are twofold: higher availability of system resources, and faster and easier sharing of information and resources among nodes.

If a DBMS is installed initially on a stand-alone computer that later becomes a node in a cluster, the DBMS installation has to be modified for the clustered environment. Suppose that a stand-alone computer C_1 is clustered with a second computer C_2 to form the cluster CL. Then the following steps are needed:

1. Back-up all system and temporary files of the DBMS on C_1.

2. Back-up all data and index files on C_1.

3. Shut down the DBMS on C_1 as a stand-alone system (ORACLE command: IOR SHUT).

4. Reinstall the DBMS on C_1 as a node with C_2 in the cluster CL (ORACLE commands: INSTALL, followed by CREINIT).

5. Assign logicals for the system.

6. Load data dictionary and all other DBMS products on the cluster CL.

7. Make operational changes such as adjusting LOGIN.COM file, granting database access, and changing passwords.

8. Load all data and index tables and system and temporary files into CL.

9. Link all applications that use the DBMS on C_1.

10. Install the DBMS on C_2 as the second node in CL.

Usually, the backup process takes the most time. The actual clustering lasts about 30 minutes, depending on the machine. During this process the DBMS remains unavailable to the users.

9.9.2 Backup and Recovery

The contents of a database (e.g., relations, view definitions, indices) are copied onto tapes on a daily basis for backup. This process ensures that in the case of any type of system failure, no data are lost. Normally, full backup of a database occurs weekly and incremental backups take place daily. Also, whenever an update operation takes place, a record containing the old and new values of the changed item is written to a special data set called the *log file*. ORACLE calls this file the *Before Image* or *BI file*. In case of a system failure, two possibilities arise with respect to the recovery process:

1. The database itself is damaged (e.g., a head crash occurred on the disk). In this case the database is restored by loading it from the most recent archive copy and then using the log to redo all changes made since that archive copy was taken.

2. The database is not damaged but its contents are unreliable (e.g., a program terminated abnormally somewhere in the middle of performing a sequence of logically related updates). In this case the database is restored to a correct state by using the log to undo all ''unreliable'' changes. The archive copy is not needed in this case.

ORACLE calls the backup and recovery of databases the process of export and import. The full database *export* backs up all the table definitions, table data, clusters, indices, grants, views, synonyms, and space definitions in the database. Export produces a user-named file at run time that stores all the exported information. This file acts as a master file for restoring data, when needed. *Import* is the recovery utility in ORACLE. It restores data and also decreases fragmentation. It tries to store the entire data set in a single physical location on the disk. When such a sequence of contiguous blocks of storage space is not available, the import utility looks for additional chunks of storage.

In general, when a record is deleted from a table, the space used by the record is not immediately made available. Hence the process is called a *logical delete*. A flag is raised with a logically deleted record so that it is not retrieved by any data retrieval command. On a regular basis such records are physically deleted in order to reclaim the unused space and reduce fragmentation in the database. ORACLE achieves this goal in a sequence of three operations: full database export, run IOR INIT command, and a full database import. The export utility transfers data from the database into a file, IOR INIT then initializes the database by creating empty table structures, and the import utility uses the file created by export to load data back into the empty tables. The entire cycle can take several hours or even almost a day to finish, depending on the size of the database.

9.9.3 Database Performance

The database performance issues involve efficiency of storage usage and quick response time for both update and retrieval. At the conceptual level of a database, the appropriate tools to be used to achieve good performance are indexing, clustering, space usage clause in CREATE TABLE commands, and efficient formulation of queries (see Chapter 5). At the internal level, database performance can be improved in three ways:

1. Defragmentation of database storage (e.g., system and data partitions in ORACLE)
2. Optimal configuration of database files
3. Installation of selected executable files in memory

By ensuring item 1, we can avoid a long chain of pointers to retrieve and update data, thereby resulting in quick response time. By implementing item 2 we can reduce internal fragmentation of database files and distribute these files among separate disks. By implementing item 3 we can eliminate I/O delays that would be caused by invoking and copying DBMS utilities corresponding to these executable files. We discuss these issues in the next three subsections.

(a) Defragmentation of database storage.   The database administrator or DBA (see Section 9.10) should monitor the use of storage space within the database on a weekly basis. The purpose of the monitoring is to determine the amount of free space remaining for the current database, to monitor the amount of fragmentation on each partition, and to identify the tables that are causing the fragmentation. Both the DBA and the users will see several benefits if the DBA is vigilant in this monitoring. Some of the benefits are listed below.

1. The DBA will know in advance when space is running out and can take the appropriate action for adding storage before users begin to encounter problems.
2. By constantly looking for fragmentation and eliminating it, response time can be kept at an optimal level and the DBA can avoid having to export, reinitialize, and import the entire database. Tables that are determined to cause fragmentation can be individually exported and imported in a matter of minutes rather than the hours it takes to export/import the whole database.
3. As tables are identified to be causing fragmentation, the table owner can be contacted and the problem explained. The DBA can work with the user to define proper space definitions for his or her tables so that the problem can be avoided altogether.

In ORACLE the fragmentation of database storage can be tracked as follows:

1. Create a view FREE-SPACE defined by

```
CREATE VIEW FREE-SPACE
(NAME, BLOCKS-FREE, PIECES, AVG-SIZE, LARGEST-SEGMENT)
AS SELECT PAR$NAME, SUM(SPM$ENDBLOCK - SPM$STARTBLOCK
+ 1), COUNT(*),
AVG (SPM$ENDBLOCK - SPM$STARTBLOCK + 1),
MAX (SPM$ENDBLOCK - SPM$STARTBLOCK + 1)
FROM SYS.PARTITIONS, SYS.SPACEMAP
WHERE PAR$ID = SPM$PID
GROUP BY PAR$NAME;
```

You must have DBA privilege to use this feature.

2. Run the command

```
SELECT * FROM FREE-SPACE;
```

The following is an example of a sample report generated by this process:

NAME	BLOCKS-FREE	PIECES	AVG-SIZE	LARGEST-SEGMENT
SYSTEM	739	42	17.5952381	90
ACCOUNTING	1000	1	1000	1000

It shows that we have 1739 free Oracle blocks and that 1000 of them are in a contiguous segment for use by the Accounting partition. We can also see that there is some fragmentation on the System partition and that we should probably consider an export/import to remedy the situation and/or take a closer look to determine which tables are causing the fragmentation.

We close this subsection with some general recommendations about how to avoid excessive *disk chaining*. Whenever a user creates a table that will have either a large amount of data initially loaded into it, or one that is expected to grow over time, the table should be created using a space definition. Every table uses a space definition at the time of creation. If the user does not specify a space at creation time, the default space definition is used to determine initial storage allocation and incrementation storage allocation. The default space definition works fine for small and even some moderately sized tables. But if users do not create customized spaces for their larger tables, the initial storage allocation will be exceeded quickly, causing disk chaining. *Disk chaining* occurs when a user exceeds the initial allocation for a table. When this occurs, ORACLE must get an additional group of blocks from its free block list and allocate them to the table. Most of the times this new set of blocks will not be a contiguous segment, thus causing more overhead to identify the location of the blocks. When a table stores its data in several noncontiguous locations on a disk, we say that that table is causing fragmentation. The problem is compounded when several tables have exceeded their initial storage allocation (known as initial extents).

(b) Optimal configuration of database files.   Since the optimal configuration of database files under any DBMS is always specific to that DBMS, it is difficult to provide general recommendations without mentioning a specific DBMS. Consequently, the discussion in this section involves ORACLE's file configuration. Each ORACLE database consists of one before-image file (BI) along with one or more database files (DBS).

The database logically consists of one or more partitions. Partitions in turn are composed of one or more files. We assume that each partition has one file. A default ORACLE system will have one partition, called the SYSTEM partition.

In a single partition database system, the single database (DBS) file contains all user/application data, the system data dictionary, and the temporary tables. The BI file is used for transaction rollback and read consistency during update operations.

Further partitioning of the database file can result in less internal fragmentation of the database, which in turn will improve performance. In addition, ORACLE performance can be increased by proper distribution of database and before image files, because more reads and writes can occur concurrently. However, the disadvantage of distributing the ORACLE files is that all of the database (DBS) and before-image (BI) files must be available for the ORACLE system to be up and running. If any one of the disks is unavailable, the ORACLE system will be unavailable.

To optimize performance the database file configuration should consist of three generic partitions:

1. One system partition for data dictionary tables
2. One temporary partition for temporary tables
3. One or more data partition(s) for data and index tables for the applications using ORACLE RDBMS

Each partition should consist of one file, so that we get three or more files under the foregoing schema. In addition, there is one before-image (BI) file set up for each database. These files should exist on different disks to prevent excessive head movement.

The configuration above will maximize performance. Each data manipulation command (i.e., inserts, updates, and deletes) will write to at least two of these files and possibly to all three. Thus if all the files exist on the same disk, there will be much more head movement to scan from one file to the next than if they are on separate disks. By having the files on separate disks, the head movement is reduced and writing to several separate files can take place simultaneously.

There are two reasons for separating the single DBS file into system and data partitions:

1. Reduction of the number of head movements
2. Reduction of the fragmentation of data dictionary tables

As a result of the configuration above, whenever more space is needed for any table, ORACLE locates and uses the first set of contiguous blocks available in the table's partition. Since the space definitions cannot be modified for data dictionary tables, they will typically need a large number of extents. If the data dictionary has its own partition, these extents will not be interspersed within the application tables and thus be located more contiguously.

During operations such as updates, ORACLE must create temporary tables. These tables are usually created in the system partition. Under this arrangement, a large amount of data entered could fill up the system partition and "freeze up" the database. The advantage of having a separate temporary table partition is that an appropriate amount of free blocks is reserved for temporary tables regardless of how many additional data are entered. This ensures that the database does not "freeze up."

The only disadvantage of this configuration is that it uses four or more disks with one partition per disk. Hence ORACLE becomes unavailable if any one of these disks goes down or is damaged. Each disk used should have a relatively light load without the ORACLE files, because very busy disks cannot offer the improved performance.

If two different versions of ORACLE RDBMS are running on the same computer, there will be a minimum of eight files (double the above). Again, an optimal distribution of these files would be to distribute them over eight separate, lightly loaded disks. However, realistically, this is not always a feasible solution. If it is necessary to put more than one file on a particular disk, it is best to "double up" two files, one being from one ORACLE RDBMS and the other being from another. This will maintain the distribution of files within each system, and they will compete with one another only when both RDBMSs are getting heavy use.

Generally, the Data Partition Database file and the Before Image file will be the largest and most heavily used files, followed by the System Partition Database file, and lastly by the Temporary Partition Database file. So, if doubling up of files is required, it would be preferable to double up a System or Data Partition file with a Temporary Partition file, rather than doubling up two System or Data Partition files.

Another placement consideration is that ORACLE-based application code should be placed on the same disks that hold the RDBMS. This minimizes application downtime. For example, it would make sense to put applications using RDBMS 5.1 on the same disk as the database using RDBMS 5.1. If one of the disks goes down, then both the applications on it, and the ORACLE system, would not be available. However, if the application was on one disk and the

ORACLE system on another, a failure of either disk would make the application unavailable.

(c) Installation of utilities in memory.   Performance of DBMS utilities (e.g., forms generator, report generator, precompiler) can be increased by installing their executable files into shared global memory. When not installed in shared memory, and a user invokes a utility, the user's process copies the executable into its area of memory, and then runs it. But when it is installed in shared memory, it is not necessary for the user's process to copy the executable into their memory area, because it is accessible from shared global memory.

There are two major benefits:

1. The image is invoked faster because the user process can access it directly without any copying.

2. User processes use less memory space, since they can access the image from shared global memory.

As shared memory is limited, not all images can be installed. The best images to install are those that are most heavily used.

9.9.4 Database Security

Database security procedures protect the database against unauthorized retrieval or update of data. Such protection may be applied either to the entire database, or at individual relations level, or even at the designated tuples and attributes level. For example, a user may be allowed access only to a horizontal subset or a vertical subset of a given relation.

User authorizations are handled through the *user profile* or the *object profile*. In a user profile a record is maintained for each user that identifies the relations or subsets thereof that the user is authorized to access and the operations (e.g., SELECT, UPDATE) that the user can perform on these relations. In an *object profile* a record is maintained for each object (i.e., a relation or a subset thereof), specifying the users who are authorized to access that object.

The set of all user profiles and object profiles constitutes the *authorization matrix* for the database users. The cell $A(i, j)$ of the authorization matrix A represents the set of all user authorization rules that apply to user i with respect to object j. Thus row i of A constitutes the user profile for user i. Also, column j of A represents the object profile for the object j. The granularity of the objects for which columns may exist in A is one measure of the sophistication of the system concerned.

There are various categories of user authorizations, as listed below:

1. *Value-independent control.* Authorization is based purely on the names of objects and the user is allowed access on an ALL or NONE basis.

2. *Value-dependent control.* Authorization rule includes an access predicate that allows the user to access only a subset of an object based on the values of some attributes in the object. Views are used to implement this type of control.

3. *Context-dependent control.* Authorization rule contains an access predicate that refers to system variables such as the time of the day, user's password, and terminal address. For example, a user may be allowed to access certain objects only between 9 A.M. and 3 P.M., or only from a certain secure/classified terminal.

4. *Statistical control.* Authorization rule contains a built-in statistical function, such as AVG, MAX, or SUM, so that the user can retrieve only the average of some attribute values, not the individual values. For example, in the LHUDB database, a user may compute the average grade point (2.8, 3.5, etc.) for a course but may not see the grades of individual students in that course.

To enforce the authorization rules the DBMS uses a *security enforcer* or an *arbiter* that has unconstrained access to the entire database, checks each access request, and then grants or denies permission, as appropriate. Given a request $R(i, j)$ for some type of access from user i to object j, the arbiter examines the cell $A(i, j)$ of the authorization matrix A and goes through a sequence of tests to determine whether to grant or deny the request. Each test after the first in the sequence is performed only if the preceding test returns a negative answer. The arbiter reaches its final decision as soon as a test returns an affirmative answer. If all tests return negative answers, the arbiter informs the user that the request is denied. In this case the arbiter can take a variety of actions, depending on many factors, such as the nature of the attempted violation, the sensitivity of the data, whether the request came from an on-line user or a batch program, and so on. In particularly sensitive situations it may be necessary to terminate the program or to lock the terminal keyboard; in less critical cases it may be sufficient merely to return an appropriate exception code to the user. It may also be desirable to record attempted breaches of security in the log ("threat monitoring"), to permit subsequence analysis of such attempts, and also to serve in itself as a deterrent against illegal infiltration. In general, required violation responses will be specified as yet another component of the authorization rule entries in the authorization matrix.

As noted above, the view mechanism of the DBMS can restrict user access to specific horizontal and/or vertical subsets of relations. However, it does not specify the operations that authorized users may execute against such subsets. In ORACLE the authorization scheme is implemented through GRANT and REVOKE commands. The GRANT command creates ORACLE users with three types of privilege:

1. *CONNECT privilege.* A user with this privilege can
   a. Access ORACLE.

    b. Retrieve another user's data if the owner of the data has GRANTed SELECT access on the data to the user.

    c. Create views and synonyms.

2. *RESOURCE privilege.* A user with this privilege can

    a. Perform all operations given by CONNECT privilege.

    b. Create tables, indices, and clusters.

    c. GRANT or REVOKE to other user privileges on objects that he or she owns.

3. *DBA privilege.* A user with this privilege can

    a. Perform all operations given by RESOURCE privilege.

    b. Access any user's data and execute any SQL statement on it.

    c. GRANT and REVOKE database access privileges.

    d. Create PUBLIC synonyms (make objects available to all users).

    e. CREATE and ALTER partitions.

    f. Perform full database exports.

    g. Change a user's password.

There is no limit to the number of DBAs that an instance of ORACLE can have.

    The REVOKE command works in the opposite direction of GRANT. By using REVOKE for a user the privileges that are specified in the REVOKE command are withdrawn from the user and also from all other users to whom this user has GRANTed these privileges.

9.10 DATABASE ADMINISTRATOR

We have discussed the implementation and maintenance of a relational database in Sections 9.8 and 9.9. Since these activities require a consolidated and continuous effort, a separate position is created to handle this responsibility. Usually, the title of database administrator (DBA) is assigned to this position. The DBA works both as a manager and as a technical person. As such, he or she has to work diplomatically at various times to resolve conflicting needs and demands from a diverse group of people who can be categorized into the following five classes:

1. Management

2. End users

3. Applications developers

4. System software and operations staff

5. Vendors for software and hardware

Each of the foregoing five interfaces is a two-way communication. We now elaborate on each class separately.

9.10.1 DBA and Management

The DBA is not always placed in a managerial slot in the organization. As a result, he or she may not be in a direct line of communication with management. This situation poses a severe limitation on the DBA's effectiveness. The following five issues comprise the main items of communication between the DBA and the management:

1. Short- and long-term goals of the organization and their impact on the databases in both production and development functions
2. Time constraints on various projects, both current and future, that involve databases
3. Staff requirements for the DBA at both ideal and feasible levels
4. Procurement of new software and hardware to improve the database performance
5. Analysis and feedback on project status report from the DBA to management

9.10.2 DBA and End Users

The DBA's primary responsibility is to keep the end users satisfied by providing for them a highly tuned database environment. The DBA should remain in constant communication with the end users in order to get their input for data requirements and system performance. The following five issues are of major importance in this respect:

1. Frequency of use and response time
2. Access privilege and database security
3. Training needs of the end users
4. Proposed changes and future applications
5. Appropriate tools to make the end users more productive

9.10.3 DBA and Application Developers

The database performance of any application software depends on two factors: efficient design of the database at the conceptual level and efficient maintenance of the database at the internal level. The DBA should work in close coordination with the application developers on both issues. More specifically, the following items deserve special attention:

1. Logical design of the database for each application

2. Physical implementation of the logical database for each application
3. Maintenance of security as needed by the end users
4. Enforcement of data integrity for each application
5. Database backups and recovery procedures
6. Schedule for application development

9.10.4 DBA and Systems and Operations Staff

The systems and operations staff are involved with the daily maintenance of all the applications and system software. The DBA communicates with them on the issues of database maintenance and performance. The following items are of prime importance:

1. Current and new software and hardware required to support the database
2. Performance constraints, such as the response time, that affect the system
3. Responsibility of the staff for implementing the database
4. Storage and system capacity requirements
5. Availability of the database during prime time
6. Initialization and relinking of the database
7. Security enforcement procedures
8. Reports of operational problems of the database

9.10.5 DBA and Software/Hardware Vendors

The DBA must communicate with the vendors for his or her database requirements. Special application generators using databases, tools for managing disk space and reducing fragmentations, performance improvement tools in a transaction processing environment, and so on, are procured from the vendors. The DBA keeps track of these new tools. As such, the following issues are to be addressed:

1. Selection process of DBMS-related tools
2. Training and support provided by the vendors for new products
3. Available documentation supplied by the vendors
4. Hardware and software requirements for the database
5. Future expansion possibilities to match the projected growth of the database

9.11 DATA DICTIONARY

In a database environment common data are shared by multiple users. So control of data usage and data structure is necessary. A *data dictionary* (DD) provides such control by containing complete documentation of all data in the database.

Thus a DD is really a database about the database. A DBMS normally contains the software that creates and maintains an integrated data dictionary.

The data dictionary stores such information about the data as its origin, description, format, relationship to other data, usage, and access privileges. For example, the ORACLE data dictionary contains a group of tables and views that contain information about the database. The DD is created at the time of database creation and describes tables, columns, indices, clusters, users, access privileges, and data synonyms. ORACLE automatically updates the DD whenever anyone creates or drops a table or view, grants or revokes a privilege, creates or drops an index, and so on. Figure 9–3 gives a complete list of the tables and views in ORACLE's data dictionary.

The main advantage of the data dictionary is that it makes information about the database available in a central location. Data descriptions exist only once in the system and are stored in the data dictionary. The latter can be queried using standard SQL commands to derive information about the database. With the help of a report generator one can produce detailed nicely formatted reports using the contents of the data dictionary. Such reports can become very valuable tools for documentation purpose.

Some authors (Atre [1, p. 65]; Gorman [4, pp. 130–131]) call a data dictionary by the name *meta database*, or simply *metabase*. Gorman [4, p. 66] has described the metabase as a database application that contains all the data about the database project. His comments on metabase are quoted below [4, pp. 130–131].

While the metabase system is important for standard data processing systems, it is absolutely critical for database systems. Typically, a database application's documentation exists in at least a dozen large binders, and that does not include the DBMS-related documentation or the actual program designs or listings. It is clearly impossible to manage this monumental amount of paper effectively in any unautomated way.

The metabase system must store, update, maintain, report, protect, and preserve all these data in the most accessible form. This is best done with a DBMS. Most DBMS vendors have recognized this fact and have implemented their metabase, also called data dictionaries, using their own DBMS as the main source of power. Typically, vendor-provided metabase packages address only the data processing portion of the metabase requirements, so they must be greatly expanded to include all the artifacts of the database project.

Designs do exist for metadata databases, and there have been some very successful implementations when the following considerations have been kept in mind:

- Canned data dictionary packages or DBMS-based systems must be capable of expanding in terms of data and reports to suit the peculiar needs of the organization.

- Successful metadata database projects require high-level organizational attention,

TNAME	Remark
Reference date	ORACLE catalog as of May 10, 1984, installed on ⟨date/time⟩
AUDIT_ACCESS	Audit entries for accesses to user's tables/views (DBA sees all)
AUDIT_ACTIONS	Maps auditing action numbers to action names
AUDIT_CONNECT	Audit trail entries for user log-on/log-off (DBA sees all users)
AUDIT_DBA	Audit trail entries for DBA activities (for DBA use only)
AUDIT_EXISTS	Audit trail entries for objects that do NOT EXIST (DBAs only)
AUDIT_TRAIL	Audit trail entries relevant to the user (DBA sees all)
CATALOG	Profile of tables accessible to user, excluding data dictionary
CLUSTERS	Clusters and their tables (either must be accessible to user)
CLUSTERCOLUMNS	Maps cluster columns to clustered table columns
COL	Specifications of columns in tables created by the user
COLUMNS	Specifications of columns in tables (excluding data dictionary)
DBLINKS	Public and private links to external databases
DEFAULT_AUDIT	Default table auditing options
DTAB	Description of tables and views in ORACLE data dictionary
EXTENTS	Data structure of extents within tables
INDEXES	Indexes created by user and indexes on tables created by user
PARTITIONS	File structure of files within partitions (for DBA use only)
PRIVATESYN	Private synonyms created by the user
PUBLICSYN	Public synonyms
SESSIONS	Record of log-in sessions for user
SPACES	Selection of space definitions for creating tables and clusters
STORAGE	Data and index storage allocation for user's own tables
SYNONYMS	Synonyms, private and public
SYSAUDIT_TRAIL	Synonym for system audit trail (for DBA use only)
SYSCATALOG	Profile of tables and views accessible to the user
SYSCOLAUTH	Directory of column-level update grants by or to the user
SYSCOLUMNS	Specifications of columns in accessible tables and views
SYSDBLINKS	All links to external databases (for DBA use only)
SYSEXTENTS	Data structure of tables throughout system (for DBA use only)
SYSINDEXES	List of indexes, underlying columns, creator, and options
SYSPROGS	List of programs precompiled by user
SYSSTORAGE	Summary of all database storage (for DBA use only)
SYSTABALLOC	Data and index space allocations for all tables (for DBAs)
SYSTABAUTH	Directory of access authorization granted by or to the user
SYSTEM_AUDIT	System auditing options (for DBA use only)
SYSUSERAUTH	Master list of ORACLE users (for DBA use only)
SYSUSERLIST	List of ORACLE users
SYSVIEWS	Quotations of the SQL text upon which system views are based
TAB	List of tables, views, clusters, and synonyms created by the user
TABALLOC	Data and index space allocations for all users' tables
TABQUOTAS	Table allocation (space) parameters for tables created by user
TABLE_AUDIT	Auditing options of users' tables and views (DBA sees all)
VIEWS	Quotations of the SQL statements upon which views are based

Figure 9–3 Tables and views in ORACLE's data dictionary.

input, review, and guidance—roughly analogous to the effort expanded on other critical data processing systems.

- The best results are achieved when the metadata database has been integrated into the work process that designs, implements, maintains, and operates automated systems.

9.12 SPECIAL USES OF THE DATA DICTIONARY

Some DBMS vendors have produced specially designed software that can manipulate the data dictionary in order to perform special functions. Two such functions are (1) transparency of changes in database structure, and (2) reverse engineering. These two issues are discussed in the next two subsections.

9.12.1 Transparency of Changes in the Database Structure

When a database is restructured by altering the structures of its existing relations, all the applications dependent on the old database have to be modified in order to access the new database (see Section 9.5.2). Ideally, we would like to impose an extra layer of software on top of the data dictionary in such a manner that this software insulates the underlying database structure from the applications. This means that the applications use the table definitions belonging to the data dictionary by means of a given set of commands that refer to the database structure and that remain the same even when the structure of the database changes. This phenomenon is known as the *transparency* of changes in database structure for applications.

The VAX *common data dictionary* (CDD) belonging to the VAX Information Architecture introduced by Digital Equipment Corporation is an example of the type of software described above. Using the CDD, the DBA can perform the following functions:

1. Create shareable definitions in a data definition language understood by many VAX programming language compilers and VAX Information Architecture products.
2. Store those definitions in the CDD database.
3. Modify those definitions in the dictionary without editing the programs and procedures that use the definitions.
4. Document the creation and use of the definitions in the dictionary.
5. Specify user access to individual definitions.

The programmers and other users can:

1. Copy definitions from the dictionary into programs at compile time.

2. Use VAX Information Architecture products to create CDD definitions automatically.
3. Document the use of a definition by making an entry in the definition's history list.
4. Maintain an area of the dictionary that contains data definitions for their private use.

The CDD is organized as a hierarchy of dictionary directories and dictionary objects. *Dictionary directories* are similar to VMS directories: They organize information within the hierarchy. *Dictionary objects*, located at the ends of the branches in the hierarchy, are like the files in a VMS directory: They contain the data definitions stored in the dictionary. These definitions include:

1. Record descriptions that can be copied into application programs
2. Definitions required by VAX Information Architecture products

The CDD's hierarchical structure is like a family tree. Dictionary directories are the parents and their children include other directories and dictionary objects. Using the *CDD Data Definition Language* (CDDL), the DBA creates and modifies record definitions. The command CDDL/REPLACE replaces an existing record definition with a new one as follows:

1. Create a new CDDL source file that contains the path name of the record definition that is being modified.
2. Compile the new source file with the command CDDL/REPLACE.

The CDDL compiler processes the new source file and performs the following functions:

1. Removes the original definition and replaces it with the new version.
2. Keeps the original access control list and history list.
3. Creates a new history list entry documenting the change.

Programmers who want to copy the record definitions into their application programs search the CDD for these definitions. Once found, the definitions can easily be included in the program at compile time. For example, a COBOL programmer can use COBOL's COPY statement in the Data Division of the program to include the required record definitions. The COBOL compiler retrieves the definitions from the CDD and compiles them as COBOL object code. In case a record definition changes, the new definition is copied into the program so that there is no need of changing the code.

9.12.2 Reverse Engineering Using the Data Dictionary

Reverse engineering means taking existing applications and their associated database or file descriptions and deriving the specification (''what'') level of the application from its implementation (''how'') level. In a database environment the reverse engineering process takes the definitions of views, relations, indices, and clusters from the data dictionary and creates a full documentation of the underlying database. In case of undocumented applications the reverse engineering allows the DBA to have appropriate database design reports. These can then be used for a database restructure project, if needed.

The *SQL Design Dictionary* (SDD) offered by ORACLE provides such reverse engineering capability that is called the *SDD retrofitting feature*. This is implemented via a set of utility programs that take one or more existing ORACLE databases and load them into SDD. The DBA or any other user of SDD interacts with the system by means of a set of menu hierarchies. However, SDD, like any other CASE tool, can retrofit only those pieces of information that have already been entered via SDD. If, for example, the information on functional dependencies and normalizations has not been entered beforehand, SDD cannot generate any report dealing with these issues.

9.13 SUMMARY

In this chapter we have dealt with the design, implementation, and maintenance of relational databases. The design issues have been treated under the broader perspective of system life cycle. The implementation and maintenance issues are described in two stages for each: the theoretical part and illustrations using ORACLE version 5.1.24. The role of DBA is crucial in all three areas and the data dictionary provides a mediocre-to-excellant tool, depending on its sophistication, for the DBA to manage these functions.

The database design issues arise during the detailed system design phase of the system life cycle. There are two approaches used: the *synthetic approach* if no prior database exists, and the *analytic approach* if an existing database is to be restructured to meet current needs and/or improve performance.

The synthetic approach starts with a complete identification of entities, attributes, and keys. Conceptually, an entity corresponds to a relation. There are three types of entities: kernels, associations, and characteristics. In the terminology of entity–relationship data model, an association resembles a relationship relation, a characteristic is a weak entity relation, and a kernel is a regular entity relation. For a given entity type, its attributes describe the entity and its keys uniquely identify entity tuples. A pseudo DDL, designed to simulate SQL statements, is then introduced to record the design information under the synthetic approach.

The analytic approach starts with the existing database structure and strives to improve it by using normalization principles at the conceptual level and indexing and clustering principles at the internal level. It is necessary to capture the information on the existing database structure in a common data dictionary. Peak performance can be achieved in a restructured database only by optimizing both the conceptual and the internal levels. The actual implementation of a relational database is dependent on the DBMS used.

We next addressed a variety of database maintenance issues, such as daily operation, backup and recovery, performance, and security. Actual examples from ORACLE are used to discuss these concepts.

A database administrator (DBA) is responsible for the creation and maintenance of databases. He or she plays a dual role as an administrator and technical consultant by interfacing with end users, management, application developers, system and operations staff, and outside vendors for hardware and software. Each interface is a two-way communication.

The chapter closes with a discussion of the data dictionary, which is often described as a "database about the database." It stores such information about the data as its origin, description, format, relationship to other data, usage, and access privileges. The information is stored in the form of relations that can be queried by using the query language provided by the DBMS. Some DBMS vendors offer special software that can use the data dictionary to perform reverse engineering or to insulate application programs from changes in the database structure.

KEY WORDS

analytic approach
arbiter
association
attribute
authorization matrix
before image (BI) file
CDD data definition
  language (CDDL)
characteristic
cluster
clustered environment
clustering
common data dictionary
  (CDD)
control, context
  dependent
control, statistical

control, value dependent
control, value
  independent
data base administrator
  (DBA)
data dictionary
data independence
database partition
database performance
database restructure
defragmentation
denormalization
dictionary directory
dictionary object
disk chaining
entity
entity integrity

entity subtype

entity supertype

entity type

entity-relationship
    diagram

export

foreign key

functional dependency

import

indexing

kernel

log file

logical delete

meta database

metabase

n-ary association

node

normalization

object profile

partition

primary key

pseudo DDL

retrofitting

reverse engineering

security enforcer

SQL Design Dictionary
    (SDD)

standalone environment

subtype

supertype

synthetic approach

system development

system life cycle

third normal form

transparency of change

type hierarchy

user profile

REFERENCES AND FURTHER READING

The following references contain additional materials related to the topics covered in this chapter.

1. S. ATRE, *Database: Structured Techniques for Design, Performance, and Management,* Wiley, New York, 1980.
2. C. J. DATE, *Introduction to Database Systems,* vol. I, 4th ed., Addison-Wesley, Reading, MA, 1986.
3. C. J. DATE, *Relational Database Selected Writings,* Addison-Wesley, Reading, MA, 1986.
4. MICHAEL M. GORMAN, *Managing Data Base,* QED Information Sciences, Wellesley, MA, 1984.
5. H. F. KORTH and A. SILBERSCHATZ, *Database System Concepts,* McGraw-Hill, New York, 1986.
6. DAVID S. KROENKE, *Database Processing,* Science Research Associates, Chicago, 1977.
7. SITANSU S. MITTRA, *Structured Techniques of System Analysis, Design, and Implementation,* Wiley, New York, 1988.
8. JEFFREY D. ULLMAN, *Principles of Database Systems,* Computer Science Press, Rockville, MD, 1982.

Atre [1] and Kroenke [6] have discussed the issue of database design in greater detail than have Date [2], Korth and Silberschatz [5], and Ullman [8], who have limited their discussions to the normalization theory alone. Mittra [7] has discussed the database design in the context of business system life cycle. A detailed discussion of the synthetic and analytic approaches is available in Date [3, Chapter 19].

The discussion of the functions of the DBA is adapted from Atre [1, Chapter 2]. Gorman [4, Chapters 3 and 4] has dealt with the DBA function in the broader perspective of staffing viewpoint and data administration. Date's discussion [2] is quite sketchy, but he includes the basic functions of this position.

Atre [1, Chapter 3] and Gorman [4, Chapters 6 and 8] have discussed the concept of data dictionary from a conceptual viewpoint. This should be augmented by the more technical discussions contained in Date [2, Chapter 7]. However, Date's treatment is specific to DB2 implementation.

The ORACLE commands used throughout this chapter can be found in the appropriate SQL manuals published by Oracle Corporation of Belmont, California. Similarly, discussions of CDD software are available from the CDD manuals published by Digital Equipment Corporation.

REVIEW QUESTIONS

1. Explain the concept of system life cycle. At what phase does the database design enter the cycle? Why?

2. Describe the two approaches to the design of a relational database. Which approach is suitable for what type of problems?

3. Define and give examples of the three types of entities used in the synthetic approach. How do you correlate them with the components of an entity–relationship model?

4. What is the need for primary and foreign keys in designing a database?

5. What is a pseudo DDL? Why is it designed with a SQL-like snytax? What syntax would you choose in a non-SQL environment?

6. Why do you need a database restructure? How do you perform this task?

7. Comment on the statement: The performance of a database depends on the efficiency of both the conceptual and the internal levels.

8. What role does a common data dictionary play in database restructure?

9. Define entity subtypes and supertypes. What is a type hierarchy?

10. Discuss some of the major issues related to database maintenance.

11. What is meant by the clustered environment for a computer? How does it affect the performance of the DBMS?

12. Discuss the importance of backup and recovery of a database. How are ORACLE's export and import processes related to the backup process?

13. What is meant by fragmentation of database storage space? Why is it bad for performance?

14. In ORACLE, how does the space definition clause help in reducing fragmentation?

15. Describe the partition mechanism used by ORACLE for the physical storage of data.

16. What are the benefits of installing database utilities in memory?

17. Describe the structure and use of the authorization matrix to enforce database security.

18. Discuss the functions and responsibility of a DBA.

19. Define a data dictionary and explain its role in a database environment. Why is it called a meta database by some authors?

20. How is a data dictionary used for performing reverse engineering?

EXERCISES

You must have access to database installation to perform the following exercises.

1. Assume that you have a database with the three LHUDB relations UNIV, INSTR, and STUDNT. Restructure the database to optimize the design efficiency.

2. Implement the restructured database using a relational DBMS.

3. Using the methodology of Section 9.9.3(a), monitor the fragmentation of the database storage over a period of time, say six months. Check the fragmentation on a weekly basis.

4. Perform a database backup process using your restructured database.

5. Examine the data dictionary to find out the structures of the relations in the new database.

6. If you have reverse engineering capabilities, retrofit the relations from data dictionary into your account.

CHAPTER 10

CONTEMPORARY TOPICS IN RELATIONAL DATABASE SYSTEMS

10.1 SCOPE OF THE CHAPTER

In this chapter we discuss a set of heterogeneous topics dealing with current and future trends in relational database systems, although some of these topics also apply to nonrelational databases. The topics are listed below.

1. Transaction processing systems
2. Distributed databases
3. Database machines
4. Natural language as query language
5. Intelligent databases
6. Object-oriented databases
7. PROLOG database systems
8. Future trends

10.2 FEATURES OF ON-LINE TRANSACTION PROCESSING SYSTEMS

On-Line Transaction Processing (OLTP) represents an application in which a common database is available to interactive terminal users for both inquiries and updates. The database contains all the data used for the application. A transaction represents an activity that causes an update of the database (e.g., receipt of a shipment, change of a customer name) or involves data retrieval from the database in consequence of an inquiry.

The airline reservation system introduced in the mid-1960s was the first application using OLTP. Additional applications were started during the mid-1970s, some of which are:

Hotel and motel reservations

Car rentals

Large-scale banking applications such as demand/deposit teller support, automatic teller machines, and electronic funds transfer

Credit authorization systems

Trading and brokerage systems

OLTP systems exhibit the following characteristics:

1. Many terminals access and update a large database in real time.
2. The latest information in the database is the basis for real-time business decisions.
3. Each terminal accesses the database in a random fashion.
4. The system processes many small and unrelated requests for data.
5. The system will be required to grow or diversify unpredictably.
6. The system should support and maintain a consistent level of performance.

10.3 DEFICIENCIES OF RELATIONAL DATABASES IN AN OLTP ENVIRONMENT

Relational databases are decidedly superior to nonrelational databases for problem definitions, ad hoc queries, and unanticipated changes to the database structures. However, their perceived disadvantage pertains to the area of OLTP environment. The reason is that OLTP places enormous demands on all resources—software and hardware alike. The software demands include:

1. *High throughput:* high transaction rates and consistently fast response times
2. *High concurrency:* the ability to handle concurrent access by potentially hundreds of users
3. *High availability and fault tolerance:* guaranteed system uptime, such as 24 hours a day, seven days a week
4. *Large database support:* the capability to access and administer databases up to several gigabytes in size

In addition, this database must also be available for management decision support activities: the traditional "information center" role of a DBMS system. Because these demands have overwhelmed relational systems in the past, OLTP applications have traditionally used hierarchical and network DBMSs. But while these nonrelational systems may have met performance requirements, their rigid framework has made application development and maintenance a grueling process. Also, nonrelational systems have virtually prohibited upper- and midlevel managers from getting ad hoc access to the database.

When a relational DBMS processes a transaction (i.e., a retrieval or an update request), the following sequence of actions takes place:

1. Conversion of a 4GL command into a DBMS request through input parsing
2. Verification that the requested data exist in the database
3. Establishment of the data access method through the query optimization process
4. Execution of the data access method
5. Return of control to the calling program with the data

Since all of the steps above are executed at run time for each transaction, performance suffers in an OLTP environment using a relational DBMS.

10.4 MEASUREMENT OF PERFORMANCE IN OLTP

In 1985 a benchmark was introduced to measure and compare the throughput and price/performance ratios of various OLTP systems. It was comprised of three generic operations (Caniano [2, p. 51]):

1. Single interactive transaction forming the basis of a transaction-per-second (tps) rating as well as a cost-per-transaction figure
2. Minibatch transaction that updates small batches of records
3. Utility that performs batch data movement

The first operation has since been used to simulate a debit/credit transaction in a banking application and has been called TP1. However, the TP1 has not been standardized. Often vendors include only those portions of TP1 in their benchmark studies that show their particular products in the best light and omit or modify other portions without regard for the preservation of the original TP1 definition.

Since 1987 several relational DBMS vendors have used a fairly consistent version of TP1, simulating a banking transaction where a deposit or a withdrawal is made. For example, Oracle Corporation has used a TP1 that consists of updates to three relations containing account balances for each bank branch, each teller, and each account, and an insertion of a transaction record into a history relation. Update activity is randomly distributed across the database. The goal of the test is to estimate maximum throughput. Different sizes of databases have been used to compare results.

10.5 FEATURES OF RELATIONAL DBMS REQUIRED IN AN OLTP ENVIRONMENT

An OLTP system is a multiuser system and should be supported by multiple CPUs instead of a single CPU, since the latter configuration severely limits the throughput of the system. When the OLTP system using a relational DBMS executes a transaction (i.e., an update or a retrieval), the following events affect system performance negatively:

1. When a user updates a record in a relation, the entire relation, or at least the page containing the record, is locked, preventing other users from accessing that relation for retrieval or update.
2. Each update is implemented via a disk write operation in a relational database environment. Since disk I/O is slow, update-intensive OLTP applications lead to slow response time.

To make relational DBMSs more efficient for OLTP applications, the following steps should be taken:

1. Use a multiprocessing architecture to take full advantage of the CPU power of multiprocessor hardware such as VAX 6200 and VAX 8800 series, IBM 4381 and IBM 3090 mainframes, and multiprocessor UNIX platforms from vendors such as Sequent and Pyramid. Other possible configurations are VAX clusters having shared disks and multiple computers that are networked together.
2. Implement locking at the record level instead of at the block, page, or relation level. This minimizes *data contention* among users by providing the finest possible lock granularity: namely, at the record level. When one user is updating a set of records in a relation, other users can still access the remaining records of the relation for retrieval or update purposes.
3. Minimize the number of physical disk write operations because disk I/O is slow compared to memory speed. It is advisable to perform as much work as possible in the memory and postpone disk I/O operations. When a page is eventually written to a disk, it will contain updates, insertions, and deletions from multiple transactions instead of just one.

10.6 IMPLEMENTATION OF OLTP CAPABILITIES WITH RELATIONAL DBMS

As of now (December 1988), the following three vendors offer OLTP capabilities with their individual relational DBMS products: (1) Sybase, Inc., (2) Oracle Corporation, and (3) Informix Software, Inc. We shall discuss each effort separately.

(a) Sybase, Inc. In May 1987, Sybase, Inc. of Berkeley, California, marketed a distributed SQL-based relational DBMS equipped to handle OLTP applications. Data Server and Data Toolset are the two components of Sybase's product. Together they support multiuser, data-intensive, and "mission critical" applications characterizing the OLTP environment. Data Server uses a multithreaded disk I/O that results in substantial performance gains. The Data Server in a single process controls and optimizes many multiuser functions, such as task switching, scheduling, indexing, and transactions processing, that usually would fall to the computer's operating system.

This results in substantial performance increases and a decrease in CPU use. Moreover, the Data Server is multithreaded, which means that it can process SQL statements concurrently instead of lining them up to be processed at a later time. Again the performance improvement is dramatic.

Sybase's Data Server is also equipped to store and manage predefined, fully compiled procedures, including SQL queries, transaction control, and flow-logic control. The stored procedures let Sybase control data integrity and transaction logic not in the application as is usually the case, but in the database itself. The consequent reduction in network traffic adds up to an approximately 80 percent reduction in time spent on query processing.

(b) Oracle Corporation. Oracle Corporation of Belmont, California introduced their new product called TPS (Transaction Processing System) in May 1988. TPS is a part of their RDBMS version 6.0. It improves performance for OLTP applications by offering the following four capabilities:

1. *Multiprocessor support.* In a multiprocessor system TPS uses every CPU to deliver better performance. The CPUs may be clustered and share common disk storage but with separate memory for each CPU, or else they may share common disk storage and common memory and function as an integrated system.

2. *Row-level locking.* TPS locks only rows for update instead of locking blocks or pages. As a result, multiple users can retrieve and update different rows of a table at the same time. No lock escalation takes place (i.e., during the actual replacement of data during an update the lock is placed only on the affected rows).

3. *Multiversion read consistency.* If data are altered during a read operation, TPS remembers and uses an earlier version of the data to satisfy the request.

This means that update operations in OLTP environment are never blocked for executing read operations.

4. *Reduction in disk I/O.* Instead of reading from or writing to a disk during a transaction, TPS stores copies of the data in memory. Transactions then read from or write to memory. When a page is full with updates from multiple transactions, it is written to the disk. This is called a *deferred write process* and it significantly reduces disk I/O operations. Thus multiple transactions are committed in a single write operation.

In a report published in July 1988, Oracle Corporation claimed that the TP1 benchmark test showed the rates of 48.6 transactions per second (TPS) on VAX 6240 VMS, and 124.3 TPS on Sequent 5890-600E MVS. These TPS rates are claimed to be the highest ever reported by a relational DBMS with this test. To add credibility to their claim, Oracle Corporation had an expert from the Codd and Date consulting firm to direct and audit the tests.

(c) Informix Software, Inc.   Informix Software of Menlo Park, California, announced a product called INFORMIX-TURBO in September 1988. This database engine has been specially designed for OLTP applications. It has a performance monitor and some built-in tuning capabilities that can be applied to any OLTP application to custom tune it for peak efficiency. It includes the following features:

1. *Multiprocessor support.* In a multiprocessor system programs do not run faster, but they provide better response time and greatly delay the thrashing point for heavily loaded CPUs. These machines achieve better response time by spreading the workload across the available processors.

2. *Software process architecture.* INFORMIX-TURBO uses a two-process architecture, consisting of a database server process for each corresponding requester process. The database server accepts retrieval and update requests, and interacts with a memory buffer pool and disks to perform the requested operations. The requester processes handle all user interface activities, including formatting reports and processing interpreted or compiled application code.

3. *Usage of shared memory.* By using shared memory on high-volume machines such as multiprocessor systems, INFORMIX-TURBO allows for common data buffer pooling. Thereby it consolidates many small buffer pools into one large buffer pool that contains more disk data and reduces the number of overall disk accesses.

4. *Reduction of disk I/O.* INFORMIX-TURBO uses advanced internal and disk data structures and several tunable parameters, such as the size of the shared memory. It controls the basic unit of disk I/O in the form of a logical page instead of allowing the operating system to control this basic unit. Page size

is set according to the capabilities of the CPU on which INFORMIX-TURBO will operate and can range from 1 to 4 kilobytes in size. Thereby it allows the database server to behave in a fashion optimized for the particular machine.

10.7 DISTRIBUTED DATABASE SYSTEMS

A *distributed database system* is a database that is not stored in its entirety at a single physical location, but instead is spread across a network of locations that are geographically dispersed and connected via communication links. A distributed system consists of a collection of sites or nodes, connected into a communication network. Each site, in turn, constitutes a database system in its own right in the sense that the site has a separate database of its own that is handled by the copy of the DBMS installed at the site. As such, each site enjoys a very high degree of autonomy. Thus a distributed database system is really the union of a set of individual centralized databases, one at each site. The sites of a distributed database system may be distributed either over a large geographical area (such as the United States) or over a small geographical area (such as a single building or a number or adjacent buildings). The former type of network is referred to as a *long-haul network*, while the latter is referred to as a *local-area network*.

Since the sites in long-haul networks are distributed physically over a large geographical area, the communication links are likely to be relatively slow and less reliable than with local-area networks. Typical long-haul links are telephone lines, microwave links, and satellite channels. In contrast, since all the sites in local-area networks are close to each other, the communication links are of higher speed and lower error rate than their counterparts in long-haul networks. The most common links are twisted pair, baseband coaxial, broadband coaxial, and fiber optics.

Architecturally, a distributed database system is designed as a graph, where the sites are the nodes of the graph and the communication links are the edges of the graph. This representation satisfies the algebraic definition of a graph. Two sites *A* and *B* are connected if there exists a path in the graph between the nodes representing the sites *A* and *B*. Depending on the connectivity requirements imposed on the graph by its underlying network topology, we can have a distributed system having a fully or partially connected network, a tree-structured network, a star network, or a ring network. Figure 10–1 shows examples of all these networks.

If a node fails in distributed system graph, that site becomes unoperational. Also, if an edge fails (i.e., if the communication link between two sites fails), those sites may become temporarily disconnected from the rest of the network. It is possible for a distributed system graph, which is originally connected, to degenerate into a set of disconnected subgraphs such that each subgraph is connected, but no edge exists connecting any two nodes from two different subgraphs.

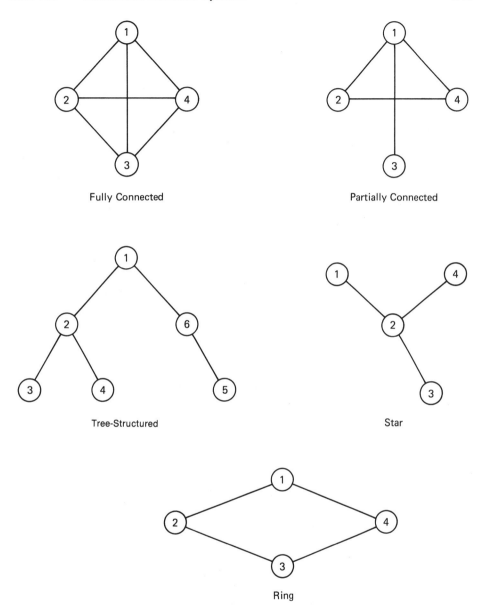

Figure 10–1 Examples of networks.

We now give an example of a distributed database system. Assume that Long Hill University maintains three satellite campuses, at Nashua, New Hampshire; New York City; and Washington, D.C. Consequently, LHUDB is fragmented so that each campus maintains its own database but any campus can access any other location via the distributed system. The attribute SECNO in the relation

CRSLST identifies the location of the campus as follows:

00–50	Boston
51–60	Nashua, N.H.
61–80	New York City
81–99	Washington, D.C.

Let us suppose that the Registrar's Office wants to print a student list for course CS579, Database Management, for fall 1988. The following query is run:

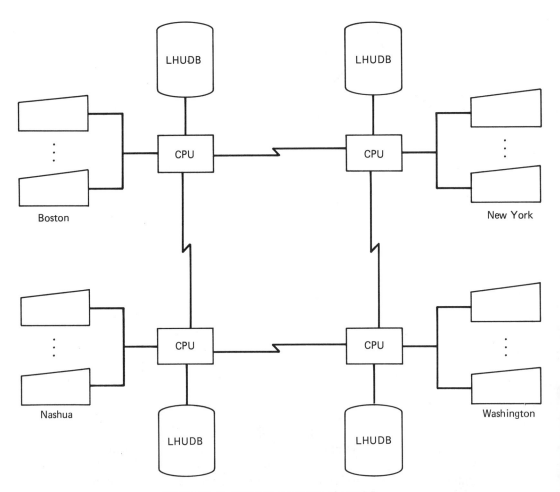

Figure 10–2   Distributed version of LHUDB.

```
SELECT SNAME, MAJOR, DEGREE FROM
  STUDNT, CRSLST WHERE
  CRSLST.SID = STUDNT.SSNO
  AND CRSLST.CNO = 'CS579'
  AND CRSLST.OFRNG = 'FALL 88'
ORDER BY CRSLST.SECNO;
```

To process this query it is necessary to retrieve data from copies of the relations STUDNT and CRSLST kept at each satellite campus and at Boston main campus. Data communication links connecting Boston with the three satellite locations are used to transmit the retrieved data to Boston, where the query is generated. Figure 10–2 shows the distributed LHUDB configuration.

10.8 OBJECTIVES OF A DISTRIBUTED DATABASE SYSTEM

Two primary objectives of a distributed database system are: (1) location transparency, and (2) replication transparency. We discuss each item separately.

10.8.1 Location Transparency

Location transparency means that the user need not know where a specific data item resides within the distributed system. When a user logged in Boston, for example, enters the query of Section 10.7, he or she does not need to know whether the data to be retrieved reside in Boston or Nashua or New York City or Washington. The query is processed as if all of the required data reside locally in Boston. The data dictionary of the distributed system keeps track of the location of each data element and uses that information to process the query. Data residing at a remote location are accessed via the data communication link. Three scenarios are possible:

1. Remote data are moved to Boston and are processed there.
2. Remote data are processed at remote site(s) and results are fetched to Boston.
3. A combination of scenarios 1 and 2 occurs.

In all cases the logic of the application program is simplified and data can be moved from one location to another, depending on the data usage pattern without necessitating any reprogramming.

10.8.2 Replication Transparency

Data *replication* means that a given logical data element can have multiple stored values at different locations within the distributed system. *Replication transpar-*

ency requires that the maintenance (i.e., location, updating, and synchronizing) of the replicated data elements will be handled by the system and not by the user. If the data are replicated in a distributed system, the system must support replication transparency. When data are replicated, we get both improved performance and improved data availability, since applications can use local replicas and hence do not depend on data communication links, which are often responsible for slow response time due to traffic volume along the links.

Location and replication transparency problems involve the internal level of the database as opposed to the external or conceptual levels. Distribution does not have any effect on the user's view of the data, the specific language used, or the logical database design.

10.9 REQUIREMENTS OF A DISTRIBUTED DATABASE SYSTEM

To meet the objectives described in Section 10.8, a distributed system should have the following features:

1. *Reliable communications.* Message from node A should be delivered to message at node B without any garbling and only once and in the order that it was sent from A. Proper communication software ensures these requirements.

2. *Data fragmentation.* Data may be partitioned into row-and-column subsets (called *subrelations*) of a given relation by means of projection and selection. This is necessary if logical data elements are replicated in physical storage. A subrelation is called a *horizontal* or a *vertical* fragmentation according as it is derived from the parent relation through selection or projection, respectively. The parent relation can be constructed from its subrelations by join or union operations, as discussed below.

Let a relation R be decomposed into m horizontal fragmentation $R_1, \ldots,$ R_m, defined by

$$R_i = R \text{ WHERE } P_i, \quad i = 1, \ldots, m$$

where P_i is the predicate of the selection condition producing R_i. Then

$$R = \overset{m}{\underset{i=1}{\text{UNION}}} R_i$$

Similarly, let $S_1, \ldots, S_n$ be n vertical fragmentations of R derived by taking appropriate projections of R. Then we can write

$$R = \overset{n}{\underset{i=1}{\text{JOIN}}} S_i$$

where it is assumed that attributes are properly repeated among $S_1, \ldots, S_n$, so that the join operations can be performed. If, however, such repeated attributes do not exist among $S_1, \ldots, S_n$, the system should add a hidden attribute, called *tuple identifier*, to each tuple in R. Each projection $S_i, i = 1, \ldots, n$, must contain this tuple identifier as a common linking attribute. Then the joins can be performed using the tuple identifier. This attribute is globally unique so that no two different tuples can have the same value of the identifier. For example, ORACLE RDBMS assigns a hidden attribute called ROWID to each tuple in a relation. But ROWID is not displayed in a SELECT statement such as

```
SELECT * FROM. . .
```

ROWID is displayed only when the SELECT statement explicitly mentions it. The ROWID is represented as a hexadecimal number that contains the address of the tuple. It provides the following three pieces of information necessary to locate a tuple:

a. Logical partition block number identifying the logical block containing the tuple within the partition

b. Row sequence number identifying the location of the tuple within the logical block

c. Partition ID giving the name of the partition

    3. *Transaction management.* A *transaction* is a logical unit of work that is initiated by an *agent*. An agent is a process executing a transaction at a specific node. As an agent executes, it may cause other agents to start executing at other sites, and so on. For example, a transaction using data from multiple nodes requires that the system recognize these nodes as logically related. The system treats all these nodes as a unit for recovery and concurrency control. Thus a query on CRSLST at Nashua and at New York involves two agents, one at Nashua and one at New York, which must be locked together during the execution of the transaction.

10.10 SUITABILITY OF THE RELATIONAL DATA MODEL FOR DISTRIBUTED DATABASE SYSTEMS

Most of the DBMS packages, relational or nonrelational, that are available today (December 1988) provide little or no support for distributed database systems. However, the present trend indicates that distribution of data over geographically dispersed sites will become crucial in the near future. Relational data models are specially suitable for implementing distributed databases due to the following reasons (Schmidt and Brodie [22, p. vii]):

    1. Relational databases offer great decomposition flexibility when planning how a database is to be distributed over a network of computer systems. Tables may be sliced vertically or horizontally, and they may be glued together by joins and unions (by contrast, databases based on the network or hierarchical models are constrained in their decomposition by the entanglement of their navigation links).

2. The relational operators provide great recomposition power for dynamic combination of decentralized information (by contrast, the network and hierarchial models do not possess operators of comparable power).

3. The concise high-level languages of relational systems offer considerable economy of transmission compared with the record-at-a-time languages of nonrelational systems.

4. The concise high-level languages of relational systems make it feasible for a node to analyze the intent of a transaction and speedily decompose it into three parts that can be handled locally and into parts that will have to be shipped off to other nodes.

10.11 ADVANTAGES OF A DISTRIBUTED SYSTEM

A distributed database system offers the following advantages:

1. *Local autonomy.* A distributed system is suitable for an organization that is physically distributed over multiple locations. It allows the local users to have more control over their own data instead of depending on another remote location. It also allows them access to data at other locations.

2. *Capacity and incremental growth.* It is possible to add one or more sites to an existing distributed system to meet any expanded usage. This is easier to do than a total restructuring of an existing centralized system.

3. *Reliability and availability.* The system continues to function at a reduced level even when an individual site is down or when an individual communication link is not available. This is not possible for a centralized system. If data are replicated, replicated entities are available as long as at least one copy of these entities is available.

4. *Faster query processing.* If a query involves data at several sites, as in the example in Section 10.7, it is possible to split the query into subqueries that can be executed in parallel by several sites. This speeds up the query processing. If the query involves data that are replicated, the system can direct queries to the least heavily loaded sites to provide quicker processing of the query.

10.12 DISADVANTAGES OF A DISTRIBUTED SYSTEM

The primary disadvantages of a distributed system involve the communication system that is used for transmitting data, messages, and query results, as discussed below.

1. Communication links are rather slow compared with access times of local storage devices such as disks. ARPANET has a data transfer rate of 25,000 bytes/second, whereas a disk drive has a data transfer rate of 1,000,000 bytes/second.

2. Communication systems have a high access delay time.

3. Messages are expensive in terms of CPU instructions executed. To send a message and get the acknowledgment involves 5,000 to 10,000 instructions of the operating system and communication control code.

4. Different communication systems have widely different characteristics. Data transfer rates can vary by as much as three orders of magnitude and access delay by as much as six. It may or may not be possible to propagate updates to all copies of an object in real time. It is generally true that in a centralized system the main performance objective is to minimize the number of disk accesses, whereas in a distributed system the goal is to minimize the volume of data and the number of messages transmitted across the communication lines.

10.13 SPECIAL ISSUES FOR DISTRIBUTED DATABASE SYSTEMS

In this section we discuss two special issues related to a distributed system: (1) query processing, and (2) update propagation.

10.13.1 Query Processing

In Section 10.11 we briefly mentioned the advantages that a distributed system can provide in processing a query that involves data in multiple sites. The data may be replicated or fragmented or both. Depending on how we determine the strategy to access the required data at multiple sites, the processing cost can vary enormously. Date [4, pp. 303–305] has given an example where the communication time needed for moving data around can range from 1 second to 2.3 days under a set of assumptions on relation sizes and communication time.

Let us examine the query of Section 10.7 once more. This query is used in Boston, but data for the query reside at Nashua, New York, and Washington. Possible communication strategies can be listed as follows:

1. Transmit all the data from the three satellite campuses to Boston and perform the joins in Boston.

2. Transmit data from New York to Nashua and perform the joins at Nashua; transmit data from Washington to Boston and perform the joins in Boston; finally, transmit the result from Nashua to Boston and produce the final result after eliminating duplicate rows, if any. Note that the join processing at Nashua can be done concurrently with that in Boston, resulting in reduced response time.

3. In a variation of strategy 2, joins are processed at sites other than Nashua and Boston.

The communication time depends on the extent of data replication and fragmentation among the sites. Since communication time is slower than disk access time, the goal in deciding an optimal strategy is to reduce the size of the result processed locally before transmitting it to another site. Thereby the volume of data to be transmitted is reduced, resulting in reduced communication time. As a rule of thumb, the following formula can be used to estimate the communication time:

$$\text{communication time } = \text{ total access delay } + \frac{\text{total data volume}}{\text{data transfer rate}}$$

Using the process of semijoin (Korth and Silberschatz [14, pp. 420–422]), we can reduce the number of tuples that are not needed in computing a future join. Such unneeded tuples are then not transmitted to another site. The theory of semijoins is beyond the scope of the present discussion.

10.13.2 Update Propagation

If data are replicated in a distributed database, each time a data element is updated at one site it must be updated at every other site where it is stored. This process of update is called update *propagation*, since the updated value must be propagated to multiple storage sites. If a relation is fragmented horizontally or vertically so that a given data element is replicated, update propagation ensures that all affected fragments are updated.

The primary problem with implementing update propagation is that one or more of the sites where the data have to be updated may be unavailable because the sites are down or the communication links to those sites are down or both. To solve this problem, we can proceed as follows:

Suppose that a data element X is stored in sites $S_1, \ldots, S_n$ in a distributed system. Let X be updated to Y and let us assume that sites S_i and S_j are unavailable at the instant of update. Then update X to Y at the remaining $n - 2$ locations that are available, and keep a list showing that S_i and S_j are not yet updated. As soon as S_i and S_j are connected to the rest of the system, update X to Y at these sites. However, do not allow the updated value Y to be available at any site until all n sites have been updated. This all-or-none approach ensures data integrity.

10.14 DISTRIBUTED DATA DICTIONARY

In a distributed system the data dictionary (see Section 9.11) includes not only the usual information on relations, clustering, indexing, user access, and so on, but also all the necessary control information about the location, fragmentation, and replication of data in the relations. As a result, when a query is processed for retrieval or update of data, the data dictionary can provide the necessary information regarding location and replication transparency, as well as update propagation. The distributed data dictionary is stored in a variety of ways, depending on the DBMS and its vendor. Usually, an arbitrary subset of the dictionary is stored in a given site depending on that site's requirements. The full data dictionary can then be retrieved by taking a union of all the local copies of the dictionary. It is understood that some overlaps exist among the different local copies stored at different sites. Sometimes a *caching mechanism* is employed to improve the efficiency of repeated access to dictionary entries stored at remote sites. Under this scheme a reference from a local site L to a dictionary entry E stored at a remote site R causes a copy of E to be retrieved from R and kept in a cache at L; subsequent references to E from L can be directed to that copy instead. However, the caching mechanism itself leads to additional overhead, because the cached copy at L must be discarded if the original remote entry at R is updated.

10.15 GATEWAY COMPUTER SYSTEM

A *gateway computer system* is a device (i.e., computer and operating system) providing access to different manufacturers' networks and computers. The *gateway* is a connection between two or more computer systems such that it understands the protocols on both sides, transfers information to and from systems, and participates in system-level reliability. The gateway computer interfaces with heterogeneous systems and allows diverse DBMSs to participate in a distributed network. Thus the gateway computer provides automated access to other computers and other computer networks and databases, whether stored locally or at remote sites. If two or more of the computers accessed via gateway were not designed to communicate with one another, they are called *incompatible hosts*. A gateway system allows incompatible hosts to share data and communicate back and forth. The user gets a single entry point into other computers and databases. The software underlying the gateway system is transparent to the user except for the messages displayed on the terminal when accessing other systems. A variety of communication networks, such as DDN, Tymnet, and Decnet, can be used for communication purposes. We now give two examples of gateway computer systems.

10.15.1 Intelligent Gateway Processor

The Intelligent Gateway Processor (IGP) was prepared by Control Data Corporation under contract to Lawrence Livermore National Laboratory in 1986. IGP is a complex software that allows the user to connect to other computers using the IGP's connectivity feature and to transfer files of information between IGP and other systems. The software has often been described as a "limousine service" between the user's system and the remote system that is being accessed. This means that by logging at his or her local system, the user is connected to the remote system.

The whole process takes place in three stages (see Figure 10–3):

1. The user connects to the remote system.
2. The user logs on the remote system.
3. The user transfers files to the remote system from his or her local system.

We now describe each stage separately in more detail (see Figure 10–4):

1. *Connection to Remote System*
   The user can connect to the remote system in three different ways:
   a. Select an option number or a system name from the IGP Main Menu.
      Option 10 of the IGP Main Menu contains a list of remote systems accessible from the user's local system. By selecting this option a submenu is displayed on the user's terminal showing a list of codes in the form 10.X (e.g., 10.1, 10.2, . . .) and a list of corresponding remote sys-

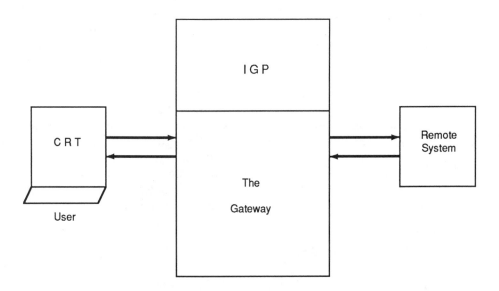

Figure 10–3 Overview of IGP operation.

tem names. The user enters a code or a system name of his or her choice from the displayed menu and then presses carriage return (CR). In response the IGP displays several lines of message identifying the remote system with which the connection is requested. The last line of the display must be a prompt for the USER NAME at the remote system to signify that connection has been established.

b. Use the CONNECT command and the system name.

The submenu at Option 10 of the IGP Main Menu (see step (a) above) displays a list of remote system names. The user can select any one of them and enter the following command at his or her terminal

CONNECT system-name

followed by (CR). In response the IGP displays several lines of acknowledgment message that ends up with

CONNECTION ESTABLISHED TO system-name

to signify that the remote system is now accessible.

c. Use the DIAL command.

To use this option the user must know the phone number of the remote system to be accessed. He or she enters the command DIAL at the terminal and presses (CR). In response the IGP displays a set of available options such as phone number, baud rate, parity, etc. The user enters the response to each option and presses (CR) at the end. IGP displays several lines of acknowledgment message that ends up with the full name of the remote system indicating that it is now accessible.

2. *Logon to Remote System*

Once the connection is established to the remote system, the log-in prompt for the remote system is displayed. The user enters his or her user name and password for the remote system in response to the prompt. If they are invalid, IGP disconnects the user from the remote system and displays the following message

⟨⟨⟨Press RETURN to continue⟩⟩⟩

Otherwise, the user is logged on the remote system and is ready to transfer files between the local and the remote systems.

3. *Transfer of Files to Remote System*

The user proceeds as follows to transfer a file from one location to the other:

a. User types (ESC) followed by (CTRL-a) or tilda(˜) followed by (CTRL-a), depending on his or her local system.

IGP asks for the terminal type of the user.

b. User enters the type of terminal such as VT 100, TVI 950, etc. and presses (CR).

   IGP asks for the name of the file to be transferred.

c. User enters the name of the file and presses (CR).

   IGP displays the contents of the file on the terminal of the user.

d. User types (ESC) followed by (CTRL-a) or tilda (̃) followed by (CTRL-a), depending on his or her local system, to close the file.

   IGP displays the message "... Output stopped." and disconnects the user from the remote system.

10.15.2 ASCENT

ASCENT software package was developed by Control Data Corporation (CDC) during the mid-1980s. It provides more capabilities than does the IGP software described above. ASCENT is an integrated suite of products that include AS-CENT∗ gateway, ASCENT∗ mail, and ASCENT∗ plus. These components can function independently or together to integrate an organization's hardware and software needs. ASCENT∗ gateway allows any user to access any host from any terminal and use that host as a native user. It provides connectivity for multiple terminal types and for noncompatible hosts operating under multiple communication disciplines which can be remotely located. If any existing software is upgraded or any additional hardware is procured, the gateway will link together the new and existing systems. No changes to current databases or software will be needed.

ASCENT∗ plus furnishes a menu-driven common user interface that allows any user to access any resource with a single command or menu selection. Multiple log-ins and passwords are not needed. Users can move data among different systems at different sites, updating existing files and creating new ones. Full control of data security is ensured. ASCENT∗ mail performs electronic mail functions.

ASCENT is based on UNIX operating system. However, it allows the system managers to perform the following tasks without a thorough knowledge of UNIX:

1. Add, delete, and modify user accounts.

2. Manage the daily activities necessary to keep a UNIX system running smoothly.

3. Control the access of individual users or user groups.

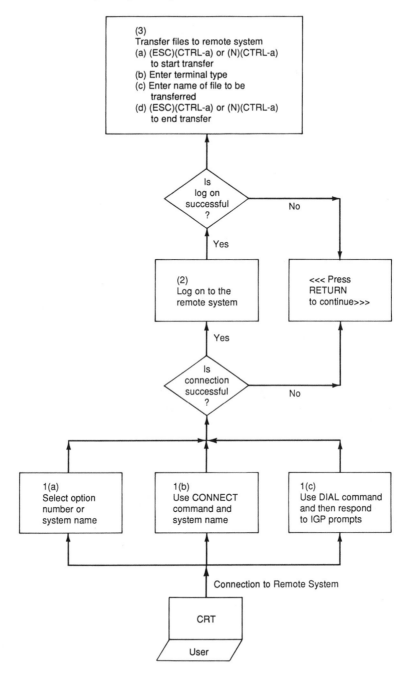

Figure 10–4   File transfer via IGP.

4. Develop multiple menus that permit only authorized users to perform specific functions.

CDC provides the following four kinds of service to a customer:

1. Preimplementation analysis of information processing requirements, system requirements, user needs, and training needs
2. Implementation service
3. Customization service
4. Ongoing support service

Access to ASCENT is provided through a hierarchy of menus. The user selects an option and is prompted for more information for the next level of action. Each menu contains submenus that offer a group of functionally related options. The ASCENT menu option numbers, consisting of alternating numerical and alphabetic characters, appear in the left column on each menu. To access a specific option the user types the option number at the ASCENT prompt "⇒" and presses ⟨CR⟩. Depending on the ASCENT option requested, the option number may display another menu or activate an ASCENT resource. The ASCENT commands appear in lowercase letters on the right side of each menu. The command name

---

CONTROL   DATA   CORPORATION

A S C E N T

Type ? for Help	Type q to Quit

Type OPTION or COMMAND   ===>

OPTION	RESOURCE	COMMAND
+	Main Menu	plus
1	Gateway	gateway
2	Electronic Mail	mail
3	Converse with Others	converse
4	Desk Top	desk
5	Time Manager	time
6	System Utilities	utilities
7	Custom Applications	applications
8	Help	help

Figure 10–5 ASCENT main menu.

acts in the same manner as the option number. Depending on the ASCENT option requested, the command may display another menu or activate an ASCENT resource. The user may type the command in lowercase letters at the "$\Rightarrow$" prompt and press $\langle$CR$\rangle$.

When a user logs in, the main menu (see Figure 10–5) appears with a list of eight options. The user selects any one of them and is directed to the next level of functions.

10.16 DISTRIBUTED DATABASE SYSTEM IN A CLUSTERED ENVIRONMENT

A *cluster* is defined as a set of CPUs linked together via local-area network (LAN) and sharing a common disk farm for storage. The CPUs are called the nodes in a cluster and they do not share memory. Instead, the nodes communicate with one another via messages. The distributed database system in a clustered environment avoids the problems of a long-haul network associated with a geographically distributed database system. Thus in a clustered environment the access times are dominated by disk access time instead of by data communication time. Consequently, a different type of architecture called *requester server design* has been proposed for distributed databases in a clustered environment (Gray [8, p. 48]).

Let us assume that a clustered database environment consists of two clusters, CL1 and CL2. The scenario works in exactly the same way for more than two clusters. The application using the database is called the *requester* and must reside on both CL1 and CL2. The DBMS and the database are called the *server* and should reside on only one cluster, say CL1. Thus CL1 contains both the requester and the server, whereas CL2 contains only the requester. Now suppose that a query (retrieval or update) is issued at CL1. Since the database is local for CL1, the query is processed as in a nondistributed environment. But if the query is issued at CL2 for which the database on CL1 is remote, the requester–server model of communication is invoked. Under this scheme the necessary data for the query are first requested and then retrieved through the communication links. Appropriate LAN and networking software for the DBMS must reside on both CL1 and CL2 in order to implement the requester–server model.

Oracle Corporation marketed the networking software SQL*Net to implement the foregoing scenario, except that the model is called *client–server* instead of requester–server. SQL*Net must reside on CL1 and CL2 and a database link must be created on CL2 so that the link points to the database on CL1.

10.17 DATABASE MACHINES

A *database machine* is defined as a dedicated, backend processor with auxiliary disk storage, attached to one or more host computers running applications. It is usually perceived as a conventional processor with a stripped-down operating system and a full-fledged DBMS. The original motivation for the database machines was essentially to improve system performance. But that goal has not yet materialized. As of now (December 1988), the database machine's real potential appears to be as a database server in a LAN, where the host computers are of different types. The database machine offloads some or all of the DBMS activities from the host computer to the backend processor. Its basic operation consists of the following steps (see Figure 10–6):

1. An application program executing in the host issues a database request in the normal manner.
2. The host interface code intercepts that request and ships it to the backend machine.
3. The backend interface code receives the request and passes it to the DBMS.
4. The DBMS executes the request and produces a result.
5. The backend interface code intercepts the result and ships it back to the host.
6. The host interface code receives the result and passes it to the application.

A database machine environment offers a flexibility of configuration in that it can consist of:

1. One host connected to several database machines if the overall system is very heavily database oriented
2. One database machine connected to several host computers, resulting in a distributed database environment, thereby permitting these hosts to share data and database management functions

There are two major categories of database machines: (1) dedicated by conventional backend computer, and (2) specialized hardware device known as associative disks. These two categories are described in the following two subsections.

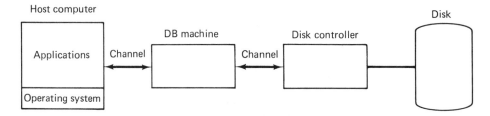

Figure 10–6 Operation of a database machine.

10.17.1 Dedicated Backend Computer

The *dedicated backend computer* database machine consists of a conventional general-purpose computer running a relational DBMS. The primary goal is to improve performance by increasing throughput, although the response time gets longer due to additional communications between the host computer and the backend machine. A rule of thumb known as the *offloading theorem* is often used to examine the cost-effectiveness of the configuration. The theorem is stated below (Date [4, p. 348]):

For offloading to be cost-effective, the amount of work offloaded should be an order of magnitude greater than the amount of work involved in doing the offloading.

The DBMS on the backend machine supports its own file system for the internal level of the database. The portion of memory not occupied by the DBMS is dedicated to buffers that are managed by the DBMS using algorithms that utilize the DBMS's knowledge of data access patterns. The I/O operations consist of:

1. Acceptance of an input message carrying a database request
2. Transmission of an output message carrying the result of such a request

10.17.2 Associative Disk Approach

The basic idea behind *associative disks* is to apply some hardware search logic directly to the data as they are read from the disk. As a result, the amount of data transmitted across the channel to the host computer is reduced so that the amount of processing to be done by the software is reduced also. For example, a conventional disk can be augmented by incorporating a microprocessor with each read/write head of the disk. Every such microprocessor then applies some simple selection logic to the data as they pass under the corresponding read/write head. When all these processors work in parallel, several tracks of data can be searched simultaneously.

Associative disks are good for a specific type of processing known as the library search problem. This type of processing involves very complex queries, but these queries have the property that every record can be identified as being, or not being, a hit by inspecting nothing other than the record itself. For more conventional applications which involve queries that can only be satisfied by inspecting multiple record types, associative disks are not found to be cost-effective.

10.17.3 Commercially Available Database Machines

XDMS (Experimental Database Management System), the first backend system, was produced by Bell Laboratories at Piscataway, New Jersey, in the early 1970s.

Its host was a UNIVAC-1108 and the backend was a Digital Scientific META-4 minicomputer. ADABAS Database Machine, the first commercially available machine, was produced by Software AG of America in 1980. Its host was IBM/370 and the backend could be any machine compatible with the host.

Britton Lee, Inc. of Los Gatos, California, has been a major vendor of database machines. In 1980 they marketed IDM 500 (Intelligent Database Machine) as a hybrid system consisting of a backend machine together with some optional associative disk hardware. Input to IDM 500 is a user request in SQL-like query language. A front-end machine receives the request, converts it into parsed form and submits to the backend machine. The backend machine then performs the database functions. More recently, in the mid-1980s they introduced BL300, a low-end system that can work as a shared database machine for use in a diverse network of PCs and workstations. The vendor claims that a benchmark test showed that BL 300 performs three-and-a-half-times faster than a VAX 11/782 running INGRES. Britton Lee is currently developing a high-end database machine called BL8000 scheduled for release in early 1989. The vendor prefers to call it a shared database system instead of a database machine.

Teradata, Inc. of Los Angeles is another major vendor of database machines. The product is called DBC/1012 and supports several relational DBMS products. It works in a parallel processing environment and uses the vendor's Ynet intelligent network linking interface processors, communications processors, and access module processors. It currently provides a cumulative 265 MIPS via 260 parallel CPUs. The host can be an IBM mainframe or a compatible Amdahl V8. Britton Lee currently claims 850 installations compared to fewer than 100 users for Teradata. But Teradata's users are far larger and have parallel processing.

Charles River Data Systems of Framingham, Massachusetts introduced in 1989 a database machine called the Relational Accelerator. It is a dedicated database engine that enhances the performance of ORACLE applications in a VAX/VMS environment. It can be attached to an existing VAX computer and allows the VAX to run application software while the Relational Accelerator performs backend ORACLE RDBMS processing.

REAL Database Corporation of Sunnyvale, California introduced in 1989 two database machines called the ServerCharger 50 and the ServerCharger 100. Both of them are used in multiple platforms such as VAX superminis, IBM mainframes, UNIX minis, and LAN-based workstations and increase the performance and reliability of the ORACLE RDBMS based applications running on these computers. They are attached directly to the computers and, according to the vendor, increase the throughput of the ORACLE RDBMS by 50−200 tps. The ServerCharger 50 is described as an entry level machine. The base configuration consists of four to eight loosely coupled processors that integrate with the existing ORACLE environment. The components of the ServerCharger 50 are: DBA Processor, RDBMS Processor, Network I/O Processor, and Disk I/O Processor. The ServerCharger 100 is intended for more extensive use and can be configured for a distributed database system. It uses the same four basic processors as does the ServerCharger 50, but the base configuration consists of five to twelve loosely coupled processors resulting in more processing power than the ServerCharger 50.

10.18 QUERY PROCESSING USING NATURAL LANGUAGE

A nonprocedural query language such as SQL is a far cry from the plain English language used for querying a relational database. With the current advances in natural-language representation (a branch of artificial intelligence), a trend is emerging to provide a limited form of English as a query language. An end user would normally like to query the database in English rather than using a nonprocedural query language. To implement such queries, the DBMS must have an extra layer of software to process the English language queries. The software must have the following components:

1. *Query analyzer*. The primary functions of the query analyzer are to:
   a. Scan the query and extract all the keywords that belong to a user-defined dictionary available to the system.
   b. Examine the meaning of each keyword given in the dictionary and then interpret the meaning of the query.
   c. Ask the user for the meaning(s) of keyword(s) that do not exist in the dictionary and incorporate these words in the dictionary if the user so desires.
   d. Recognize the basic query from a set of seemingly infinite English variations of the same.
2. *Dialogue handler*. This part carries on an interactive dialogue with the user to determine if its interpretation of the user's query is correct.

The above is only a theoretical framework. Any RDBMS with a natural-language query capability always includes a query analyzer with at least the first three of the four capabilities listed above, and also a dialogue handler. The fourth capability of the query handler is still an active area of research, because the capability of establishing the equivalence of a variety of English statements, whether in imperative form or interrogative form, requires a deep semantic analysis of the statements. The dialogue handler's capability depends on that of the query analyzer. As a minimum, the dialogue handler displays the interpretation of the user's English language query. Once the user signifies approval, the DBMS processes the query and displays the result.

As an example, let us process the following query:

Tell me which instructors are associate professors or professors.

Conceptually, the following steps are taken:

1. Query analyzer
   a. Extracts the three keywords "instructor," "associate professor," and "professor" from the query
   b. Searches the user-defined dictionary to find the "meanings" of these keywords
   c. Finds "associate professor" and "professor" as values for the attribute RANK
   d. Searches the data dictionary and finds out that RANK is an attribute in the relation INSTR
   e. Determines that a search of the INSTR relation is needed to process the query
   f. Supplies the SQL reserve words SELECT,FROM, and WHERE in proper slots within a SQL query template
   g. Formulates the SQL version of the user's query in the form

   ```
   SELECT * FROM INSTR WHERE
   RANK = "AssocProf" OR
   RANK = "Professor";
   ```

   h. Transfers control to the Dialogue Handler
2. Dialogue handler
   a. Displays the English version of the query above, say, in the form

      Find all fields from records of instructors whose rank is associate professor or professor.

   b. Asks the user if that interpretation is valid.
3. User responds "No" and indicates that he or she wants only the names of the instructors with those ranks.
4. Dialogue Handler transfers control to the Query Analyzer for final processing.
5. Query Analyzer formulates the revised version of the query, namely,

   ```
   SELECT INAME FROM INSTR WHERE
   RANK= 'AssocProf' OR
   RANK= 'Professor';
   ```

If the user selects any other version of the query, the query analyzer follows the same procedure and finds or does not find the solution, depending on the complexity of the query. During the scanning process the query analyzer ignores irrelevant words such as "tell me," "give me," and "what are." This process of keyword matching was used in some of the earlier natural-language interfaces, such as ELIZA, MENTOR, and PARRY (see Colby [3] and Martin [17]). Of course, they did not involve any database query language.

10.19 IMPLEMENTATION SOFTWARE FOR KEYWORD MATCHING

Several DBMS packages currently available support the natural-language queries. Examples are: CLOUT, INTELLECT, SAVVY, THEMIS, NATURAL LINK, and METAMORPH. The technology used in them can be described as follows:

1. Natural-language processors interactively retrieve all information about the relations and tuples used in the queries.
2. It then examines the user-defined dictionary of words to interpret the meaning of the query.
3. It allows the user to change interactively any definition displayed on the screen.

Depending on the DBMS used, the user can type the query in plain English. CLOUT, SAVVY, INTELLECT, and METAMORPH use this approach. Alternatively, the user can formulate the query by linking together different words and phrases (e.g., nouns, connectors such as AND and OR, qualifiers, etc.) from various windows displayed on the screen. Each window on the screen contains a different type of word. NATURAL LINK uses this approach.

10.20 SEMANTIC ANALYSIS BY DATA TALKER

Data Talker, a software by Natural Language Inc., provides a natural-language interface to the database query processing by performing a true semantic analysis of the query instead of a mere keyword matching. Its main features are summarized below (adapted from Manferdelli [16]).

1. *Front end:* performs spelling correction, morphology analysis, dictionary lookup, and constructs the word lattice used by the parser.
2. *Parser:* converts the sentence as represented in the word lattice into a grammatical structure similar to a sentence diagram.
3. *Semantic interface:* translates the diagrammed sentence into the internal representation language. The latter is a hybrid of semantic network and predicate logic. This representation distinguishes Data Talker from other keyword-based systems.
4. *Generator:* converts into English statements in the representation language.
5. *Interpreter:* contains the deductive reasoning capability of the system. It is

called by the semantic interface to help resolve references, decide among multiple possible interpretations, and perform certain noun and verb transformations.

6. *Database interface:* translates statements in the representation language into database queries.

7. *Conversation monitor:* guides the conversation between the user and the system. It is comparable to the dialogue handler discussed earlier.

8. *Dictionary:* contains English words, currently numbered at about 9000. It is possible to add more.

9. *Concepts:* consist of the internal notions of predicates, named objects, and statements. Set and membership hierarchies are maintained in this structure.

10. *Rules:* consist of the "facts" that make up the rule base of the system. Rules can handle quantification, sets, and general logical constructs.

10.21 INTELLIGENT DATABASES

Intelligent databases represent an attempt to merge the relational database technology with the knowledge engineering. The goal is to develop expert systems that can interface with existing large databases to allow users to derive conclusions that cannot be drawn directly from the databases. The basic approach is to build a separate knowledge base consisting of the rules that use the data in the databases to arrive at conclusions.

An *intelligent database* is defined to be an application that combines a relational database consisting of relations, a knowledge base consisting of rules, and an inference mechanism that is activated by queries from end users and draws conclusions by using data from the relations to execute rules in the knowledge base. The main problem in developing intelligent databases is structural in nature. Relational databases emphasize syntax or format over semantics or meaning, whereas knowledge bases stress semantics over syntax.

Expert systems are currently gaining popularity in business environment. Intelligent databases can be used to enforce rules and policies of an organization in a computer-oriented work environment. Schur [23, p. 27] describes the process as follows: "Data is extracted into information that is used to make policy decisions. Policies are incorporated into a knowledge base imbedded into core business applications. These applications govern the database, which provide policy data, and so on, in a closed feedback loop."

10.21.1 Architecture of Intelligent Databases

An intelligent database consists of the following components:

1. A relational database containing corporate data

2. A knowledge base containing company policies as rules

3. A user interface allowing input of queries by users and display of conclusions in report and/or graphic format

4. An inference mechanism that draws conclusions by combining components 1, 2, and 3

    The rules in the knowledge base are in IF-THEN format (See Section 10.21.2 for examples). The user interface appears as the human window to the application. Usually, it is menu driven and allows the user to communicate with the application via responses to prompts. The inference mechanism provides the processing logic for the application. It interprets the user input, identifies the relevant rules in the knowledge base, retrieves the necessary data from the database, fires the rules using these data, and displays the result for the user. The user interface and the inference mechanism together constitute an intelligent front end for the application (see Figure 10–7).

    The front end can be built by using a forms package that comes with the relational DBMS. For example, ORACLE provides SQL∗Forms as a forms utility

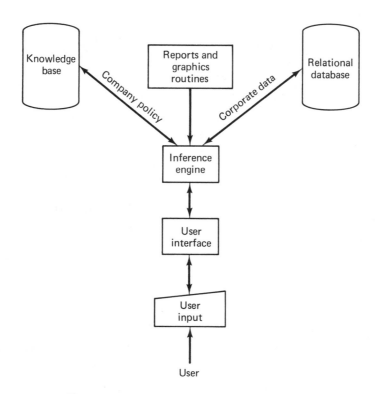

Figure 10–7 Architecture of intelligent database.

that can call the data-based routines, as well as the procedural language code, as "user exists" from a form.

10.21.2 Example of Intelligent Databases Using LHUDB

We shall use the data in LHUDB and build a knowledge base containing three rules in order to show how "intelligent" conclusions can be drawn from LHUDB. Let us assume that the user wants to print a graduation list for the coming commencement session. We introduce the following rule:

Rule 1. If degree status of a student is NDEG, do not include his or her name in the graduation list.

Rule 1 embodies the university policy that a nondegree student does not graduate and thus provides an initial screening of the eligible students. Of course, many additional screenings will be needed to ensure that all the graduation requirements have been satisfied for preparing the final list.

Next, suppose that the user wants to print a list of instructors who are eligible to teach a given course. The knowledge base can contain a rule of the following form:

Rule 2. If an instructor has specialty code X, he or she is eligible to teach courses $X_1, \ldots, X_n$.

To use Rule 2, the application has to use a lookup table of the following type:

Specialty Code (X)	Course List ($X_1, \ldots, X_n$)
2	CS579
4	EN104, EN604
5	MA423, CS547
6	HS525
7	CS547, MA611
9	CS761

and so on.

The application uses Rule 2 and the lookup table above and concludes that all instructions with SPCODE = 5 or 7 can teach the course CS547. It then issues the following query

```
SELECT INAME FROM INSTR WHERE
    SPCODE = 5 OR SPCODE = 7;
```

The application returns the names

> Deb Kumar Roy
> Tom Clark

Finally, suppose that the user wants to get names of instructors who can be department heads. The knowledge base can contain a rule embodying the selection criterion for becoming a department head:

Rule 3.   If an instructor has the rank associate professor or professor, he or she can become a department head.

As before, when the rule is fired, it generates a list of instructors with rank associate professor or professor.

10.21.3 Commercially Available Intelligent Databases

In this section we report on two commercially available packages that can be used to develop intelligent databases. The first package is called *NIAL (Nested Interactive Query Language)* and was invented by Mike Jenkins of Queen's University, Kingston, Ontario. (See Jenkins [12] for more details.) NIAL combines ideas from LISP, APL, Pascal, and logic programming in one coherent system. It is designed to treat both symbolic and numeric data collections on equal footing, making it well suited for artificial intelligence applications involving a large amount of data, as in a corporate database. Jenkins has discussed an example of a roster data model [12, pp. 35–38] built with NIAL that adds a nine-rule knowledge base in predicate logic symbolism on the top of a relational database consisting of a single relation called REPORT FAMILY. The resulting application can draw simple conclusions.

The second package was developed in an MIS environment involving employee expense claim processing. It used SQL*Expert, a utility generating SQL statements that ORACLE puts through its dynamic SQL interface in order to integrate an ORACLE database with a NEXPERT-OBJECT knowledge base. (See Schur [24, pp. 52–53] for more details.)

In addition, any expert system shell that can interface with a relational database can be used to build intelligent databases. Some examples of such shells are given in Figure 10–8.

Package	Vendors	DBMS Interface
ACORN	Gold Hill Computers 163 Harvard Street Cambridge, MA 02139 (617) 492-2071	dBase III
AION/PC	Aion Corporation 101 University Avenue Palo Alto, CA 94301 (415) 328-9595	dBase III, R:base 5000
ART	Inference Corporation 5300 West Century Boulevard Los Angeles, CA 90045 (213) 417-7997	SQL System
Expert Edge	Jeffrey Perrone & Associates, Inc. 3685 17th Street San Francisco, CA 94114 (415) 431-9562	dBase III
GURU	Micro Data Base Systems, Inc. P.O. Box 248 Lafayette, IN 47902 (800) 344-5832	dBaseIII, RDBMS
INSIGHT2+	Level Five Research 503 Fifth Avenue Indialantic, FL 32903 (305) 729-9046	dBase III, Datatrieve

Figure 10–8   Sources for expert system shells.

10.22 OBJECT-ORIENTED DATABASES

Relational databases work as storage facilities for conventional data processing applications. In recent years, however, increasing emphasis is being placed on engineering- and manufacturing-related applications such as CAD/CAM, circuit simulation, and architectural design support. Such applications do not map well on the relational data model, since they use object-oriented programming, which is quite different from the standard problem-oriented programming using a 3GL. The aim of object-oriented databases is to combine the two conceptually distinct paradigms of relational databases and object-oriented programming. They offer two different viewpoints of how to structure and manipulate data. But these two viewpoints can be used together as long as a map can be made between the tuple of a relation and the instance of an object.

The premise of object-oriented databases is that the combination of object-oriented languages with the storage mechanism of relational database systems can provide an extension of the relational data model that can capture behavior instead of just structure. Object-oriented programming uses the inheritance property of objects that deals with behavior or semantics, whereas relational databases are concerned with the data structure or syntax. The object-oriented data model fills in the semantic gap existing in a relational data model. The former correlates an object, which is an item in the real world being modeled, with a relation in the database and preserves any inheritance property of the object that is used in the model.

The field of object-oriented data bases is about four years old, but researchers have already organized sessions at database conferences. Recent meetings have included the Databases session, chaired by Paul McCullogh at OOPSLA '86 (Object-Oriented Programming Systems, Languages, and Applications) in Portland, Oregon, and the 1986 International Workshop on Object Oriented Database Systems in Pacific Grove, California. OOPSLA '86 was sponsored by the Association for Computing Machinery, while the Workshop was jointly sponsored by the Association for Computing Machinery's Special Interest Group on the Management of Data (SIGMOD) and the Institute of Electronics and Electrical Engineers Computer Society. We discuss next some of the basic concepts of object-oriented programming.

10.22.1 Overview of Object-Oriented Programming

Object-oriented programming started in 1967 with the development of the language SIMULA 67, which introduced the concepts of objects and inheritance. Later in the 1970s, Xerox Research Center developed Smalltalk using the ideas from SIMULA. During the early 1980s, a LISP-based language called Flavors and a C-based language called C + + were introduced as additional examples of object-oriented programming languages.

In any language, programs have two components: a procedural part that operates on data, and the data on which the procedural component operates. The procedural component, known as a program, contains the instructions for an operation to be performed. Such components include procedures for "add," "find," "read," "write," "print," and "conditional programming statements" (such as "if this condition is true, then do that"), and so on. The data on which the program operates might typically be numbers, strings of characters, graphical shapes, documents, or files.

In conventional programming, most people consider programs as primary and the data (or objects) as secondary. In object-oriented programming, the reverse is true. The data, such as a graphical shape or document to be operated on, are of primary importance.

In object-oriented programming, rather than sending the program the name of an object to manipulate (which corresponds to providing the program with data in conventional programming), the programmer sends the *object* (or data) a *message*. A *message* is actually the name of an operation or procedure (called a *method* in object-oriented programming) to be performed. Typically, operations on the object "document" include open and close document, find print, and display it. Sending the object "document," one of these messages is like the data calling a subroutine in conventional programming.

The object is able to respond appropriately to a message because an object is defined along with a group of associated procedures that it can perform. As a result, when the object, for example, "document," receives a message, such as "display," it knows how to perform that procedure because associated with the object are the procedure instructions. To perform the same task in conventional programming, the program would call a procedure called "display," which would take the document as data, execute the display instructions, and display the document.

Inheritance is possible in object-oriented programming languages such as Smalltalk or Flavors because these languages organize programs as a hierarchical arrangement of things known as classes and subclasses. *Classes* and *subclasses* are sets of the same kinds of generic objects or components. Typically, object-oriented programs might contain classes such as numbers, character strings, graphical shapes, documents, or files. Others have classes of components such as queues or frames. The highly graphical Lisp computer user interfaces are implemented with object-oriented programming techniques. These programs would probably have classes of windows, menus, and icons.

In object-oriented programming, the most generic object in a class lattice is highest in the hierarchy. The most specific objects described by a class are lowest in the hierarchy. The relationships between objects in the hierarchy and those immediately below them are described as parent–child inheritance relationships, because some objects in the hierarchy are called "parents" and the related objects at the next-lower level of the hierarchy are their "children."

Associated with each class is a group of procedures (methods). Each class's subclasses automatically inherit these procedures from their parents unless they have their own procedures that mask out one or more particular procedures.

10.22.2 Components of an Object-Oriented Programming System

An object-oriented programming system has three main components:

1. Object memory
2. Virtual machine
3. Programming language constructs

The *object memory* stores all the objects in the system. Since objects are usually referenced in vendor order, hashing can provide a suitable device for implementing an object memory. Usually, the implementation details of the object memory are hidden from the programmer. As a result, the users of the system get the impression that a virtual space is available for creating and storing objects.

The *virtual machine* processes the message sent to an object. It reads from and writes to the object memory and ensures that the correct method is invoked when a message is sent. The machine can be implemented as a physical CPU designed for such purposes. Alternatively, it can be implemented by using a set of recursive procedures where every other procedure call is to a message procedure. The *programming language constructs* can be a pure language such as Smalltalk or a hybrid of Smalltalk-like expressions within the framework of a host language.

10.22.3 Object-Oriented Data Model

An *object-oriented data model* can be defined as a relational data model that has been adjusted to suit the object-oriented programming environment. Such a data model is composed of object-oriented entities that encapsulate data and procedures. Encapsulation separates the external interface of an object from its internal workings. End users of an object can interface with the object through its interface specification. They do not have direct access to the internal implementation details or internal data of the object. Thus the users can use an object without knowing anything about its internal structure. A relational database offers an exactly similar end-user interface. The end users are involved only with the external level of the database. The data independence provided by the user transparent external/conceptual level interface and conceptual/internal level interface shields the end users from the internal level of the database.

Figure 10–9 shows the correspondence between an object-oriented system and a relational database system. Using this mapping, we can design an object-oriented database as follows:

1. Identify classes for the object-oriented system.
2. Identify instance variables for each class.
3. Identify instance variable constraints for each instance variable.
4. Set up relations, attributes, and domains in the relational database such that the correspondences of Figure 10–9 hold. For example, a relation matches a class, its attributes match the instance variables of the class, and the attribute domains match the instance variable constraints.
5. Ensure that the class hierarchy of the object-oriented system is represented by the database schema. The concept of inheritance used in the class hierarchy can be implemented in a relational database by means of subtypes and supertypes (see Section 9.6).
6. Prepare a list of procedures involving retrieval and update of data from the relational database.

Object-Oriented System	Relational Database System
Object or class instance	Tuple
Class	Relation
Instance variable	Attribute
Instance variable constraint	Domain
Class hierarchy	Database schema
Method	Procedure body
Message	Procedure call

Figure 10–9 Correspondence between object-oriented system and relational database system.

7. Write programs to attach these procedures as methods to objects and to call the methods via messages.

As examples, adding an instance variable to a class of objects corresponds to adding an attribute to a relation; similarly, removing an instance variable from a class of objects corresponds to removing an attribute from a relation. This process requires a certain amount of reorganization of the database and a recompilation of all methods for the class and its subclasses. Methods are coded in a programming language used by the object-oriented database system and the messages are passed to methods as their arguments.

10.22.4 Problems with Object-Oriented Databases

The problems with object-oriented databases can be summarized as follows:

1. It lacks a coherent data model with a mathematical foundation such as relational algebra or relational calculus. As a result, query formulation or maintaining database integrity becomes difficult.
2. Research into storage structures for efficient storage of objects is still in its infancy. Arrays are generally used now.
3. Use of an object-oriented database from a conventional data processing language such as COBOL, C, or Pascal is difficult since these languages lack the idea of an object.
4. Although classes are matched with relations (see Figure 10–9) from an information modeling viewpoint it is still debatable whether a class is similar to data types in a programming language or to relational database (see Stein and Meier [27, p. 64]).
5. The encapsulation of data and procedure interferes with query optimization, because the latter requires global information, which may be lacking in an object-oriented system. Designing a query language for an object-oriented database is not an easy job.

10.22.5 Commercially Available Object-Oriented Database Systems

In this section we describe briefly four object-oriented database systems that are currently available commercially.

(a) BOOPS.   The Basic Object-Oriented Programming System (BOOPS) is a Smalltalk-like object-oriented environment that can enhance a multiuser relational database system with capabilities that are usually found only on dedicated single-user workstations. Without sacrificing relational features, BOOPS provides simulation, program and data encapsulation, and window interface as well as inheritance.

An advanced form of BASIC is provided to interface easily with the database. This implementation has the necessary control constructs to write fairly well structured code. It also supports indirect procedure calls through procedure variables, a feature necessary to construct the virtual object-oriented machine.

The syntax of BOOPS is similar to that of Smalltalk, with a few differences. In BOOPS, message selectors are represented as a single string

```
'PutAt:object index'
```

BOOPS also allows variable-length parameter lists in a manner similar to C.

The BOOPS compiler is basically a recursive descent parser that converts message expressions into procedure calls to 'sendmsg' in the host language. It also maps any instance variables used in a method into the appropriate references in the database record.

(b) Gemstone.   Gemstone is an object-oriented database server that has been developed by Servio Logic Development Corporation of Beavertown, Oregon. It is a DBMS that fully supports object-oriented database concepts. Its companion object-oriented language is OPAL. Gemstone/OPAL stores entities such as text, pictures, expert systems rules, and diagrams in structures predetermined to be best suited for each type of data to be stored. Each entity is stored as an object composed of structure, behavior, and value. Combined, they satisfy the requirements for object orientedness.

GemStone/OPAL supports interactive incremental development of software. Furthermore, GemStone comes with a bundled library of 44 predefined database objects and more than 600 fully tested procedures.

GemStone can be classified as behaviorally object oriented, providing the controlled shared access and permanence of data common to database systems. Unusual for database systems but increasingly common in object-oriented databases, GemStone supports object identity independent of an object's physical location or contents.

(c) POSTGRES.   POSTGRES, a research project at the University of California at Berkeley, is a relational database with extensions to support object management. POSTGRES extends the relational database model with an abstract data typing mechanism and procedures as a fundamental data type. M. Stonebraker argues that the many data models developed over the last decade exhibit widely varied concepts and that unifying these constructs into a single data model will be impossible. Stonebraker proposes developing a data model able to simulate all the various constructs. POSTGRES is an attempt to do this.

Support for abstract data types means that POSTGRES allows the user to define a new data type to define a column in a relation and to define procedures usable in a relational query that manipulates the new data type. Dates, for example, might be defined as an abstract type, together with procedures for format conversion, addition, subtraction, and comparison. A query could then ask for tuples where the date field contained any date belonging to a given range.

(d) VBASE.   VBASE is an object-oriented database system marketed by Ontologic, Inc. of Billerica, Massachusetts. Together with its companion products (compilers and others), it is a platform on which to engineer systems that have data, text, geometry, and graphics in the same database. All forms of information are treated as natural objects. There is no need to translate the conceptual design to a less of a natural-language representation. VBASE functions as both a language and a database system.

The VBASE database is composed of objects (object-oriented entities) that encapsulate data and procedures. Encapsulation separates the external interface of an object from its internal workings. Thus the client can use an object without knowing anything about its internal structure.

Language aspects of VBASE include strong datatyping, a structured schema definition language, and parameterization. The last feature supports typing members of aggregate objects. Database aspects include system support for one-to-one, one-to-many, and many-to-many relationships. A technical advantage claimed for the VBASE is its use of strong typing.

10.23 PROLOG DATABASE SYSTEM

PROLOG is a programming language based on predicate logic that was invented and developed by the researchers of artificial intelligence. PROLOG is particularly suitable for traversing a search space efficiently and is also used for knowledge representation in expert systems. The predicate logic formalism of PROLOG can be used to represent a relational database. Query processing and query optimization can be handled easily through PROLOG programs. This linkage between PROLOG and relational databases results in the PROLOG database system, a concept that has been gaining popularity since 1983. A *PROLOG database system* is a relational DBMS whose DDL and DML are implemented by means of the PROLOG language. This is done in the following manner:

1. Each row of an *n*-ary relation is represented as a predicate with *n* arguments.
2. A query for data retrieval or update is written as a PROLOG clause.
3. The processing of a query is regarded as a mechanical theorem proving process using the resolution principle in PROLOG.
4. Query optimization is handled easily by PROLOG since PROLOG can be used to implement the canonical form of the internal representation of the query.
5. An equivalence exists between functional and multivalued dependencies in a relational database (see Chapter 6) and a fragment of propositional logic that deals with Horn clauses.

The main thesis supporting a PROLOG database system can be described as follows (Li [15, p. 17]): The formulation of a query on a relational database is similar to the statement of a theorem that has the general form

```
IF X THEN Y
```

The *X* part in a query consists of the set of facts necessary to respond to the query (i.e., the relations in the database referenced by the query). The *Y* part of the query consists of the statement of the query. The processing of the query is analogous to proving the theorem using PROLOG. Hence a relational DBMS is just a general-purpose theorem proving system. Recent development in automated reasoning has led to increasing use of PROLOG as a high-level programming language and as a language for description and manipulation of relational databases.

10.24 FUTURE TRENDS IN RELATIONAL DATABASE SYSTEMS

In the preceding sections we have discussed seven topics, each of which comprises an active research area in the relational database systems. In this section we list a variety of statements, reflecting some of the additional future trends for relational databases.

10.24.1 Relational Front End with SQL

Since SQL has been accepted as the industry standard for nonprocedural query languages, many vendors of inverted list and hierarchical/network data models are offering relational front ends for their nonrelational database systems. SQL appears as the query language in such cases. Examples of this trend are IDMS/

R from Cullinet, DB/2 from IBM, and Model 204 from Computer Corporation of America. In addition, several vendors of relational DBMS packages that did not offer SQL as the query language are now modifying their products to include SQL. Examples of the latter category are INGRES, which used QUEL as its initial query language; UNIFY, which initially offered a menu-driven front end for data definitions and queries; dBase III Plus, which has a separate query language; and SQL/DS from IBM.

In all such cases, the vendors either use the existing DBMS as an access method to implement the new databases, or put a relational front end onto an older DBMS to obtain relational-style access to existing databases. The second alternative is much more difficult to implement than is the first one.

10.24.2 Application Generators with Relational DBMS

DBMS vendors are offering application generators as a self-contained suite of products. For example, Oracle Corporation has marketed SQL* Plus, SQL*Forms, SQL*Calc, SQL*Menu, and SQL*ReportWriter as a set of tools to build applications. Also, some vendors are introducing new procedural languages that combine SQL with structured programming laguages. PL/SQL from Oracle Corporation and UNIFY/ACCEL from Unify Corporation are examples of such efforts.

10.24.3 PC Version of Relational DBMS

When the relational DBMSs were introduced on the market, they needed a large memory to be operational. Also, performance was a major obstacle. With current research techniques involving relational databases, performance is no longer a significant issue. Also, with the advent of high-powered PCs, vendors are introducing more and more PC-based relational systems. A definite future trend will be the appearance of two types of relational DBMSs: PC-based and mainframe/supermini-based. An industry survey in 1987 estimated that there would be 800 PCs for every mainframe and 13 or 14 minicomputers for every mainframe. This ratio would be reflected in the number of PC-based and mainframe/supermini-based DBMSs in use in the country.

10.24.4 Semantic Data Modeling

The entity–relationship data model of Chen has been extended to a *semantic data model*. Such a model is depicted graphically as a series of nodes connected by arcs. Each node is a *class* or a *concept*. Each arc is a *relationship*. A class corresponds to an entity, and a concept corresponds to a tuple. An arc can represent a strong or a weak relationship.

Semantic data modeling and semantic DBMS originated from the notion of object-oriented programming. Several vendors, including Unisys and Computer

Corporation of America, are currently building semantic technology. Semantic systems attempt to capture the knowledge relating to the application of the data, not just the storage of it. Although works in semantic data modeling started in the late 1960s by M. R. Quillian, G. G. Hendrix, and J. B. Mylopoulos, it was not until recent years that these systems have begun to arouse widespread interests.

Within a semantic database system, classes of data are organized into a hierarchical structure such that each level of hierarchy is associated with a set of rules applicable to that class. This set of rules is called *constraints* and they are applied to all data within the class. In addition to having their own constraints, lower-level classes inherit constraints from the higher-level classes to allow the system to make well-defined and accurate decisions regarding the manipulation of data. In a conventional database system, constraints exist only within an application and must be encoded each time a new application is designed using the same data. This is not the case with a semantic database system since the data already have their associated constraints.

A semantic data model is similar to an object-oriented data model in that a class corresponds to an object and a constraint corresponds to a method. Semantic database systems offer great potential. But no such system is available yet commercially. It is important to become aware of the developments that may lie ahead in the field.

10.24.5 Parallel Computers and Relational Databases

Architecturally, a parallel computer consists of multiple processors sharing a common memory and a single copy of the operating system. In multiuser applications, the parallel architecture remains completely transparent to the user and automatically balances process loads across the multiple processors. Since a parallel computer executes tasks concurrently instead of sequentially, the performance is dramatically improved.

Parallel computers can be used to implement relational databases in large applications. They are specially suitable for OLTP environments (see Sections 10.2 through 10.5). In the future, such machines will be used increasingly for implementing a transaction processing system (TPS) with relational databases.

Sequent Computer Systems introduced the Symmetry series of parallel computers in May 1987 using the operating system DYNIX, which is Sequent's implementation of UNIX. The Symmetry series was used in conjunction with INGRES, a relational DBMS marketed by Relational Technology, Inc., in a benchmarking test of the throughput rate of INGRES running on parallel computers. The result was published in the report "The Silver Bullet Benchmark" in May 1988 (see Sequent Computer Systems [26]). The report concluded that parallel computers could deliver an improved price/performance ratio and high system uptime needed by an OLTP environment.

In a continuation of the above joint venture of Sequent Computer Systems and Relational Technology a new mechanism called Parallel Data Query Optimizer (PDQO) is currently being developed and is expected to be released in two phases in 1990 and 1991. PDQO partitions a query processing involving joins into two or more components and then processes them simultaneously on a parallel computer system so as to reduce the total execution time. For example, let us consider the query involving the join of the two tables UNIV and INSTR (see Section 5.4). In a nonparallel system, the selection is done first, then the Cartesian product and the further selection, followed by the projection that retrieves the required data from the tables (see Figure 5–3). Under the PDQO algorithm on a parallel computer, the two selections would be done on two separate processors and the Cartesian product would occur on a third processor, all in parallel. The final projection would then return the desired data. The execution time of the whole process in a parallel system can take about one-third of the time on a nonparallel system.

Oracle Corporation is currently working with NCube Inc. on a joint venture to introduce a parallel processing RDBMS platform that does not use shared memory. In October 1989 they released preliminary information about the ORACLE NCube port. When fully developed and made available in 1990, this product will be called ORACLE for the NCUBE 2 and will port the ORACLE RDBMS to NCube's Hypercube platform by using the direct memory access channels on the CPU itself to handle the interprocessor communication. Each of the 14 pairs of channels on each processor in the Hypercube will be capable of passing 2.5MB of data in and out of the processor. Oracle Corporation anticipates that this tool will accommodate up to 8,192 processors and will demonstrate over 1000 tps performance.

10.24.6 Distributed Databases

The distributed relational database system of the future will consist of global networks of disparate systems and dispersed data with which a user can interact as if he or she were dealing with a system all his or her own. Such a system will allow the user of any type of machine in a network an easy access to data stored on any other machine in that network, no matter who is the vendor of the machine or whatever operating system it uses. The concept of gateway computer system (see Section 10.15) is a step in the right direction. However, the final goal of a communications network with a collection of individual nodes tied together, each having its own stand-alone database, is yet to be realized.

Carnegie–Mellon University of Pittsburgh plans to use INGRES-STAR from Relational Technology, Inc. (RTI) to integrate 6000 to 7000 workstations with its central computer operations. By 1990 the university will tie together as a distributed systems its 1500 micros, 2000 Macintoshes, about 75 VAXes, eight DEC 2060s, 400 Micro VAXes, 200 RTs, and over 100 Sun Micro-systems workstations. The databases residing on these different machines will talk with one another.

10.24.7 Object-Oriented Databases

Significant research is going on in the areas of object-oriented database systems and related languages. Important research areas include data models, object versions across time or through the use of "what if" to create alternative revisions, object identity, high-level language interfaces, protection and locking mechanisms for objects and subobjects, long transactions (transactions running for hours or days, a major problem for engineering applications), and database design and administration tools.

Some of these areas are not unique to object-oriented databases, but in the context of an object-oriented database their importance becomes accentuated. In the near future, object-oriented database technology will become another accepted and commonly used data model and take up a position alongside the relational model as the subject of research efforts and commercial products.

In anticipation of the future potential of object-oriented databases, a five-generation classification scheme of the database technology has been attempted in a manner similar to that for the computer languages. The five generations of the database technology are:

1. First Generation   : File processing system
2. Second Generation : Hierarchical database system
3. Third Generation   : CODASYL (Network) database system
4. Fourth Generation : Relational database system
5. Fifth Generation   : Object-oriented and Extended Relational (RM/T) database system

Browsing through the OOPSLA proceedings (see Section 10.22) one finds articles on applications developed using object-oriented technology, such as interactive time series analysis, data flow analysis, interactive VLSI simulation, rule-based production systems, discrete event simulation, and spreadsheets. Experience with these and other implementations of large complex systems will further refine the technology.

The promised productivity gains will be realised; whether it will be a factor of 2, 10, or more remains to be seen. Compilation and other optimization techniques will be applied to systems that are largely interpreted. Systems that use a compile and link methodology will provide mechanisms, such as incremental linkers, to allow for rapid prototyping and modification.

10.25 SUMMARY

In this chapter we have discussed several heterogeneous topics that represent current research areas in relational database systems. *Transaction processing systems* (TPSs) support relational database applications in an OLTP environment. A TPS requires high throughput, high concurrency, high availability and fault tolerance, and large database support. Until 1987 TPS was not regarded as an appropriate domain for a relational DBMS because of performance reasons. Since then, several DBMS vendors (e.g., Oracle Corporation, Sybase, Inc., and Informix Software, Inc.) have marketed their versions of TPS by improving performance. The main features used by these products are (1) multiprocessing architecture, (2) record-level locking, and (3) minimization of physical disk I/O operations, all of which result in quick response time.

A *distributed database system* may conceptually be regarded as a collection of databases located in geographically separate areas with data partitioned among these areas. An end user's query for retrieval or update can access the required data irrespective of their location(s) in a manner that is totally transparent to the user. This is called location transparency. If, in addition, the maintenance of the replicated data elements is also undertaken by the system, we get replication transparency. These are two major objectives of a distributed database system. Data communication plays a major role in such systems. Both long-haul and local-area networks are used.

Relational data models are especially suitable for distributed systems because they offer great decomposition flexibility. Relations can be sliced horizontally or vertically and then can be "glued" together by joins and unions. Local autonomy, capacity of incremental growth, and better availability of data are three main benefits of distributed systems. The data dictionary of the system is usually distributed too. Gateway computer systems developed recently provide access to different manufacturers' networks and computers. As a result, by using this device a distributed database system can access multiple databases on diverse machines running under disparate operating systems and DBMSs.

A *database machine* is a dedicated backend processor with auxiliary disk storage, attached to one or more host computers running applications. Its purpose is to improve system performance by offloading database works from the host computer. In reality, it functions as a database server in a LAN, where the host computers are of different types. There are two main types of database machines: (1) dedicated but conventional backend computer, and (2) associative disks.

Several DBMS vendors are currently offering natural language as a query language. Consequently, users can query the databases by means of a somewhat limited form of plain English. The DBMS includes a query analyzer and a dialogue handler in order to process a natural-language query. Keyword matching is used in the processing of the query. Since the same query can be posed in multiple ways in English, the query analyzer must be able to establish the equivalence of all these versions. This still remains the major obstacle in implementing natural-language queries. Tools from artificial intelligence to handle syntax and semantics of a natural-language query are used by the query analyzer.

Intelligent databases represent a combination of the relational database technology with knowledge engineering. Such databases access data from corporate relational databases and make inferences by processing these data against a knowledge base. The latter contains rules that are fired whenever the condition part of a rule matches data values from the relational database. Intelligent databases provide an interface between expert systems and relational databases. As such they include a user interface and an inference engine.

Object-oriented databases offer a new data modeling concept that adjusts a relational data model to suit object-oriented programming environment. An object-oriented program is different from a conventional program in that programs are primary and data are secondary in the latter, whereas the reverse is true in the former. Thus, in object-oriented programs, the programmer sends the object (i.e., data) a message that is the name of an operation or procedure (i.e., program) which has to be executed with the data. A variation of the object-oriented data model is called a semantic data model.

A *PROLOG database system* is a relational DBMS whose DDL and DML are implemented by means of the PROLOG language. Each tuple of an *n*-ary relation is represented as an *n*-argument predicate. The processing of a query is regarded as a mechanical theorem-proving process that can be handled very efficiently by PROLOG. The query optimization is implemented through PROLOG since the canonical form of the internal representation of the query uses predicate forms.

The final section of the chapter includes a list of statements describing some of the future trends of the relational database market.

KEY WORDS

agent	database machine
application generator	dedicated backend computer
ASCENT	deferred write process
associative disk	dialogue handler
benchmark	distributed database system
BOOPS	edge
caching mechanism	expert system
class	expert system shell
client server model	fault tolerance
cluster	functional dependency
concept	gateway
concurrency	gateway computer system
constraints	GEMSTONE
data contention	graph
data dictionary, distributed	horizontal fragmentation
data fragmentation	incompatible host

inheritance

instance variable

intelligent database

Intelligent Gateway Processor (IGP)

keyword matching

knowledge base

local area network

local autonomy

location transparency

locking

locking, row level

long haul network

message

method

multi-processing architecture

natural language

Nested Interactive Query Language (NIAL)

node

object

object memory

object oriented data model

object oriented database

object oriented programming

offloading theorem

On Line Transaction Processing (OLTP)

parallel computer

POSTGRES

PROLOG database system

query analyzer

query optimization

relational front end

replication transparency

requester-server design

semantic analysis

semantic data model

semijoin

subrelation

throughput

TP1

transaction

transaction management

transaction processing system (TPS)

tuple identifier

UNIX

update propagation

VBASE

vertical fragmentation

virtual machine

REFERENCES AND FURTHER READING

The following references contain additional materials related to the topics covered in this chapter.

1. R. G. Bowerman and D. E. Glover, *Putting Expert Systems into Practice*, Van Nostrand Reinhold. New York, 1988.
2. S. Caniano, All TP1s Are Not Created Equal, *Datamation*, August 15, 1988, pp. 51–53.
3. K. Colby, *Artificial Paranoia,* Pergamon Press, Elmsford, NY, 1975.
4. C. J. Date, *Introduction to Database Systems,* vol. II, 3rd ed., Addison-Wesley, Reading, MA, 1983.
5. C. J. Date, *Relational Databases Selected Writings,* Addison-Wesley, Reading, MA, 1986.

6. J. M. Davis, Database Requirements for the CASE Environment, *Database Programming and Design,* October 1988, pp. 62–71.

7. J. Gomsi and M. Desanti, BOOPS and Relational Database, *AI Expert,* November 1987, pp. 60–66.

8. J. Gray, Database Transparency, *Database Programming and Design*, March 1988, pp. 46–52.

9. E. Gregory, Database Machines: The Least Cost Route, *Datamation,* November 1, 1988, pp. 85–86, 90.

10. K. Horak, Turbo PROLOG and dBase III Plus, *AI Expert,* June 1988, pp. 26–33.

11. Informix Software, Inc., *SQL Based Products for Multiprocessor Machines,* Technical Paper, 1988.

12. M. Jenkins, Intelligent Databases and NIAL, *AI Expert,* March 1987, pp. 32–39.

13. R. Knaus and C. Jay, A Single PROLOG DBMS, *AI Expert,* April 1988, pp. 13–21.

14. H. F. Korth and A. Silberschatz, *Database System Concepts,* McGraw-Hill, New York, 1986.

15. D. Li, *A PROLOG Database System,* Research Studies Press, Hertfordshire, England, 1984.

16. J. L. Manferdelli, *Natural Language Interfaces: Benefits, Requirements, State of the Art and Applications,* Natural Language Inc., Berkeley, CA, 1987.

17. J. Martin, *Design of Man–Computer Dialogues,* Prentice-Hall, Englewood Cliffs, NJ, 1973.

18. E. D. Myers, Distributed DBMSs: In Search of Wonder Glue, *Datamation,* February 1, 1987, pp. 41–48.

19. D. R. O'Connell, A Matter of Semantics, *Datamation,* December 15, 1988, pp. 51–54.

20. Oracle Corporation, *ORACLE Performance Report,* July 1988.

21. R. W. Peterson, Object-Oriented Database Design, *AI Expert,* March 1987, pp. 26–31.

22. J. W. Schmidt and M. L. Brodie, *Relational Database Systems,* Springer-Verlag, New York, 1983.

23. S. Schur, The Intelligent Database, *AI Expert,* January 1988, pp. 26–34.

24. S. Schur, Intelligent Databases, *Database Programming and Design,* June 1988, pp. 46–53.

25. E. Sciore and D. S. Warren, Integrating Databases and PROLOG, *AI Expert*, January 1988, pp. 38–44.

26. Sequent Computer Systems Inc., *Sequent/INGRES Performance Report,* May 1988.

27. J. Stein and D. Meier, Object-Oriented Data Management, *Database Programming and Design,* April 1988, pp. 58–67.

28. Sybase Corporation, *SYBASE for Online Applications, Data Server, and Data Toolset,* 1988.

29. J. D. Ullman, *Principles of Database Systems,* Computer Science Press, Rockville, MD, 1982.

References 2, 11, 20, and 28 contain discussions about the benchmarks TPS and TP1 to test transaction processing systems. The last three of these four references describe three specific products and explain how each implements the transaction processing mechanism by means of a relational DBMS. Currently, more and more DBMS vendors are introducing transaction processing capabilities within their products. These are announced primarily in the trade journals.

References 4, 8, 14, 18, 22, and 29 relate to distributed databases. Of these, 4, 14, and 29 treat the subject from a textbook approach and discuss a variety of related issues. Reference 22 gives a justification for using relational databases instead of nonrelational databases as the appropriate vehicle for implementing distributed concepts. Reference 8 discusses the location transparency issue in a requester/server mode of distributed databases.

References 4, 5, and 9 discuss database machines. Although reference 4 dates back to 1983, the information provided is relevant. Reference 9 addresses cost-comparison issues of database machines with several industry examples.

References 12, 23, and 24 deal with intelligent databases. Reference 1 is a good source of information on expert systems that is needed to understand the concept of intelligent databases.

References 6, 7, 21, and 27 discuss the object-oriented data model. More information on BOOPS, GEMSTONE, POSTGRES, and VBASE can be found in references 6, 7, and 21. Reference 19 discusses the semantic data model, which is a variation of the object-oriented data model.

References 10, 13, 15, and 25 talk about the PROLOG database system. Reference 15 gives the most detailed treatment. Reference 10 discusses an application integrating PROLOG with dBase III Plus on IBM PCs.

Reference 26 is a good source of information of using parallel computers with relational databases for improved performance.

CHAPTER 11

RELATIONAL DBMS PACKAGES

11.1 INTRODUCTION

In this chapter we briefly discuss the following seven commercially available relational DBMS packages, the first six being mainframe/supermini-based and the last being PC-based: (1) INFORMIX®, (2) INGRES™, (3) LOGIX®, (4) ORACLE®, (5) RIM®, (6) UNIFY™, and (7) dBase III Plus™. The discussion of each DBMS will address a general description, data definition, data manipulation, and application development. The goal is to provide an overview of each package rather than detailed knowledge.

11.2 INFORMIX

(a) General description. INFORMIX is marketed by Informix Software, Inc. Although initially targeted for UNIX environment, the vendor now supports other computers, such as IBM, DEC, AT&T, and Data General. The basic DBMS products provided by the vendor are INFORMIX-SQL, INFORMIX-ESQL/COBOL, INFORMIX-4GL, and INFORMIX-ESQL/C. Thus the products support the query language SQL in both interactive and embedded modes. Both INFORMIX-4GL and INFORMIX-SQL offer a form generator and a programming language based on SQL. But INFORMIX-4GL does not have the separate REPORT component that INFORMIX-SQL has. INFORMIX-ESQL (the "E" stands for "embedded") allows a programmer to write programs in the host language C or COBOL using blocks of SQL statements for retrieval or update purposes embedded within the programs.

(b) Data definition.   INFORMIX provides both menu-driven and command-oriented interfaces to define databases. The user can create, modify, and delete tables in a database through a menu-driven interface, through RDSQL commands entered interactively (RDSQL is a SQL-based query language), or through RDSQL commands included in a 4GL program. The menu-driven interface is helpful for a beginner but may appear too slow for an experienced user. However, one nice feature of the menu-driven interface is that it allows a user to ask INFORMIX to create an RDSQL command file based on the interactive input from the user. This file can then be saved and modified using a text editor during the database design phase, which is iterative in nature. This option is much faster than going through a long interface session each time.

(c) Data manipulation.   INFORMIX offers two methods for data manipulation: a form-driven interface and a command-oriented interface. The form-driven interface involves generating a default form with the INFORMIX form generator and then processing it with a PERFORM statement. This displays a menu on the screen with options such as QUERY, ADD, UPDATE, and RE-MOVE, which can then be used to retrieve or updata data. The command-oriented interface uses standard SQL commands such as SELECT, INSERT, DELETE, and UPDATE. The user enters these commands interactively for retrieving or updating data. INSERT adds one row at a time unless it is used with a SELECT clause. Natural joins can be handled in either way.

The user can create and drop views with RDSQL commands. A table can be updated through a view except in the following two situations:

1. The view depends on multiple tables.
2. The view definition involves joins, the clause GROUP BY, the keyword DISTINCT, or a built-in aggregate function such as SUM, AVG, or COUNT.

(d) Application development.   As with data definition and data manipulation, INFORMIX offers two methods for application development. One method uses the form generator to generate a form and then executes the form using the PERFORM command. Appropriate validation routines can be added using control blocks with the form. However, this method has the following four limitations:

1. Only one form can be executed at a time, allowing no hierarchy of forms.
2. Menus presented on the form cannot be customized.
3. Complex computations and logic cannot be included.
4. No database access statements can be included.

The other method uses host language interface programs using COBOL or C as the host language. This approach has a disadvantage in that screen I/O has to be handled through COBOL or C code. The form generator cannot be used from a host language program.

11.3 INGRES

(a) General description.   INGRES (INteractive Graphics and REtrieval System) is currently marketed by Relational Technology, Inc. (RTI) of Berkeley, California. It started as a research project at the University of California at Berkeley in 1973 and used the UNIX operating system. At present INGRES is available for other operating systems, such as VMS, VM/CMS, and MVS. It operates as a multiuser DBMS. A PC-based version is also available.

RTI offers a basic system called INGRES Kernel and several add-on components. The major components of Kernel include the following:

RDBMS (relational DBMS)
INGRES/Menu (Menu Generator)
INGRES QBF (Query By Forms)
INGRES VIFRED (Visual Interactive Forms Editor)
INGRES/REPORTS (Report Generator)
INGRES/REPORTS RBF (Report by Forms)
INGRES ISQL/IQUEL (Interactive SQL/QUEL Terminal Monitor)
ESQL/EQUEL (Embedded SQL/QUEL) Preprocessors for C

Among the add-on components we can mention

INGRES/PCLINK
INGRES/GRAPHICS
ESQL/EQUEL Processors for COBOL, BASIC, Ada, Pascal, FORTRAN, and PL/I
ABF (Application by Forms)

INGRES offers two query languages: SQL and QUEL (see Section 10.24). Unlike SQL, QUEL is based on tuple relational calculus.

(b) Data definition.   A database is created by using the command CREATEDB at the operating system level. Both menu-driven and command-driven interfaces are available to define and delete relations. A combination of several commands from the command-driven interface must be used to add an attribute, delete an attribute, change the data type of an attribute, or rename an attribute. Thus relational definitions cannot be modified from the menu-driven interface.

The user can access the menu-driven interface by selecting the TABLES option from INGRES/Menu. The command/driven interface is available from ISQL. The user can enter one or more SQL statements on a blank screen and ask ISQL to execute them. Limited editing facilities are available within ISQL.

(c) Data manipulation. INGRES provides two tools for data manipulation: QBF, which is form oriented, and ISQL, which is command oriented. The user can work with a relation in a Simple Field format, which displays one row at a time, or in a Table Field format, which displays multiple rows at a time. The latter allows the user to scroll the displayed rows vertically and horizontally.

If the user selects the QBF route and chooses a relation, a blank form corresponding to the relation appears on the screen. The user can insert new rows by entering data on the screen. To delete or modify existing rows, he or she retrieves them by entering appropriate selection criteria on the screen, and then makes changes as needed. The form used by QBF must already have been generated with VIFRED. The form can be created from scratch or the user can ask VIFRED to generate a default form that he or she can edit.

If the user selects the ISQL route, the standard SQL commands, such as SELECT, INSERT, DELETE, and UPDATE, are used. INSERT adds one row at a time unless the user uses the SELECT clause with it. DELETE and UPDATE work on a group of rows based on the criteria specified by the user.

INGRES supports two methods for handling joins. The first is with the SELECT statement (command oriented) executed from ISQL. The second method is with entities called Joindefs, defined and manipulated from QBF (form oriented). A *Joindef* includes the definition of a join, a form for querying, adding, changing, or deleting data in the underlying tables and certain rules for updating and deleting.

The user can define views by using the SELECT statement from ISQL. In general, INGRES supports updates to data through a view only if it can be guaranteed (without looking at actual data) that the result of updating the view will be identical to updating the corresponding relations. This puts some restrictions on updating tables through views. Updates to data through views are not permitted if any of these conditions apply:

1. The view has more than one relation.
2. The update affects a column that is in the search condition of the view definition.
3. The update affects a column in the view that is not a database column. For example, the column might be the result of a set function (e.g., max, min, avg) or computations.

QBF allows users only to retrieve data through views. It is not possible to add, change, or delete data in a view from QBF; it must be done through ISQL. One cannot build indices on views.

INGRES provides three methods of report generation: default reports, reports generated by RBF, and reports generated with the report writer. A default report includes all rows and columns for a selected table. To include a subset of the data in a table, the user creates a view or a permanent table based on the original table and uses the new table or the view for the report. He or she can select the output style to be column, block, or wrap. The output can be directed to the terminal, printer, or file.

RBF provides some customization over the default report but not as much as provided by the report writer. RBF allows the user to specify the report specification in a form mode. RBF works very much like VIFRED. An RBF report works on a table or a view as opposed to a SELECT statement. The user first asks RBF to generate a default report and then edits it. The default report contains six formal elements: title, column heading, data shown on the detail line, headers for breaks and pages, page footers, and break footers. The user can edit only the first three elements.

To generate a report with the report writer, the user first writes a report specification file containing report writer commands that specify the data to be reported and the way they will appear. After the file is created it is loaded into the database before it can run. INGRES performs certain validity checking while loading the file.

(d) Application development.   INGRES provides two tools for application development: ABF and ESQL. ABF is suitable for forms-oriented applications, and ESQL is suitable for both forms- and non-forms-oriented applications.

1. *ABF.* The highest-level object known to ABF is an application. ABF maintains a list of components for each application. An application consists of two types of components: *frames* and *procedures.*

ABF supports four types of frames: user-defined, QBF, VIGRAPH (not on PC), and Report. A *user-defined frame* consists of a form and 4GL specification. A 4GL specification is a module written in ABF's programming language, known as Operation Specification Language (OSL). A *QBF frame* consists of a form. A *VIGRAPH frame* consists of a graph and, optionally, the name of an output file and command line flags from VIGRAPH. A *Report frame* consists of a report specification file, an optional output file name, and an optional form for passing parameters to the report specification file. A *procedure* for ABF is written in the OSL or in a 3GL such as C, Pascal, or FORTRAN, and can be called from a form's 4GL specification or from another procedure.

ABF provides a menu-oriented application development environment. From within ABF the user can invoke VIFRED, VIGRAPH, and the designated editor. ABF provides a top-down environment for application development. This facility allows running and testing frames at each level before moving to the next-lower level in the application hierarchy.

2. *ESQL.* ESQL allows the user to write programs in 3GLs such as COBOL, C, Pascal, FORTRAN, PL/I, and Ada and embed database access and forms control statements. All the form control capabilities available to 4GL applications are also available through these programs. Unlike a 4GL application, where data can be passed directly between database columns and form fields, in an ESQL program the user has to go via program variables. ESQL modules have to be run through a preprocessor provided by INGRES. The preprocessor converts the embedded statements into the 3GL statements being used. The forms also have to be preprocessed. All preprocessed modules and forms are then compiled and linked to create a load module that can be run from the operating system.

11.4 LOGIX

(a) General description.   LOGIX is marketed by Logical Software, Inc. It runs under the UNIX operating system. Compared to INGRES, LOGIX offers much fewer capabilities. There are three components of LOGIX:

1. LOGIX commands entered directly from the operating system level
2. Interpreted "quick query" (QQ) language
3. C interface that allows the user to access LOGIX from compiled C programs

There is no menu-driven interface. An end user who is knowledgeable in both LOGIX and UNIX can freely alternate between LOGIX and UNIX commands and use shell facilities such as I/O redirection and shell parameter substitution. Frequently used LOGIX and UNIX commands can be saved in command files for ready reference.

LOGIX provides mechanisms that ensure the integrity of data stored in a relation, and will report items that violate user-specified integrity constraints. It also allows for networking between specific databases. Users may share data from one database, and the database owner can specify which users or groups have access to particular items of a relation.

(b) Data definition.   LOGIX does not use SQL. Figure 11–1 gives a list of LOGIX commands. The user creates a database directory with the command MAKEDB. Within that directory a relation is defined with the DEFINE command. However, before using this command the structure of the relation (i.e., column names and formats) must be defined in a separate file RELATION.s, created with a text editor, where RELATION is the name of the relation to be DEFINEd subsequently.

Database Maintenance

    logix   *Set up LOGIX environment*

    lxecho   *Display the LOGIX environment*

    makedb   *Create a database*

    removedb   *Remove a database*

Relation Maintenance

    copy   Copy a relation

    define   Define a relation

    domainof   Display domains of elements of a relation

    dumpr   Dump a relation to a text file

    format   Test the format for *load* or *addto*

    index   Create one relation which indexes another

    keyof   Display the type of a key

    remove   Remove a relation from the database

    rename   Rename a relation

    show   Display relations in a database and their features

    typeof   Display the structure of a relation

    verify   Analyze and restore a *dumpr*ed relation

Item Manipulation

    addto   Add items from a text file to a relation

    append   Add items of one relation to another nondestructively

    delete   Delete items from a relation

    load   Load a relation from a text file

    fred   Interactively edit the items of a relation

    update   Add items of one relation to another preserving new items in conflicts

Relation Output

    display   Print a "boxed" listing of a relation

    flist   Produce a fancy listing

    list   List the items of a relation

Relational Operations

    join   Construct the join of two relations

    project   Construct a vertical slice of a relation

    sort   Sort a relation

    common   Set theoretic intersection of two relations

    union   Set theoretic union of two relations

    select   Create a relation with some items of another

    qq   Process an interpreted query

Aggregation Operations

    avg   Average columns over groups of items

    count   Compute sizes of groups of items

    max   Find maxima of columns over groups of items

    min   Find minima of columns over groups of items

    sum   Sum columns over groups

Comparison Operations

    compare   Compare two relations

    conflicts   Report on items with common keys but different residual col

    diffa   Report differences from one point of view

    diffb   Report differences from another point of view

    merge   Construct a relation containing information from two other relations

Figure 11–1   LOGIX command summary.

Dated Relations

chrone	Create a relation describing the history of another
clone	Copy a dated relation retaining its history
date	Print the date in a congenial format
flash	Flashback to another time
log	Give a synopsis of a relation's history
rollback	Restore a relation to an earlier state

Figure 11–1   (cont.)

In a LOGIX database every relation must have a key consisting of one or more attributes. The key is declared in the .s file as follows:

1. The list of key attribute(s) appears first followed by a colon(:).
2. All nonkey attributes then follow and are separated from one another by blanks, commas, or newlines.

The data contained in a relation named RELATION, say, are stored in a file RELATION.d.

(c) Data manipulation.   The user can retrieve the full contents of a relation via a DISPLAY, FLIST, or LIST command. Qualified retrieval according to user-specified condition(s) can be done by the SELECT command. Other retrievals are done via the commands JOIN, PROJECT, COMMON, UNION, MERGE, and so on. (See Figure 11–1 for a complete list.) Updates of a relation are made with the commands APPEND, DELETE, LOAD, and UPDATE. The LOAD command allows bulk loading of data from a text file into a relation. LOGIX supports the five aggregation functions AVG, COUNT, MAX, MIN, and SUM. It should be noted that the SELECT command in LOGIX is much less powerful than the same command in SQL, because LOGIX provides separate commands to perform joins, projections, unions, and so on, whereas SQL performs all these functions with the single command SELECT. The SELECT in LOGIX performs the selection operation of relational algebra (see Section 3.2.2). The dated relations form a special feature of LOGIX (see Section 2.9).

(d) Application development.   LOGIX does not provide a 4GL application generator for application development. The programmer has to write programs in C to implement application components such as multilevel menus, screens, and reports. LOGIX commands and calls to the QQ language within LOGIX form a part of the programs. The C interface of LOGIX allows the programmer to develop such applications using compiled C programs.

11.5 ORACLE

(a) General description.   ORACLE is marketed by Oracle Corporation of Belmont, California. ORACLE was the first commercially available relational

DBMS offering SQL (then called SEQUEL) as the query language. The DBMS runs on a variety of hardware and operating systems such as IBM/MVS, IBM/VM-CMS, VAX/VMS, VAX/ULTRIX, and PRIME/PRIMOS. The basic ORACLE products include RDBMS (the kernel), SQL*PLUS query language, SQL*Forms screen formatter, SQL*Report report writer, SQL*Loader bulk data loading facility, export/import utilities for database backup and recovery, and host language interfaces for specific 3GLs, such as COBOL, C, FORTRAN, and Pascal. Additional utilities are SQL* Menu menu formatter, SQL*Calc spreadsheet software, SQL*Net networking tool, SQL*Design Dictionary CASE tool, and SQL*Graphs graphics package.

All software titles prefixed with "SQL" are interactive and command driven and therefore are meant for experienced users. By contrast, product titles prefixed with "Easy" (e.g., Easy*SQL) indicate full-screen products that guide users through their work, offering them choices via menus and detailed on-line help. They are intended for new or infrequent users of ORACLE. Easy*SQL is the menu-driven interface of ORACLE. Host language interfaces are prefixed with "Pro," as in Pro*C and Pro*FORTRAN.

(b) Data definition.   Tables in an ORACLE database are created using the CREATE TABLE command. It includes the following information:

1. Name of the table
2. Name of each column
3. Type of data to be stored in each column
4. Width of each column
5. Other optional information, such as NOT NULL, to indicate that the designed column cannot accept NULL values

The command contains three optional clauses:

1. SPACE: specifies a storage space definition that is to govern the table's location and disk storage allocation.
2. PCTFREE: specifies the percentage of space to keep free for updates. When a row is inserted into the table, ORACLE allocates a new block for storing the row if inserting it in an existing block will leave less than PCTFREE percent free space in that block.
3. CLUSTER: specifies that the table is to be included in the designated cluster.

(c) Data manipulation.   ORACLE allows data manipulation (retrieval and update) in three ways:

1. Menu-driven interface (Easy*SQL)
2. Command-driven interface (SQL*Plus)
3. Form-driven interface (SQL*Forms)

In method 1 the user selects menu options and responds to the prompts posed by the software. In method 2 the user uses standard SQL commands, such as SELECT, INSERT, DELETE, and UPDATE. Simple and qualified retrievals are possible. Complex retrievals and updates can use nested queries in which the processing starts with the lowest query in the nest and moves upward. INSERT adds one row at a time, while INSERT AS SELECT adds multiple rows that are returned by the predicate of SELECT. DELETE and UPDATE work on a group of rows based on the criteria specified by the user.

In method 3 the user retrieves data by performing a query on a form based on the table(s) where the data reside. Updates are done using a blank form corresponding to the table(s) to be updated. Triggers can be attached to a form for validation purpose. Thus referential integrity can be enforced by means of triggers. ORACLE does not have a JOIN command, so that joins are done by properly phrased SELECT statements.

Views are defined from one or more tables with CREATE VIEW command and are retrieved in the same way as tables. ORACLE allows updates of tables through views in the following cases:

1. Rows may be deleted from a table through a view if the query used to define the view observes these restrictions:
   It selects rows from only one table.
   It does not contain a GROUP BY clause, a DISTINCT clause, a group function, or a reference to the pseudo-column ROWNUM.
2. Rows may be updated in a table through a view if the query used to define the view observes both of the restrictions above and the following:
   It does not define any of the updated columns with an expression.
3. Rows may be inserted in a table through a view if the query used to define the view observes all three of the foregoing restrictions and the following:
   Any NOT NULL columns defined in the underlying table are represented in the view.

Reports can be generated in three ways:

1. Using reporting commands in SQL*Plus
2. Using the utility SQL*Report, which is completely procedural, or SQL*Report Writer, which is menu driven and screen based
3. Using a 3GL interface such as Pro*COBOL or Pro*C.

Highly complex reports cannot be developed using method 1. The programmer should use method 2 or 3.

(d) Application development.   ORACLE-based applications are best generated by using a combination of its utilities. For example, menus and screens can be developed with SQL*Forms, and reports can be generated with

SQL*Report or SQL*ReportWriter. Alternatively, the programmer can use host language interface programs consisting of 3GL code and blocks of embedded SQL statements. ORACLE RDBMS version 6.0.27 offers PL/SQL, a procedural language containing blocks of nonprocedural SQL statements used for retrieval and update of data in tables. ORACLE allows the same commands to be used in both interactive and embedded modes.

SQL*Net allows networking of ORACLE tables in a distributed database environment. However, a user can only retrieve data from a remote location. Update of remote tables is still not available from SQL*Net.

SQL*Design Dictionary (SDD) is a CASE tool without graphics. It offers a menu-driven and prompt-oriented environment for the analysis and design of an application. SDD has been augmented with graphics capability and is called CASE.

11.6 RIM

(a) General description.   RIM, an acronym for Relational Information Management, was developed by Boeing Commercial Aircraft System under contract to the National Aeronautic and Space Agency as part of the Integrated Program for Aerospace Vehicle Design. It was initially developed to satisfy the data-handling needs of design engineers; as such it was required to handle vectors and matrices and be relatively easy to use. A further design intention was portability. The RIM was developed on a CDC Cyber and then adapted to other computers, such as CYBER, CRAY, IBM, VAX, PRIME, DATA GENERAL, and UNIVAC computers.

In early 1980 RIM was made available as a public domain program and the source code could be obtained for the cost of material and handling—generally less than $500. By the summer of 1982, Boeing Computer Services formally adopted the RIM as a commercial product. Boeing Computer Services have expanded the RIM with such features as plot and edit capabilities, added a precompiler, and enhanced the report writing. Boeing Computer Services subsequently upgraded the documentation.

RIM offers a menu-driven interface and a command-driven interface for the user. Both support the following three options:

1. Create a new database.
2. Update an existing database.
3. Query an existing database.

The menu-driven interface is geared toward the beginner or an infrequent user of RIM. It is significantly slower than the command-driven interface, because the user has to select menu options and respond to prompts at every step in order to continue the dialogue.

The command-driven interface consists of three modules: DEFINE, LOAD, and RETRIEVE. They are used respectively for defining a database, loading data into a database, and querying (retrieval and update) a database. RIM does not have separate screen formatting or report generation utilities. It offers host language interface commands for FORTRAN 77.

RIM does not require that every relation be normalized and supports matrix type data where a matrix can be of type $m \times n$. Also, SQL is not the query language for RIM, although some of the commands syntax of RIM resemble those of SQL.

(b) Data definition.   A RIM user in a command-driven interface defines a database using the DEFINE submodule commands in the following sequence:

1. DEFINE database-name
2. OWNER password
3. ATTRIBUTES list-of-attributes
4. RELATIONS list-of-relations
5. PASSWORDS password-clauses
6. RULES rule-clauses
7. END

Commands 5 and 6 are optional. The user specifies a ''database-name'' under command 1 to which his or her ''password'' applies, as in command 2. Additional passwords at individual relation level can be assigned by command 5. Using command 3 the user lists *all* the attributes belonging to *all* the relations in the database. Each attribute is assigned a name, a type (which can be scalar or matrix), a length, and a designator KEY if that attribute is a primary key. Using command 4 the user indicates which attributes belong to which relations. The syntax is

```
relation-name WITH attribute-list
```

Using command 6, the user can introduce a set of validation conditions both among attributes within a relation and among attributes belonging to multiple relations. All attributes referred to in RULES must have been defined previously via the ATTRIBUTES command and grouped into relations by the RELATIONS command. The command END signifies the end of the data definition phase.

(c) Data manipulation.   A database must be OPENEd via the ''OPEN database-name'' command in order to perform any data manipulation. In the command-driven interface, data retrieval is done through a variety of commands as follows:

1. The SELECT, TALLY, PROJECT, and SUBTRACT commands permit re-

trieval of data by a single attribute or combination of attributes. A WHERE clause, coupled with the SELECT, TALLY, PROJECT, and SUBTRACT commands, permits retrieval of data by rows based on attribute value. The first three commands operate on a single relation, while the last command uses two relations.

2. The INTERSECT and JOIN commands are similar in that each command combines two relations. The INTERSECT command restricts the newly formed relation to specified attributes, while the JOIN command lists all attributes of the two relations in the join. The JOIN further permits logical operations such as EQ, NE, GE, LE, LT, and GT, which the INTERSECT does not.

3. The LISTREL ALL command displays the definitions of all relations in the database.

4. The EXHIBIT command takes up to 10 attribute names as arguments and displays the names of all relations containing one or more of these attributes.

5. The user can use the built-in functions COUNT, MIN, MAX, AVE, and SUM as a part of the generic COMPUTE function that performs mathematical computations.

6. The BUILD KEY command changes an attributes from nonkey to key. The DELETE KEY command reverses the result of BUILD KEY. Data may be retrieved based on single keys, multiple keys, and nonkey attributes. Data cannot be retrieved on concatenated fields.

7. Data may be moved from a file, external to the relational database, to the relational database via the INPUT command. Data may be moved from a relational database to an external file via an OUTPUT command. Data may be moved from/to files to/from relational databases via FORTRAN application programs. Data and Database Schema may be moved to/from other RIM databases.

Data update is performed as follows:

1. The LOAD command adds rows to a relation.
2. The DELETE command deletes rows from a relation.
3. The CHANGE command changes attribute values in a relation.

New relations may be created from two given relations via INTERSECT, JOIN, and SUBTRACT commands, and from a single relation via the PROJECT command. RIM does not support SQL. As with LOGIX (Section 11.4), the SELECT command in RIM is a truly relational algebra operation and as such is much more limited in capability than is the SELECT command of SQL. Also, RIM does not support views. Simple reports can be generated within the command-driven interface by using a set of formatting commands, BLANK, TITLE, DATE, LINES, and WIDTH.

(d) Application development. RIM does not have special application generators using 4GL commands and/or interactive screen input. Its host language interface routines for FORTRAN 77 are the only tools for developing applications. Form-oriented input screens are not supported. However, reports of any level of complexity can be produced.

Any programming language that can call FORTRAN subroutines can access and modify a predefined RIM database through FORTRAN-callable subroutines contained in the RIM application program interface library (RIMLIB). Data are accessed one row at a time. The RIM data access subroutines store data in and retrieve data from an array that the programmer provides in the program. The programmer can use one array for accessing each, or all, relations, depending on the program logic. In either case, the array used must be large enough to hold a complete row for each relation accessed.

The application program interface requires the programmer to manage the database files. The database files must exist on three properly named logical files before the program can be executed.

11.7 UNIFY

(a) General description. UNIFY is marketed by Unify Corporation of California and runs with the UNIX operating system alone. The basic product, called UNIFY RDBMS, is heavily oriented toward menus and prompts. During the database design, implementation, and modification phases the user merely selects options from menus and responds to prompts. The product allows the user to design data entry screens using a screen painter and to generate complex reports using a report processor. The user can perform ad hoc queries in SQL by selecting the option, SQL-Query/DML Language, from UNIFY Main Menu. Alternatively, the user can perform query by forms in a manner analogous to QBF of INGRES.

ACCELL Integrated Development System is an application generator built on top of UNIFY RDBMS. As such, ACCELL consists of the following five components:

1. *UNIFY RDBMS:* the basic product
2. *ACCELL application generator:* includes a form painter to enter and validate data definitions
3. *ACCELL procedural language:* allows a programmer to develop applications using looping, branching, and assignment statements and supports three types of variables: attributes in relations, screen fields, and general purpose variables
4. *ACCELL window driver:* overlays multiple windows (forms) on a screen, displays context sensitive help messages, screens, and function key assignments, and displays database status

5. *ACCELL development environment:* supports interactive definition of database design, forms, 4GL scripts, and menu-driven application development

(b) Data definition.   UNIFY does not have any DDL statements. A database is designed entirely through menu options and prompts. Internally, UNIFY stores all data in a single repository called file.db and stores the schema of the database in another repository called unify.db. The latter contains additional information, such as record relationships, record change list, and field change list. In effect, unify.db contains the data dictionary for the user.

A user can implement a database as follows (see Figure 11–2 for UNIFY menu map):

1. Select option 1 (Design and Create a New Database) from the Main Menu.
2. Enter the name, expected number of records, and a long name (optional) for each record type. Note that a file is called a record type in UNIFY.
3. For each record type, enter the name, type, length, long name (optional), key (if applicable), and reference (if applicable) for each field.
4. Answer 'Y' to the following five questions displayed on the screen:
   a. Print database design?
   b. Create database?
   c. Create data entry screens?
   d. Create menu?
   e. Are these choices OK?

At the end of step 4, UNIFY creates the empty database structure, containing all record types and their respective fields, detailed data dictionary information formatted for printing, a separate data entry screen for each record type, and a new item, labeled option 8 (Data Entry Screens) on the Main Menu.

UNIFY allows a variety of design modifications after the initial database has been created. For example, a user can add new fields to an existing record type, modify the type/name/structure of a field in a record type, change information in key and reference columns, and so on. However, the modification process is quite cumbersome and time consuming, due to the menu/prompt-oriented interface of UNIFY. The user proceeds as follows to modify an existing database (see Figure 11–2):

1. Select option 6 (Database Design Utilities) from the Main Menu.
2. Select option 1 (Modify Database Design) from the submenu. (The screen displays a list of all the record types in the current database.)
3. Enter the number of the record type you want to modify. [The cursor moves to the CMD (command) column for the record type selected.]
4. Enter an appropriate command (e.g., 'f' to modify a field, 'a' to add a new record type, etc.). Follow directions to make modifications. At the end press 'CTRL U' to incorporate these changes into the database.

MENU MAP

Main Menu

1. Design and Create a New Data Base
2. Create or Modify Screen Forms
3. SQL-Query/DML Language
4. Edit SQL or RPT Command Files
5. Add, Modify or Delete Menus
6. Data Base Design Utilities
7. System Administration

Create or Modify Screens Forms

1. Paint Screen Forms
2. Register Screen Form with ENTER
3. Register Screen Form with SQL
4. Check Screen Form Coordinates
5. Display List of Screens
6. Test Screens
7. Compile Screens
8. Restore Screen to Data Dictionary
9. Create Default Screen Form

Data Base Design Utilities

1. Modify Data Base Design
2. Print Data Base Design
3. Create Data Base
4. Write Data Base Backup
5. Reconfigure Data Base
6. Add, Drop B-Tree Indexes
7. Advanced Field Attributes

System Administration

1. Transaction Logging Status
2. Data Base Maintenance
3. Security Maintenance
4. Create or Modify Help Documentation
5. Describe Program to System
6. Program Loading
7. Data Dictionary Reports

Data Dictionary Reports

1. Print Data Base Design
2. Print Menus
3. Print Screens
4. Print Group Privileges
5. Print Individual Privileges
6. Print Help Documentation
7. Print List of Programs

Data Base Maintenance

1. Write Data Base Backup
2. Read Data Base Backup
3. Add, Drop B-Tree Indexes
4. Rebuild the Hash Table
5. Rebuild Explicit Relationships
6. Define Data Base Volumes
7. Print, Display Data Base Statistics
8. Display Hash Table Statistics.
9. Print, Display B-Tree Statistics

Security Maintenance

1. Modify System Parameters & Security
2. Add or Modify Group Privileges
3. Add or Modify Individual Privileges
4. Print Group Privileges
5. Print Individual Privileges
6. Field Security Maintenance
7. Process Field Passwords

Figure 11–2   UNIFY menu map.*

* Reprinted with permission from Unify Corporation

302

The changes made during the database modification stage as described above are not yet reflected in the database itself. To do so, proceed as follows:

5. Select option 4 (Write Database Backup) from the submenu in step 2. (This action stores the premodification version of the database on tape or diskette and displays a message 'Backup complete' at the end.)

6. Select option 5 (Reconfigure Database) from the submenu in step 2. (This action reconfigures the database to incorporate the modifications and displays a message: 'Process complete. Backup the database.')

7. Repeat step 5 but select a different tape or diskette from the one before. Copies of both versions of the database are thereby retained.

Instead of storing each record type in a separate data file, as is done in most other DBMS packages, UNIFY stores all of them in a single file called file.db. This makes the reconfiguration of a database after schema modifications a really cumbersome process. The reconfiguration program is often described as unstable and time consuming. The "hardwired" linkage that UNIFY establishes among the repeated fields makes the database structure very rigid with respect to changes. One cannot easily remove or change record types in the database until their respective linkages are adjusted. From this aspect UNIFY behaves more like a network DBMS instead of a relational DBMS.

(c) Data manipulation.   UNIFY handles data manipulation through the menu-driven interface, although SQL commands can be entered for ad hoc queries. Such queries include both retrieval and update of records. In addition, two screen painter options, ENTER and PAINT, are available for data entry using default screens or modified screens. We divide the discussion into four parts: (1) data loading, (2) ad hoc queries, (3) report generation, and (4) host language interface.

1. *Data loading.* The user proceeds as follows:

a. Select option 8 (Data Entry Screens) from the Main Menu. (A new menu is displayed with the names of the record types already created.)

b. Select option 1 to enter data into the first record type. (A screen form is displayed with the name of the record type at the top and the name of each field listed vertically). A prompt appears at the bottom with four options:

```
(I)NQUIRE
(A)DD
(M)ODIFY
(D)ELETE
```

c. Select option 'A' to add data into the record. (The cursor moves to the first field on the screen.)

d. Enter data into each field and press RETURN. Repeat this process until you have entered data into all the fields in this record.

e. Repeat step 2 by selecting option 'N' to enter data into the 'Nth' record type. Then repeat steps 3 and 4 to enter data into all the fields within each record type.

2. *Ad hoc queries.* UNIFY supports SQL for generating ad hoc query reports. Each row in a table is referenced by two field names: FIELD and LONG NAME. FIELD must be unique for each field and can be up to eight characters. LONG NAME is *not* unique and can be up to 16 characters. If a field is repeated among tables for linkages, its FIELD value must be unique for each table, while its LONG NAME must be the same in each table. SQL uses the LONG NAME values to process ad hoc queries and to join multiple tables via common fields. FIELD values are not recognized by SQL.

To produce an ad hoc query report, perform the following steps:

a. Select option 3 (SQL—Query/DML Language) from the Main Menu. (The SQL-prompt 'sql' appears.)

b. Enter the appropriate SQL command for the query. UNIFY supports the following SQL clauses:

select	information from the database
from	specific record types
where	a condition is true or false
group by	specific fields
having	a true or false condition
order by	specific fields
into	an ASCII file
insert	records into the database
update	fields in existing records
delete	records from the database

Also, it is possible to send the output of a SQL query to an ASCII file by using the 'select . . . into' command and to add new records from an ASCII file to a database by using the 'insert into' command. In the latter case, the complete path of the ASCII file must be given.

3. *Report generation.* UNIFY provides a report processor, called RPT, which allows the user to design a multilevel tabular report. The data for the report can come from a SQL query, QBF query, a user program, or an ASCII file. RPT needs the following files to produce a report:

a. *Input file:* contains the data to be used in the report

b. *Report script file:* contains the RPT commands describing the format of the input lines and the format of the report

RPT reads the data in the input file and uses the commands in the report script to produce the report.

4. *Host language interface.* UNIFY offers only the language C as a host language. The programmer proceeds as follows to use this interface:

a. Write C program.

b. Ensure that the program has the command

```
#include "file.h"
```

as a processor macro.

c. Compile using UCC utility of UNIFY.

d. Link and load the image with UNIFY and C libraries.

(d) Application development.   ACCELL IDS is the application generator for UNIFY. It is an extra layer of software built on the top of UNIFY. The database creation is still to be done by UNIFY either prior to invoking ACCELL or invoking it from within ACCELL.

Once the database is implemented using UNIFY, ACCELL works as an application developer. An application consists of a set of forms that supply the relevant data to the application and a language script that contains the programs to generate the application.

ACCELL links the forms in a multiform application by means of repeated fields among them and displays these linked forms as overlapping windows on the screen. The user can quickly move from one window to another via menus and prompts.

The programmer writes the language scripts in an ACCELL-specific language that is *wrongly claimed* by Unify Corporation to be a 4GL. The language is *not* 4GL, since the programmer must specify all the programming logic, including IF-THEN-ELSE and DO-WHILE type constructs. The language is really a procedural 3GL type. The only element of nonprocedurality in ACCELL arises out of the situation that different modules in a program are not necessarily executed in a sequential manner, but instead, on as-needed basis.

In 1989 Unify Corporation upgraded ACCELL IDS to ACCELL/SQL incorporating an open system architecture.

(e) Comments.   We have described the operation of UNIFY in considerably more detail than any of the other DBMSs. The reason is that unlike these other packages, UNIFY uses menus and prompts very heavily, leaving the user a very limited scope of using SQL commands. This has both positive and negative side effects. On the positive side, this feature is helpful for the beginner or for an occasional user. On the negative side, the same feature appears to be cumbersome and unnecessarily slowing for a programmer or an experienced end user. They may find this overabundance of menus and prompts to be a drag on the system. Normally, when a DBMS provides menus and prompts profusely for beginners, an alternative route is also provided for programmers or experienced end users to bypass the menus and prompts by using a command mode. UNIFY does not offer that alternative. Some of the additional difficulties of UNIFY are listed below.

1. UNIFY has no DDL (data definition language). Database creation is slow and menu driven. There is no way to bypass except by writing a separate C program and loading it into unify.db.

2. Declaration of key attributes is less flexible. A table can have *only one* key, which can be a combination (COMB type) of two or more attributes. To define a new key or to restructure existing key requires a reconfiguration of the database. For a file with 50,000 records, each record having 60 fields, the reconfiguration takes nearly 6 hours.

3. An estimate of the number of records in a file is *required* at the time of creating the database. UNIFY allows a 60 percent overflow beyond the estimate. But after that it issues error messages. Thus an underestimate may lead to problems, and an overestimate may tie up disk space unnecessarily.

11.8 dBASE III PLUS

(a) General description.   dBase III Plus is marketed by Ashton-Tate Corporation of Torrance, California. It is a PC-based DBMS and runs adequately on the XT-class computers. On an AT-class machine with a hard disk, it is suitable for applications involving thousands of records. A multiuser version supports file and record locking on popular local-area networks.

dBase III Plus operates in two modes of operations: a menu-driven mode called The Assistant and a command-driven mode. Under the former the user accesses the system through a set of options that cover only a subset of the full functional capabilities of dBase III Plus. Under the latter the user interacts directly with the system by entering DDL and DML commands that are non-SQL. The February 1989 upgrade, dBase IV, supports SQL to create and maintain SQL databases stored in the form of standard dBase III Plus files.

Screen design and report formatting are possible by using the internal programming language of dBase III Plus. The user can create output screens of any format by directing the output to the screen with the @ command and can use special features of a particular terminal, such as highlighting or reverse video. Input screens can be created with the formatted GET command along with @ to allow the loading of an input value via a prompt from anywhere on the screen.

Reports can be produced by using any one of four methods: output commands, report generator, SET PRINT command, and formatted reports. The user can use them in a program or combine them as necessary in an application. dBase III Plus also provides interfaces to external report generators.

Finally, dBase III Plus allows application development by using combination of its internal programming language and the DDL and DML commands. Menu-driven customized business applications are fairly easy to implement.

dBase III Plus has the following limitations:

1. dBase III Plus programs are slower than compiled programs using C or Pascal.

2. dBase III Plus cannot process arrays, and data usually must be stored in files or memory variables. This limits the speed of programs and makes programming more cumbersome.

3. dBase III Plus has only limited text processing capabilities.

All of the limitations except the last can be eliminated by using either a compiler or the dBase TOOLS utilities. dBase III Plus is particularly suitable for the following types of applications:

1. Development of applications software (financial, inventory control, information management) in which a small number of files are used and only a few indices must be active at a time.

2. Prototypes of software for more complex applications of the same type that will be developed with languages such as C or Pascal.

3. Very fast data management of simple files. Examples of such applications would include compiling a mailing list for processing a form letter or managing a disk filing system for a personal computer.

4. Quick reporting and analyzing of data created with dBase III Plus or other software for management decisions.

5. Rapid design of input forms (screens) for entry of data to be used dBase III Plus or other programs.

(b) Data definition.   A relation is created with the CREATE command whose format is CREATE relation-name. After entering the command the user is prompted for entering information on each attribute under four headers: Field Name, Type, Width, and Dec (Decimal Position).

A relation must be opened with the command USE relation-name before it can be queried. The attributes of an opened relation can be viewed with the command DISPLAY STRUCTURE. Each relation is stored in a data file with the extension .DBF. At most 15 files, data and index, can remain open at any given instant. As many as 10 of these files can be .DBF files. Open files are closed with the command CLOSE file-name.

(c) Data manipulation.   When a relation has been opened via the USE command, a user can retrieve data from it by means of the commands BROWSE, DISPLAY, and LIST. The three commands are fairly similar in their scope except that the BROWSE command cannot be used to direct its output to the printer. Qualified data retrievals are possible in all cases by using selection criteria in the predicate. FOR ⟨exp⟩ and WHILE⟨exp⟩ are used to select records, where ⟨exp⟩ is any valid dBase III Plus expression.

There are two ways to print with the LIST command. One alternative is to use the TO PRINT option with the command. The other is to use the SET PRINT ON command before issuing the LIST command. If SET PRINT ON is used, the output will be directed to the printer.

The DISPLAY command is similar to LIST except that dBase III Plus pauses every 20 records and asks if the user desires to continue. In addition, on DISPLAY the scope does not default to ALL. If the user omits the ALL, dBase III PLUS displays only the current record. With both commands the user can use the SET HEADING ON command to print headings.

The DISPLAY command can be used to display a structure memory variable list, or system status using DISPLAY STRUCTURE, DISPLAY MEMORY, or DISPLAY STATUS, respectively. The LIST command can be used in the same way. dBase III Plus supports the JOIN command to combine two relations to form a third relation based on specified criteria.

Primary key attributes in a relation can be indexed via the command INDEX ON attribute-name. Multiple attributes can be included in an index by connecting their names with a plus (+) sign. The commands FIND and SEEK can be used to retrieve records by indexed access. FIND takes only a character string as its argument, whereas SEEK can be used with any expression. The command LO-CATE is used for sequential access only.

New records can be added to a relation via the APPEND command or the BROWSE command. Under APPEND, a blank structure of the relation is displayed with the attributes listed vertically, and the user fills in each attribute value in the proper slot. Under BROWSE, the attributes are displayed horizontally, so that a scroll to the right or to the left may be necessary to enter data for a given attribute. An existing record can be deleted with ⟨Ctrl-U⟩ with the EDIT command, or using the DELETE command in a program. The latter option is recommended since it keeps track of the deletion. The UPDATE command can be used to update relations from a separate data file that contains the key and the updating information.

The most convenient way to generate a report is by using the command CREATE REPORT report-name. This command creates the file report-name.FRM that stores the information on the format of the report and the relation containing the attributes used in the report. Only one relation can be used in a report. The .FRM file allows the user to set up a title for the report, a title for each column, number, or lines in a page (58 lines being the default), double spacing (if needed), and multiple layers of grouping for breaks and subtotals in the report.

dBase III Plus supports the function CHR( ), whereby the user can create almost any type of screen feature by supplying the argument with an appropriate ASCII code value. For example, CHR(7) can be used to "beep" the user since 7 is the ASCII bell code. Similarly, highlighting, reverse video, drawing a double-line box around a designated piece of information, and so on, can be done. All these screen formatting commands can be saved in a file with .FMT extension. The file can be called from a program.

(d) Application development.   dBase III Plus does not have any 4GL-based application generator. An application using dBase III Plus will consist of programs to generate screens and reports, create and manipulate one or more databases, perform housekeeping, and so on. Also dBase III Plus is compatible with a wide variety of programs and databases that are already created. Examples of such programs are spreadsheets such as Lotus 1-2-3, business graphics, and statistical analyzers.

dBase III Plus supports local-area networks under the model of one server and one or more workstations. A *server* is a computer system that makes all resources (files, disks, printers) available to other systems on the network. A *workstation* is a computer that uses resources on a remote server. Although dBase III Plus works with many of the available networks, the recommended networks include the PC network, the IBM Token-Ring Network, the 3Com 3Plus Network, and Novell's Advanced Netware (version 1.01 or later).

The server should have 640k of memory space, a hard disk, a monochrome or color monitor, and an 80-column printer. The workstations should have a minimum of 384k of memory (512k is better) and a monochrome or color monitor. A printer and hard disk are recommended. The user should also have all of the hardware and software necessary to support the network that is used.

11.9 SUMMARY

In the chapter we have provided an overview of seven DBMS packages, to give an outline of options generally available in the market. Basic information on each DBMS appears under four headers: general description, data definition, data manipulation, and application development. Figure 11–3 summarizes the principal features of each DBMS discussed in this chapter. An " × " in a cell indicates that the DBMS has the feature, whereas a blank entry means that the DBMS does not have the feature.

	INFORMIX	INGRES	LOGIX	ORACLE	RIM	UNIFY	dBase III Plus
SQL interface	×	×		×		×	
Other query language	×	×	×		×		×
Forms generator	×	×		×		×	×
Report writer	×	×		×		×	×
Host language interface	×	×	×	×	×	×	×
Application generator	×	×					×
Menu-driven interface	×	×		×	×	×	×
View support	×	×		×		×	

Figure 11–3   Principal features of seven DBMS packages.

KEY WORDS

dBaseIII Plus

embedded SQL

frame

INFORMIX

INGRES

interface, command-driven

interface, command-oriented

interface, form-driven

interface, menu-driven

joindef

LOGIX

ORACLE

procedure

report writer

RIM

server

UNIFY

validation conditions

workstation

REFERENCES AND FURTHER READING

The appropriate references on any DBMS are the manuals available from its vendor. In addition, newsletters from the vendors, articles in various trade journals, and seminar proceedings on specific DBMSs are helpful. The journal *Database Programming and Design* publishes papers dealing with specific products, such as INGRES and ORACLE.

CHAPTER 12

EVALUATION AND SELECTION OF A RELATIONAL DBMS

12.1 OBJECTIVES

When an organization plans to use database systems in its applications, it needs to identify a relational DBMS suitable for its use. This involves the evaluation of a set of DBMSs that tentatively satisfy the organization's database requirements and then selecting one for procurement. The entire process should be done in a fairly objective manner. The goal of this chapter is to provide a systematic way to perform this task.

12.2 METHODOLOGY

The evaluation and selection process consists of the following steps:

1. Establish a set of requirements to be met by every candidate DBMS.
2. Prepare a list of vendors who can supply the candidate packages.
3. Check with each vendor to determine if the DBMS indeed meets all the requirements.
4. Prepare a matrix showing which DBMS satisfies which requirements, and to what extent.
5. Use the matrix to prepare a score sheet that assigns a numeric score to each DBMS by using weights, if necessary, to prioritize the requirements.
6. Identify the selected candidate(s) in descending order of final score.

In Sections 12.2.1 through 12.2.6 the six steps above are discussed in more detail.

12.2.1 List of Requirements

The requirements are divided into six categories: (1) functions; (2) performance; (3) system support; (4) support for application generation; (5) data security and data integrity; and (6) user support, service, training, and maintenance.

(a) Functions

1. English-like query language (i.e., nonprocedural)
2. Integrated data dictionary
3. Retrieval of complete file, selected attributes of a relation (PROJECT), selected rows determined by selection conditions on keyed and/or nonkeyed attributes
4. Display of retrieved fields in user-specified order
5. Retrieval of combined files (JOIN, INTERSECT)
6. Logical operators (AND, OR, NOT)
7. Comparison operators ($<$, $=$, $>$, $!=$, $\geqslant$, $\leqslant$)
8. Built-in functions (SUM, AVG, COUNT, MAX, MIN)
9. Data manipulation (INSERT, DELETE, multiple MODIFY or UPDATE) on line
10. Views for relational DBMS so as to avoid storing duplicate data
11. Access control per user
12. Access control by type of access rights (e.g., READ only, INSERT/UPDATE/DELETE, USER assigns access privileges to other users)
13. Bulk load/unload from/to external devices
14. Purging relations from DB
15. I/O requirements: CRT, printer, disk, tape, graphics
16. Data types supported

(b) Performance

1. Database capacity limitations such as number of relations/database, attributes/relations, tuples/relation, characters/attribute, characters/index, characters/sortkey, attributes/index, attributes/sortkey, maximum number of indices/relation and indices/database, number of databases open
2. Conformity to ANSI standard X3H2 for SQL
3. Published benchmark tests, if available
4. Access methods for retrieval and update: for example, Is path optimized automatically? How? Does system use multiple access methods or just one?

If any key is multifield, does the system still use it to speed search on a portion of the key? Can programmer tell if up-to-date keys exist for a secondary field and then control their creation/use dynamically?

5. Run-time system: for example, Does a reduced memory and/or reduced-cost run-time system exist? Or will the vendor license additional sites at equivalent or a run-time package? Does a run-time system support ad hoc query capability?

6. Minimum memory requirements to run the DBMS?

7. Additional memory required to avoid excessive page swapping?

(c) System support

1. Language Capabilities
   a. Procedural commands?
      IF-THEN-ELSE
      LOOPS WITH NESTING (depth)
      Memory variables, Arrays (Dimensions)
   b. Compile and/or interpret?
   c. If compile, are compile and execute possible within a single execution?

2. Multiuser features
   a. Is it multiuser on mainframe/supermini? On PC?
   b. Does it support advanced record locking? What type of lock?
   c. Does each user require a complete copy of the program in their own memory partition, or is every user under the control of a resident application monitor?

3. Programming language interface (or host language interface)
   a. Are such interfaces available to Ada? C? COBOL? FORTRAN? Other languages?
   b. What languages are available on the PC version: Ada? C? COBOL? FORTRAN? Others?

4. Nature, convenience, and efficiency of interface
   a. Can a 3GL procedure be called from a 4GL procedure?
   b. Does it automatically cause a return to the OS to do so, including resulting overhead?
   c. Or can it be embedded right in same program? How?
   d. Can it pass and return memory variables?
   e. Can 3GLs access all the DBMS manipulation facilities?
   f. How (interpretive SQL versus compiled?)
   g. Can 3GLs have menu choices within a single program that will cause different screen forms/reports to be executed without returning to the OS to start again?
   h. Degree of access to OS facilities within the program?

5. Data I/O, for example:
   a. To and from ASCII fixed field format?
   b. To and from delimited format?
   c. What file transfer facilities are available?
   d. Can a table be transmitted without first unloading it from the database? Is table format published so that machine-to-machine transmission could be done by a table?

6. Data dictionary, for example:
   a. User accessible?
   b. Can database be redefined by developer once set up?
   c. Used for referential integrity?
   d. Used for active validation?
   e. Can DBA restrict valid column/field names?
   f. Length of a column name? (Is the PC version the same?)
   g. Length of column alias?

7. Software Tools Library

(d) Support for application generation

1. Forms capabilities
   a. Insert and update directly from form?
   b. Screen painting facility (to create/modify form)?
   c. Multipage forms (including control of moving to/from pages)?
   d. Windowing or other access to browsing through other table(s) on screen while processing an original form (table)?
   e. Otherwise using and/or storing information from/to two or more tables on one screen?
   f. Calculated variables within form?
   g. Automatic referential integrity?
   h. Automatic validation based on dictionary values as opposed to screen-dependent values?

2. Report generation
   a. What you see is what you get, and report painting?
   b. Default reports per table (editable)?
   c. Easy totaling
   d. Other calculations within reports: on details; on created totals?
   e. Passing memory variables to report or equivalent?

3. Menu generation
   a. Context-sensitive help text available?
   b. Can menu branching be done within one execution of the program without returning control to the OS?
   c. Basic menu capabilities?

(e) Data security and data integrity

1. Security within the DBMS itself
   a. User name/password for log-on?
   b. Read versus modify password control by table?
   c. Multiple or single valid passwords/table by field within database or within table?
   d. Data encryption?
   e. Script encryption?

2. Data integrity
   a. Journaling?
   b. Roll back?
   c. Roll forward?
   d. Failure protection—transactions immediately journaled to disk?
   e. Transaction processing?

(f) User support, service, training, and maintenance

1. Product maturity
   a. Report from users (speed, ease of use, support, etc.)?
   b. Support from vendor?

2. User training
   a. Number of hours of training provided by the vendor at no additional cost?
   b. Number of persons to be trained by the vendor at no additional cost?
   c. Additional cost for training of a given number of hours? (At what rate?)
   d. Additional cost for training a given number of people? (How many persons?)
   e. Availability of training materials from vendor?

3. Service
   a. Vendor responsiveness?
   b. Quality of available documentations?
   c. Basic purchase or lease price for RDBMS?
   d. Additional software cost for utilities?

12.2.2 Initial Vendor List

To prepare a vendor list, start by reading the reviews of relational DBMS packages by independent reviewers such as DATAPRO or Auerbach Information Management Services. Also attend seminars offered by the vendors to get overviews of different packages. Since these seminars are mostly complimentary, the presentations involve a sales pitch. Therefore, use such seminar materials cautiously and eliminate the vendors' hypes.

Asking peers who have used or know about a DBMS is another valuable source of information for preparing an initial vendor list. If necessary, conduct one or more interviews with a peer knowledgeable about a DBMS. Provide him or her a list of your requirements prior to the interview. Then, during the interview go through the list and ask for specific comments or opinions regarding each item on the list. Follow up the interview session with a written summary of your findings and share it with the peer for accuracy of your interpretation of the discussion. After appropriate screening of materials one can prepare a tentative list of vendors who offer database systems that meet most of the requirements established earlier.

12.2.3 Final Vendor List

Check with each vendor in the initial vendor list for an in-depth assessment of the software. Ideally, provide the vendors with a complete list of requirements and ask them to respond to each question in writing. In addition, ask them to give a presentation of their individual software, using your own data and applications, if possible. Also insist that technical staff be available to answer technical questions during the presentation. Ask for a list of installations of the product and contact at least three such references to get a feeling for the product's capabilities and the support provided by the vendor.

12.2.4 Requirements Analysis Matrix

A *requirements analysis matrix* is designed as a matrix in which each row represents a specific requirement to be satisfied by a candidate DBMS and each column represents the name of a DBMS. An entry in cell (i, j) of the matrix indicates how the DBMS j satisfies the requirement i, whereas a blank cell (i, j) shows that the DBMS j does not satisfy the requirement i. It is quite possible that not all of the requirements will be satisfied by a DBMS. After preparing the final list of vendors, design the requirements analysis matrix. Fill in each cell with the information gathered already and leave cells empty, if necessary.

12.2.5 Score Sheet for Final Selection

Divide the requirements into two categories: mandatory and desirable. Assign a weight of 10 to each mandatory requirement and a weight ranging from 1 to 9 to a desirable requirement, depending on the degree of desirability. A higher number indicates a greater degree of desirability. The values 1 through 10 are somewhat arbitrary and a wider range of values may be selected. By adding all the assigned values for the requirements in the list, one gets the maximum possible score that a candidate DBMS can have.

Next, take one DBMS at a time. For a given requirement in your list assign a value to the DBMS by estimating how well or how poorly the DBMS meets the requirement. If the DBMS does not satisfy the requirement, assign a value zero to the appropriate cell. After completing this exercise, add all the assigned values. The total represents the score for the DBMS.

12.2.6 Final Selection

Arrange the candidate DBMSs in descending order of magnitude of the total scores. Identify the topmost candidate as the most suitable, the next to the top as the second most suitable, and so on. The scoring process outlined above is very similar to grading students' papers in an examination. As such, it is a subjective assessment.

12.3 SUMMARY

In this chapter we have discussed a methodology for evaluation and selection of a DBMS, relational or nonrelational, to meet the needs of a particular organization. The method uses a scoring process that is somewhat subjective in nature. Establishing a requirements list for the candidate DBMS is the most crucial step in the total process.

INDEX